D1529113

The Clydesdale Motor
Truck Company

[signature]

7/4/2014

The Clydesdale Motor Truck Company

An Illustrated History, 1917–1939

Tiffany Willey Middleton
and James M. Semon

Foreword by Shirley Sponholtz

McFarland & Company, Inc., Publishers
Jefferson, North Carolina

Library of Congress Cataloguing-in-Publication Data

Middleton, Tiffany Willey, 1981– author.
The Clydesdale Motor Truck Company : an illustrated
history, 1917–1939 / Tiffany Willey Middleton and
James M. Semon ; Foreword by Shirley Sponholtz.
p.   cm.
Includes bibliographical references and index.

ISBN 978-0-7864-7587-2
softcover : acid free paper ∞

1. Clydesdale Motor Truck Company—History.
2. Trucks—United States—History.
3. Truck industry—United States—History.
I. Semon, James M. author.   II. Title.
TL230.5.C59M53 2014   338.7'6292240973—dc23   2013041042

British Library cataloguing data are available

On the front: Artwork from the cover of a
Clydesdale Motor Truck Company promotional catalog

Manufactured in the United States of America

*McFarland & Company, Inc., Publishers
Box 611, Jefferson, North Carolina 28640
www.mcfarlandpub.com*

To Jonas and Bonnie, for all of your support

In every line of business Clydesdale trucks have established records of unusual performance on seemingly impossible tasks; they have made almost unbelievable records of low cost operation. An interesting book could be written on this subject alone.

— *Clydesdale Motor Truck Company, Model 6-X Brochure, c. 1918*

Table of Contents

Foreword
by Shirley Sponholtz

A history book, by its very nature a compendium of detailed facts, tends to be rather dry and frequently boring, even when the subject matter itself is noteworthy. However, a truly good history book manages to engage the reader by telling an absorbing story that happens to be true. Tiffany Middleton and Jim Semon have accomplished this difficult feat with their history of the Clydesdale Motor Truck Company.

Clydesdale existed during a truly special moment in American automotive development, 1917–1939. Early in the twentieth century, creative mavericks ruled the automotive industry in the U.S., with independently created cars and trucks designed and built in many sheds and barns. Inventors and entrepreneurs played a game of musical chairs as they formed partnerships to produce one vehicle, then rapidly realigned themselves with another team to produce a different vehicle. Creativity and innovation bubbled over, fostering a sense that anything was possible.

When Jim Semon began collecting his Clydesdale material, he organized it into a slide presentation for *Old Time Trucks* and honored us with his program at our second truck show. His audience comprised many knowledgeable truck historians, and still Jim managed to surprise and educate all of those present. "Clydesdale" is a name most people today associate with large draft horses that pull beer wagons in television commercials, not with trucks. (Those Budweiser Clydesdales did not appear until 1933.)

Beyond the name itself, however, there are a number of other fascinating nuggets that most truck historians will be surprised to learn. Clydesdale's "Driver Under the Hood" was true cruise control, not just a governor that limited maximum speed, and it was patented in 1914. This automatic controller was a standard feature on every gasoline-powered Clydesdale truck and one of its major selling points. Another innovative feature was the radiator that was constructed with separate copper tubes and cast aluminum tanks. With no soldered seams to leak, it was very nearly indestructible. In addition to the radiator, many other components were also manufactured from cast aluminum with the obvious benefits of lighter weight and resistance to rust.

When the Clydesdale Motor Truck Company was incorporated in 1917, the United States was in the European trenches of World War I. The demand for durable, reliable, battle-ready trucks was an unprecedented and earnest challenge to American truck makers. American trucks flooded Europe as 294 truck manufacturers, including Clydesdale,

Sketch of a Clydesdale truck, by Bruce Dicken, 1995. Bruce's father, Hugh Dicken, worked for the Clydesdale Motor Truck Company as a young man.

shipped inventory overseas. Clydesdale trucks rose above the ranks, and gained a reputation for excellence as the "Liberty Truck of Europe"—from the efficient way they packed the truck chassis for shipment "better than those Ford trucks," to the way they kept on moving in the heat of battle—"it takes more than a few German shells to stop a Clydesdale." By the time the war was over, the Clydesdale Motor Truck Company had built a robust international sales market, which became the envy of many truck makers among the industry.

The Clydesdale truck features that proved successful during World War I continued to turn heads, this time at home. The "Driver Under the Hood" became the talk of the industry. Clydesdale trucks remained on the cutting edge of technology for their time and continued their forward-looking ideas into the 1930s. By that time diesel engines were beginning to gain popularity, but were not yet being widely used. Clydesdale not only embraced diesel engines, but also designed a full line of purpose-built diesel trucks.

Unfortunately, the Clydesdale Motor Truck Company met an untimely end, just as trucking was developing into the modern industry we know today. The company appeared as an accessories exhibitor, marketing their new diesel trucks and trailers, indeed semi truck trailers, at the 1937 meeting of the American Trucking Association in Louisville, Kentucky, just a few years after the organization had been founded. Clydesdale and the modern trucking industry overlapped in a very public way, but for just a brief time. Yet they laid groundwork necessary for the nascent industry to thrive in a way that even Clydesdale's forward-thinking designers and engineers never could have imagined. Today, just about every product that we use has been shipped by a truck — "If you bought it, a truck brought it," the saying goes. Trucks — the evolution of the very type of chassis that Clydesdale manufactured almost a century ago. In 2012, the commercial trucking industry hauled 83 percent of the nation's cargo and collected $650 billion in revenue. That was 5 percent of the country's gross domestic product. This translated to $4,422 generated and 2,965 miles traveled *per second*. These are staggering numbers, and the industry is only projected to keep growing over the next several decades.

Anything *this* important to the national and international landscape has a backstory worth exploring. The Clydesdale Motor Truck Company was part of this, so take a step back into this history — you just might be surprised.

Shirley Sponholtz is founding editor of *Old Time Trucks*, which has won more than 40 awards from industry organizations for excellence in communication and writing. She is the former editor of *Wheels of Time*, the flagship publication of the American Truck Historical Society, as well as a former English teacher at both the high school and college levels. Shirley lives in Richmond, Indiana.

Preface and Acknowledgments

This is the story of the Clydesdale Motor Truck Company, which existed in Clyde, Ohio, from 1917 until 1939. The Clydesdale company built a robust international sales network by fulfilling orders for motor truck chassis for World War I. Then the company capitalized on wartime service with an equally vibrant domestic sales record. If that was not enough, during the last years of their existence, the Clydesdale Motor Truck Company reinvented their brand by turning to diesel technology, which was the sharpest of cutting edges in the auto industry in the 1930s.

The Clydesdale story provides a glimpse into the bustling moment in American automotive history when independent truck manufacturers dominated the industry. It was a moment when the motor truck began to compete directly with railroads for freight hauling, and with horses for farm work. It was a moment when trucks began to carve an industry niche separate from passenger cars, so significant that national automobile shows began holding separate "truck shows." It was also a moment when auto makers gained strength to lobby for highway funding at the national level, which influenced and laid the groundwork for modern industry policy. Finally, it was a time when diesel technology was new, and while many major automakers were slow to adopt it, Clydesdale was among the first to innovate, producing an exclusively diesel truck. Most of all, the Clydesdale story is a case study of a small-town company thriving as a major player in the global marketplace. In this way, it is a modern story set in a historical time.

We will never know everything about the Clydesdale Motor Truck Company, or the chassis and trucks that they produced. In fact, virtually none of the official company records have ever been located, and most may even be lost to history. The company did not exist in a vacuum, however, but rather within a historical context crucial to its own lifespan. The story here has been meticulously researched using public photos, company advertisements and press releases, newspapers, and trade journals from the time. There were legal documents opened in archives, after decades of sitting in storage — in some cases stored in the same boxes they had arrived in from the court years ago. All of these served as portals into time past. Woven together, all of these sources tell a rich and dynamic story about an otherwise mostly unknown American truck maker.

This history of the Clydesdale Motor Truck Company is organized, for the most part, chronologically. Chapter 1 explores the company's founding and service in World War I, and discusses the years 1917–1919. Chapter 2 delves into the technical aspects of the Clydesdale truck. What, exactly, made it so special? Chapter 3 picks up after World War I, and business is booming during the 1919–1922 window. The postwar years are truly the pinnacle of success and fame for the Clydesdale truck. By 1922–1933, chapter 4, Clydesdale releases new models, including a motor coach, but a lawsuit sends the company into receivership. The company comes back, in chapter 5, with a new focus on diesel trucks in 1934, which continues until 1939. Chapter 6 and the Epilogue discuss the end of the Clydesdale Motor Truck Company in 1939, and chronicle existing Clydesdale trucks known today.

Telling the story of the Clydesdale Motor Truck Company would have been an impossible task without the assistance of several organizations. Thank you to the Clyde Public Library; Clyde Heritage League, caretakers of the Clyde Museum; and the Clyde Fire Department, caretakers of the Clydesdale fire truck, for preserving the history of Clydesdale Motor Truck Company at home in Clyde, Ohio. Thank you to all of the friends that we have made along our research journey, including: Chicago Public Library; Milwaukee Public Library, Milwaukee, Wisconsin; National Archives and Records Administration Regional Library in Chicago, where friendly archivists dusted off original court records so we could page through everything without sneezing; Sandusky County Court of Common Pleas, Fremont, Ohio; University of Michigan, particularly the folks at the Buhr Remote Shelving Facility; and the United States Patent and Trademark Office. Special thanks to Randy Dick and Robert Snyder, Bellevue Public Library, Bellevue, Ohio; Rutherford B. Hayes Presidential Center, Fremont, Ohio; Sandusky Library and Follet House Museum, Sandusky, Ohio; Harris-Elmore Public Library, Elmore, Ohio; and McCord Museum of Canadian History, Montreal, Quebec for the use of photos. The *Clyde Enterprise* archives, and in this digital age, Library of Congress, Shorpy.com, and most of all, Google Books, were also indispensable resources. We cherish the interview that we had the opportunity to do with Mr. Milton Opper, a treasure of a man whose memories of riding a Clydesdale bus to and from school provided a touchstone directly to our subject.

We also thank Bruce Dicken, Ralph Rogers, Dominic Vartorella,* Virginia Fuller Steinemann,* Dave Moyer, Roger Chapman, Norman "Jake" Warner, Georgie and Tom Ward, Roger Kuns, Leo Flory,* Jim Semon, Jr., Bob Stacy, John and Shirley Sponholtz, Ralph Dunwoodie, Bryce Manberson, Dan Ehlerding,* Mike Bushong,* and Audre Balogh.* For special assistance with images, thank you to Christie Armstrong, Photoshop wiz; and Nelcy Elder, who translated our international advertisements. Finally, none, and we mean *none*, of this would have been possible without the extraordinary dedication of Jill McCullough, and her colleagues at the Clyde Public Library, in Clyde, Ohio. Thank you.

As a final note, nearly all of the images in this book have been collected or taken over decades by one of the authors, James M. Semon. Any image that was obtained from another source has been credited appropriately.

We hope that this story shines a light on not only the Clydesdale Motor Truck Company and their trucks, but on a distinctly different era in American truck production, when independent truck makers dominated the market. The market had changed by 1930, and was transformed by 1940, with Clydesdale developing trucks until 1939. In his encyclopedic examination of early American motor trucks, author Lloyd Van Horn catalogued 1,801 independent truck manufacturers that existed in the United States prior to 1950. This is the story of one.

Deceased.

Timeline of Clydesdale Motor Truck Company

1917	Clydesdale Motor Truck Company is organized in Clyde, Ohio, following a merger of Krebs Commercial Car Company and Clyde Cars Company, also of Clyde, and Lincoln Motor Truck Company of Detroit. They begin doing business as the Clyde Cars Company, but would brand trucks as "Clydesdale."

With World War I raging in Europe, the Red Cross, headquartered in Paris, orders 52 Clydesdale trucks. |
| 1918 | Clyde Cars Company buys land adjacent to the factory, leading to an increase in railroad frontage. The company also formally changes its name to the Clydesdale Motor Truck Company.

Clydesdale trucks appear at the Sixteenth Annual Automobile Show in Boston. |
| 1919 | Clydesdale Motor Truck Company begins production at a second factory, in Toronto, Ontario, Canada.

Twenty trucks, including one Clydesdale, participate in the 3,000-mile National Motor Truck Development Tour, which traveled from Chicago, around the Midwest, and back to Des Moines, Iowa. Clydesdale trucks also appear in subsequent tours starting in Chicago and Des Moines, as well as automobile shows in New York, Chicago, Dayton, Detroit, and Boston.

Firestone Tire and Rubber Company's Ship-by-Truck campaign events include truck tours originating in Buffalo and Los Angeles. Clydesdale participates in both. |
| 1920 | Clydesdale trucks appear in automobile shows in New York, Chicago, Philadelphia, San Francisco, Boston, Los Angeles, and Milwaukee.

Ship-by-Truck campaign events expand across the country. Clydesdale trucks appear in a large truck tour traveling around Michigan.

Clyde Fire Department welcomes a Clydesdale truck into service for the city.

Clydesdale Motor Truck Company guarantees truck prices until 1921. |

1921   Clydesdale trucks appear in Wisconsin truck tours, as well as automobile shows in New York, Boston, and London.

1922   Clydesdale Motor Truck Company introduces an all-steel truck, called the Model-10.

        Company founder J.C.L. "Louis" Krebs resigns from the Clydesdale Motor Truck Company to take a position with the Collier Motor Truck Company, Bellevue, Ohio. In addition, Clydesdale Vice-President A.C. Burch resigns to take a position with the Courier Cars Company, Sandusky, Ohio.

1923   Clydesdale Motor Truck Company introduces a 6-cylinder motor coach, or omnibus. Milton Opper, at age eight, rides a Clydesdale bus to and from school.

1925   Continental Motors sues the Clydesdale Motor Truck Company for unpaid work amounting to just over $9,000. The Clydesdale company goes into receivership. Business is temporarily discontinued.

1926   The factory and contents of the Clydesdale Motor Truck company and brand are sold at public auction. Business resumes under new ownership.

1930   Clydesdale Motor Truck Company announces the planned introduction of a new line of 6-cylinder gasoline engine trucks with a distinctively modern appearance. These trucks apparently were not produced.

1932   Clydesdale engineers begin researching new diesel technologies, while the Great Depression contributes to the closing of over half of American independent truck makers.

1934   Clydesdale Motor Truck Company announces a new focus on diesel technology, and begins designing the first exclusively diesel truck. Former company Vice-President A.C. Burch returns to Clydesdale by this time to assist with the development of diesel trucks.

1936   Louis Krebs dies in Tampa, Florida.

1937   Clydesdale Motor Truck Company releases a line of 4-and 6-cylinder diesel trucks. Executives announce orders totaling $215,000 for sales worldwide, including to the U.S. government.

        The company officially trademarks the Clydesdale brand.

        U.S. Navy officials arrive in Clyde later that year to inspect the trucks. The Clydesdale diesel trucks also exhibit at the National Motor Truck Show in Newark, New Jersey, and the American Trucking Association exposition in Louisville, Kentucky.

1938   The U.S. Navy cancels the federal contract that had been awarded the previous year. Clydesdale officials attempt to reorganize and solicit support from shareholders.

1939   Clydesdale Motor Truck Company is formally dissolved.

        Lewis Snyder and Paul Beier complete the assembly of Clydesdale trucks at their Highway Garage for one outstanding order, which is later shipped to Finland.

1947   Clydesdale fire truck is decommissioned by the Clyde Fire Department and city officials authorize its sale two years later.

1948   A.C. Burch, former Clydesdale vice-president and director of sales, dies at his home in Sandusky, Ohio.

1967   City officials in Clyde recover and restore the former Clyde Fire Department's Clydesdale fire truck.

Milton Opper, 98, holding a photograph of the Clydesdale bus he rode to school in 1923 as a young student. He recalls when his school bought the bus, and remembers riding in it, down to the last detail.

1

The Crucible of War (1917–1919)

The Clydesdale Motor Truck Company was incorporated on May 1, 1917, in Clyde, Ohio. The new company's stock was valued at $500,000. Shareholders elected the company's first board of directors: Charles R. Dunbar, from Holyoke, Massachusetts, president; J.C.L. "Louis" Krebs, from Clyde, vice-president; J.B. Crockett, from New York, treasurer; Walter P. Dodge, from Springfield, Massachusetts, assistant treasurer and sales manager; Homer Metzgar, also from Clyde, secretary; and Charles F. Bowker and J.H. Baynes, also from Clyde, directors.[1]

The Clydesdale story does not start there, however, with seven directors setting out to manufacture trucks. The Clydesdale incorporation was actually a merger of three different companies: Krebs Commercial Cars Company and Clyde Cars Company, both of Clyde, and the Lincoln Motor Truck Company of Detroit. Of the three companies, the Clyde Cars Company had the most established reputation and despite its name, made the most complete trucks. The Krebs Commercial Cars Company, established by Clydesdale's Vice-President Krebs, had been in production for the longest time, and was included in a planned reorganization with the Clyde Cars Company. The two companies shared the same facility in Clyde. The Lincoln Motor Truck Company was newly incorporated in 1917, and manufactured engines. Since the two Clyde companies together boasted the largest facility, much of the Lincoln company's equipment was moved from the Detroit facility to the factory in Ohio.

Company facilities included a large factory located at 322 Amanda Street in Clyde, Ohio. The longtime manufacturing facility included over 50,000 square feet of floor space and machine equipment. The entire campus was located adjacent to railroad tracks for accessible shipping. The factory space easily transitioned into the headquarters for subsequent Clydesdale production.

For a few years, what would become known as the Clydesdale Motor Truck Company attempted to do business as the (reorganized) Clyde Cars Company, while branding their trucks as "Clydesdale." As might be expected, this created confusion, as "a great majority of mail and telegrams" were "addressed to the Clydesdale Company."[2] As a result, by the end of 1919, the company made this announcement: "The Clyde Cars Company, of Clyde, has been compelled to change its name to that of the Clydesdale Motor Truck Company simply because of the popularity of their trucks."[3] For our purposes here, this history will refer only to the Clydesdale Motor Truck Company, regardless of whether referenced events occurred before or after the formal name change.

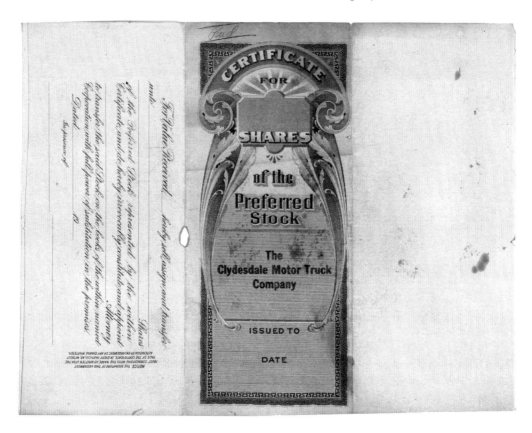

The Clydesdale Motor Truck Company was organized in 1917 following the merger of Krebs Commercial Cars Company and Clyde Cars Company, of Clyde, Ohio, and the Lincoln Motor Truck Company, of Detroit, Michigan. New company stock was capitalized at $500,000. This stock envelope held a certificate that was sold to the local Clyde Fire Department chief (*courtesy Clyde Heritage League, Clyde, Ohio*).

The name "Clydesdale" deserves explanation. It appears to be a clever moniker paying homage to two references: the home of the Clydesdale Motor Truck Company in Clyde, Ohio, and the breed of horse, known for its size and strength. The community of Clyde, according to local history, had been named after Clyde, New York, which had been named earlier after the River Clyde, which flows through Scotland. In fact, the River Clyde, which is known for sweeping valleys and views, is the ninth longest river in the United Kingdom, and even today, is a major shipping canal. A Clydesdale Motor Truck Company brochure explained the connection between the river and the horse in naming their truck products: "Clydesdale, named after the valley of the Clyde ... [and] an excellent draught horse with symmetry, activity, strength, and endurance."[4]

References to the Clydesdale breed of horse appeared early in Clydesdale Motor Truck Company advertising. Since 1933, however, the name "Clydesdale" has been most often associated with the promotional team of such horses showcased by the Anheuser-Busch Brewing Company. Clydesdale trucks had no affiliation with the Anheuser-Busch Clydesdales, and in fact, used the brand name independently during the company's entire existence, from 1917 to 1939.

At 50,000 square feet, the Clydesdale factory was spacious and modern. This photograph of the factory exterior shows the truck port where finished trucks were often parked, and the bottom of the company water tower. Railroad tracks ran adjacent to the opposite side of the building shown here for easy shipping (*courtesy Grace Luebke Local History & Geneology Department at the Harris-Elmore Public Library, Elmore, Ohio*).

Location, Location, Location

Clyde is a community in northwest Ohio, less than one hour southeast of Toledo, and two hours southeast of Detroit. At the time of the 2010 U.S. Census, the city's population was approximately 6,300 people. In 1917, it was closer to 3,000. Historian Thomas Sugrue has described this part of the country as "America's industrial heartland," a geographic belt extending from lower New England, south to Pennsylvania, and west across the Appalachian Mountains through Ohio, Indiana, and Illinois. In a study of this region's early contributions to automobile production, and its eventual concentration in Detroit, he explained, "All of the raw materials needed for automobile production were easily accessible to the city by the Great Lakes waterways and by rail."[5] Clyde, with its proximity to Detroit amid the industrial heartland, enjoyed similar access.

The city was close to shipping ports in Toledo and Cleveland, and could also transport goods via railroad. Two railroad lines traversed the city. The Lake Shore and Michigan Southern Railroad, formally part of the New York Central Railroad, was located directly adjacent to the Clydesdale factory, connecting the company to New York and Chicago. In addition to shipping and railroads, highways provided additional transportation opportunities. U.S. Route 20, today the nation's longest road, spanning the entire country, passed through the northern side of the city.

CLYDESDALE

British War Department Transport

THE CLYDESDALE WAS DESIGNED AND BUILT TO STAND THE HARDEST TEST A MOTOR VEHICLE WAS EVER PUT TO—
IT HAS STOOD THE TEST IN **WAR** AND STANDS TODAY PERFECTED FOR **PEACE**

Clydesdale Motor Truck Company promotional brochure from 1918, which spotlights the company's successful war service: "The Clydesdale was designed and built to stand the hardest test a motor vehicle was ever put to—It has stood the test in war and stands today perfected for peace." The advertisement features a Clydesdale truck used by the British War Office, as well as a Clydesdale horse in the background. This is one of few known Clydesdale advertisements that make reference to Clydesdale horses.

The city of Clyde, in 1917 still a village, might have been an ideal community in which to establish a manufacturing company such as Clydesdale. Beyond its geographic advantages, community leaders had established a tradition of welcoming new industries. The Clyde Commercial Club, by 1911, had adopted the following attitude toward new business:

> We feel that we can only give any new industries, seeking to locate in Clyde, our moral support, by assisting in procuring extensions to water, gas, and electric current lines; by using our influence, as far as it may go, in procuring enactments of village laws; by using our efforts towards seeing that they are not held up in the matter of sites, and by giving them what support we may be able to do in this line.[6]

Thus, the village of Clyde gained a reputation for welcoming manufacturing facilities, in particular. For decades before the Clydesdale Motor Truck Company put down their roots, many manufacturing companies made Clyde their home. Throughout the city's history, companies have manufactured, in addition to Clydesdale Motor Trucks, many different products, including sauerkraut, organs, church furniture, cutlery, porcelain, granite monuments, cement blocks, bricks, bicycles, and cars. Still today, the city maintains a strong manufacturing industry.

In occupying the Amanda Street facility, the Clydesdale Motor Truck Company assumed a longstanding manufacturing tradition. The same facility had been home to the Clyde Cars Company and the Krebs Commercial Car Company prior to the merger, and before that, the Elmore Manufacturing Company. In fact, a straight line might connect the histories of all of these companies to the Clydesdale Motor Truck Company. For this reason, it is worth taking a moment to explore the direct connections between the companies, and John Krebs' relationship to each.

Elmore Manufacturing Company

The founder of the Krebs Commercial Car Company, the subsequent Clyde Cars Company, and, later, Clydesdale was the company's vice-president, John C. Krebs. He often went by "Louis." The eventual automobile design and manufacturing expert was born in Clyde, on January 26, 1871, to John Krebs, a German immigrant, and Elizabeth Uthey, a French immigrant. Louis Krebs was educated in Clyde public schools, and married Louise Alberti, also from Clyde, in 1894. They had four children: Marie, Lauretta, Bertha, and Edmund.[7] Krebs was later described as "one of the best known automobile experts of the country," with "his genius and ability [putting] Clyde on the automobile map."[8]

Louis Krebs initially worked as an independent farmer in northern Ohio for approximately eight years before he took his first job in manufacturing. He began his career working at the Elmore Manufacturing Company, which operated in nearby Elmore, Ohio, from 1892 to 1893, then occupied the Amanda Street facility in Clyde prior to the Krebs Commercial Car Company, from 1893 to 1912. The company had been started in 1892 by Harmon V. Becker and operated by his two sons, James and Burton. When Louis Krebs began working for Elmore in the late nineteenth century, the company made bicycles. In 1900, however, the facilities were retooled to manufacture automobiles. By this time, Louis Krebs had earned promotion to superintendent of the factory. Under his management, the Elmore

J.C.L. "Louis" Krebs, pictured in the center with mustache, started his career at the Elmore Manufacturing Company making bicycles. He learned about engineering automobiles when the factory retooled to make cars in 1900. In 1909 he left the factory. He later founded the Krebs Commercial Car Company in 1912, where he oversaw development and patenting of the distinctive automatic controller that would become the feature of Clydesdale trucks. He founded the Clydesdale Motor Truck Company in 1917. Krebs Commercial Car Company employees surround him here: standing rear (in unknown order), James Hunt, Paul Shiebel, Fred Rhoda, Fred Broud, and an unidentified worker; middle row, Grover McKay, Rolland Reed, Levi Streeter, George Allen, Carl Whittaker, Frank Shanahan; in cab, Ralph Grimshaw and at wheel William Wells; and sitting front, from right: Fred Lynch, Mack Robinson, Fay Wilson, Howard Mason, George Conley, Louis Krebs and James Mason.

Manufacturing Company steadily grew each year, increasing car production and profits. The local newspaper described the factory as "a very busy place, and the influence of its prosperity is felt in every business channel in Clyde."[9]

The Elmore car became famous for its two-cycle engine, which was billed as "valveless." Two-cycle engines power a crankshaft in just two motions — up and down. Compared to their four-cycle counterparts, two-cycle engines did not require an intricate system of valves to direct subsequent air, fuel, and burned gas products. As the company explained, "Our contention has always been that the four-cycle engine was subversive of progress because in principle it worked away from simplicity — that the two-cycle engine was the fittest engine, which would survive, because in principle and operation it was actually elemental in simplicity."[10] Generally, two-cycle engines were powerful, yet inexpensive. They were also lighter than the common four-cycle engine.

The Elmore car's two-cycle engine became a "leading gasoline engine export from the

The Car That Has No Valves

Three Cylinder two-cycle Elmore, $1750.00.

Four Cylinder two-cycle Elmore, $2500.00.

A VALVELESS TWO-CYCLE CATECHISM

What makes a four-cycle automobile jerky?
Intermittent application of power—infrequent explosions.

How can that be overcome?
Partially by increasing the number of cylinders.

What does that accomplish?
More frequent impulses—or explosions.

But doesn't that increase complication and cost?
To a distressing extent.

Don't the valves in all these cylinders create trouble?
An incalculable amount.

Then what is the remedy?
A two-cycle valveless engine—the Elmore.

What do you gain in such an engine?
An explosion from each cylinder every time the crank-shaft turns.

What does that mean?
Unbroken power—a motion like that of a smoothly gliding boat.

What else does it mean?
Only three moving parts to each cylinder—12 moving parts against 124 on four cylinders of the four-cycle type.

What else?
More power for size and weight than any other motor in the world—pulling power developed at much less speed than any other motor.

Is that all?
Well, hardly. The valveless Elmore avoids all inaccuracy due to imperfect setting of valves, and then it will run without missing a single impulse with the engine running from 150 to 1400 revolutions a minute.

It pulls a car at so low a speed you can count the impulses . . . It develops as much or more power after 12 months' use as at the outset . . . It will start without cranking . . . It negotiates crowded streets without changing gear—climbs hills on the high speed in which other cars have to change gear.

Is that all?
No—we haven't even started—but we have no more space here. Send for the booklet—"Our Daily Mail," and incidentally ask any agent if—in spite of the facilities of this factory—he can get as many Elmores as he can sell.

Also ask any Elmore user if he were going to buy a new car if he would buy any car but the Elmore.

ELMORE MFG. CO., 1804 Amanda St., Clyde, O.
MEMBERS A. L. A. M.
In writing, kindly use the Key number given herewith.

Advertisement for the "valveless," two-cycle engine Elmore car, which appeared in *Review of Reviews* in May 1907. Clydesdale founder Louis Krebs started his career developing this car at the Elmore Manufacturing Company.

United States" in the early years of automobile manufacturing.[11] It had been patented in 1907 by Louis Krebs and Elmore colleague Frank Bachle. At least one Elmore car was sent directly to European gas engine designer Mr. J. De Beitrau, who wanted to study the Elmore car's motor, which had "attracted so much attention on this side of the water because of the revolutionary character of its construction."[12] An advertisement for the Elmore Pathfinder broadly suggested "a revolution is going on right under your eyes in the automobile world," with the city of Clyde transformed into a "mecca toward which the eyes of experts, makers and users alike are anxiously turning," thanks to "the perfect engine."[13]

Elmore manufactured three different passenger car models, with the most popular being the Elmore Pathfinder. Models ranged in price from $1,750 to $2,500, guaranteed 24 to 35 horsepower, and traveled at maximum speeds of 35 to 45 miles per hour.

By 1909, the Elmore Manufacturing Company employed 400 to 500 workers, produced approximately 1,800 cars each year, and claimed $1.5 million in annual profits. Profitable each year, and selling out of stock, the Elmore Manufacturing Company seemed to be succeeding in its promise to deliver customers "the most perfect car of its class in the world."[14] This caught the eye of William Durant, executive at newly incorporated General Motors. Through his efforts, General Motors acquired the Elmore Manufacturing Company in 1909. He agreed not to interrupt production, and the facilities remained in Clyde. Almost simultaneously, Louis Krebs announced his resignation from Elmore Manufacturing, citing business priorities outside of the factory.

Just a few years later, in 1912, General Motors moved all Elmore Manufacturing operations from the Clyde facility to Detroit, despite the company's consistent profitability. The

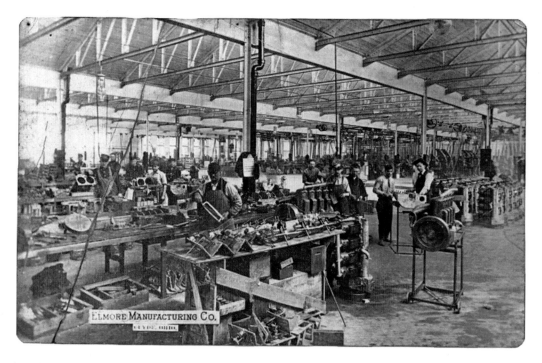

Interior of the Elmore Manufacturing Company facility. This is where J.C.L. "Louis" Krebs started his career as an automotive engineer.

The Krebs Is A "Governed" Car
Its Driver Has Nothing To Do But Steer

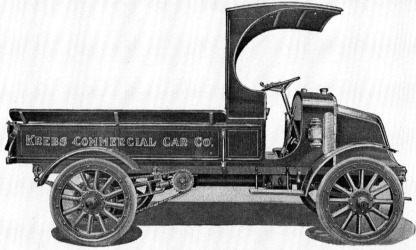

Krebs Commercial Car Model A. Guaranteed Capacity, 1 Ton. Price $1,510, with Standard Open Express Body and Cab Seat. Price for Chassis only, $1,375.

Rightly termed "The Car That Thinks," the Krebs, by means of its wonderful governor, automatically maintains the precise rate of speed that its owner desires.

A careless driver cannot mishandle the Krebs, while a careful driver finds that its governor allows him to give undivided attention to road and traffic conditions.

This is more than assurance to the car owner that his truck investment will not be abused. It is an assurance of fuel economy, and minimum cost of maintenance.

With the Krebs governor placed to give a certain rate of speed, the motor is accelerated or retarded with a greater degree of nicety than human skill can attain.

It is literally true that the action of the Krebs governor is quicker than thought; its control of gas is accurate and absolute. The exact amount needed for the required speed is supplied; never more and never less.

The Krebs is made in three models. Model A, shown above has a chain driven chassis and solid tires. Speed up to 15 miles per hour.

Model B is fitted with shaft driven chassis and pneumatic tires. Guaranteed capacity 3-4 ton. Speed up to 20 miles per hour. Price with standard delivery body, screened, $1,550.

Models A and B have our own valveless two cylinder motors. Either will be furnished with a high grade four cylinder four cycle motor if desired, for $50 extra.

Model D, chain driven, with guaranteed capacity 1 1-2 tons, has a four cylinder 30 H. P. Rutenber motor, cylinders 3 3-4 by 5 1-4. Price of chassis alone, $1,775. May be fitted with starting and electric lighting system at nominal extra cost.

We build the Krebs with special bodies for any trade or industry. Write for more complete information today, and tell us your needs.

Desirable territory for dealers who know how to handle a good thing.

THE KREBS COMMERCIAL CAR CO., Clyde, Ohio, U. S. A.

"The Krebs Is A 'Governed' Car, Its Driver Has Nothing To Do But Steer": Advertisement from the Krebs Commercial Car Company, which appeared in *Commercial Car Journal*, March 1913. The Krebs car made use of the same patented engine governor that would later become the Clydesdale Automatic Controller. It maintained speed, much like modern cruise control technology.

Krebs commercial car in use by the Smallman-Beebe Company, New Haven, Connecticut.

Amanda Street factory shutdown was a blow to the local economy. In the meantime, it became clear that Louis Krebs was working to establish his own automobile manufacturing company. After the Elmore Company vacated the Amanda Street facility in Clyde in 1912, Louis Krebs and Frank Bachle were able to buy the factory from General Motors within the same year. They retooled the facility for the Krebs Commercial Car Company, and hired many of the former Elmore Manufacturing engineers.

Krebs Commercial Car Company and the Clyde Cars Company

Louis Krebs established the Krebs Commercial Car Company in 1912, five years before merging into the Clydesdale Company. Despite its name, the Krebs Commercial Car Company manufactured trucks.[15] Krebs employed approximately 50 employees from the Elmore Manufacturing Company. They developed new trucks within several months. Local news reported: "The first of the new Krebs commercial cars made its appearance on the streets last week, and attracted a great deal of attention and favorable comment. It is a neat, light, and compact vehicle for truck work...."[16] The Krebs company produced the trucks at a rate of approximately two trucks per day.[17] Additional news reports noticed Krebs cars being shipped across the country, even to Los Angeles, and added: "The new car is getting pretty well scattered over the [United States], and is giving universal satisfaction."[18]

Krebs Commercial Car Company leaders billed their vehicles as "the car that thinks." This slogan referred to a patented engine governing mechanism employed on the trucks, which was comparable to modern cruise control. The device that left the driver with "nothing to do but steer" had been designed by Krebs engineers Frank Bachle and Walter Wells. The device used a system of springs, weights, and centrifugal force to control the speed of the vehicle. The engine "controller," as it became known, would become a distinguishing feature of the Clydesdale models, and is explored more in the next chapter.[19]

In 1917, the Krebs Commercial Car Company, which became the Clyde Cars Company, merged with the Lincoln Motor Truck Company of Detroit, to form the Clydesdale Motor Truck Company. When Clydesdale assumed operations in the factory in 1917, many of the employees, like Louis Krebs, were veteran automobile engineers who had started their careers with the Elmore Manufacturing Company. This wealth of experience and expertise left the Clydesdale Company primed for wartime manufacturing.

Going to War

The first orders to the newly incorporated Clydesdale Motor Truck Company were for trucks for use in World War I–ravaged Europe. Though the United States did not enter

When Clydesdale was incorporated in 1917, World War I raged in Europe. The company immediately began exporting inventory overseas for wartime service. This is a close-up of one of the Clydesdale Model-90 trucks in use during World War I by the British War Office.

World War I until 1917, war had been raging in Europe since 1914, and armies all over the world needed reliable trucks. Facing overwhelming demand for their product, the Clydesdale Motor Truck Company would find quick success as part of the worldwide war effort. Naturally, war trucks had to be built to perform in the harshest of conditions—and to last. The engineers at Clydesdale, according to advertisements, had worked closely with "the keenest" British and French engineers to "[make] certain changes in construction to enable it to meet better the strains of war service."[20] These relationships led to a partnership between Clydesdale and the London General Omnibus Company that would last for years after the war. Advertisements would describe the Clydesdale truck as "practically a duplicate" of the "world famed" London Omnibus trucks, and the "only truck in which all of the experience of the L.G.O. Company in building trucks has been available."[21]

The London General Omnibus Company, in fact, supplied the British army with some of the first motor transportation used during World War I. Records show that 75 buses donated by the company transported troops to battle front lines in 1914. The buses remained in service throughout the war following several adaptations: windows were removed, toolboxes and storage bins were installed, and khaki paint replaced brighter colors. In many ways, the London General Omnibus Company pioneered the use of motor trucks during World War I. Throughout the war, the British government subsidized truck production by four companies that delivered 25,000 trucks to the army. One company, Thornycroft, even developed a 3-ton antiaircraft gun, which was mounted on a flatbed to allow for 360-degree rotations.

The French army pioneered similar motor truck transportation systems, and developed significant innovations on the World War I battlefront. One, the Boulant Mobile Surgery, was a lavishly equipped operating room on wheels. Double doors in the back accommodated stretchers, while an electric light and a 200-liter water tank provided essential resources. French engineers also developed the Renault Searchlight Carrier, which allowed for battlefield illumination and long-range signaling.

The French army's use of motor truck transportation became world-famous, during the Battle of Verdun in 1916. When it appeared that the German army would capture Verdun, France, the French army strove to maintain their strategic position outside the city. The French soldiers had access to a small railroad, which commanding officer General Phillippe Petain quickly recognized as insufficient for delivering soldiers or supplies. An unpaved road, approximately twenty feet in width, ran alongside the railroad. Troops and supplies could be moved along the road via truck. During the first week of March 1916 alone, more than 25,000 tons of supplies and 190,000 troops were moved along the road, which had been dubbed "Sacred Way." At the battle's peak in June, witnesses reported that trucks passed over the road at a rate of one every fourteen seconds. When the battle ended in December, almost two-thirds of the French army had been carried entirely by motor transport along the road. Historian Brian Hanley noted, "Perhaps more so than any other material factor, motor transport—if it didn't quite win the war for the Allies—kept them from losing it at Verdun."[22]

Prior to the United States' entrance into World War I, however, trucks were not used extensively by the U.S. military. According to a 1911 article in *Infantry Journal*, the U.S. Army owned just 12 trucks, and spread them throughout the country.[23] The Army first used, and the public became aware of, trucks for official military business during the Pancho

Clydesdale trucks quickly gained a reputation for reliability in the battlefield. Armies ordered fleets. The British War Office eventually ordered 33 Clydesdale trucks.

Villa Expedition in 1916. Also known in the United States as the Mexican Expedition, the military operation was launched in 1916 in response to Mexican revolutionary Francisco "Pancho" Villa's attack on Columbus, New Mexico, during the Mexican Revolution. On orders from President Woodrow Wilson, Major General John J. Pershing led 4,800 men into Mexico with orders to stop Villa. Following disputes with the Mexican government over the use of the Mexico North Western Railway, a train-truck campaign was organized to transport supplies into the mountains of northern Mexico. It was the first use of non-rail motor vehicle transportation by the army for a military operation. The U.S. Army learned much about truck transport as soldiers encountered harsh conditions and rugged terrain. Many trucks got stuck in the mud and were abandoned. It became clear that, while the trucks themselves needed improvement, the truck as a mode of supply transport was valuable for military campaigns.

When the United States entered World War I on April 6, 1917, Pershing, now commander of the U.S. Army, ordered 50,000 trucks from American manufacturers. Army trucks, of course, would require improved performance compared to those used during the Pancho Villa expedition. Trucks were expected to perform in conditions like those at Verdun. They were also quickly regarded as practical, mobile stations that could serve soldiers remotely, in and outside of combat. Trucks could be customized into dental trucks, non-emergency medical trucks, shoe repair trucks, kitchen trucks, mail trucks, searchlight trucks, and blacksmith trucks. In response to this need, the Motor Transport Section of the U.S. Army's Quartermaster Corps, in cooperation with the Society of Automotive Engineers, developed the "Liberty Truck," a Class B truck capable of hauling loads from three to five tons. It took just 10 weeks to perfect the design in 1917. The U.S. Army contracted with 15 American manufacturers for production.

While the Clydesdale Motor Truck Company was not one of the 15 American manufacturers originally producing the Liberty Truck, company officials were studying the truck's specifications, and worked to develop additional models suitable for war service. In fact, the Clydesdale truck would eventually become known as the "Liberty Truck of Europe" by the war's end.[24]

In 1917, manufacturers and civilians alike knew that Pershing's initial order of 50,000 trucks would not be sufficient to meet the needs of the American army, much less armies around the world. Some Americans were concerned that the demand for trucks would lead to the commandeering of personal vehicles as part of the war effort. According to records from the U.S. Bureau of Public Roads, there were 4.9 million automobiles, mostly cars, registered to Americans across the United States in 1917.[25] A portion of these were increasingly popular motor trucks, with most used for commercial work or farming. A recall of these trucks for the war effort would have been devastating to businesses and farms. Companies like Clydesdale scrambled to fill orders for additional trucks, while one trade magazine reassured American car and truck owners: "The motor vehicle industry of America is prepared as no industry in this country has ever prepared before, to deliver to the army just the vehicles which it requires and in numbers sufficient for its gradually growing needs."[26]

A 5-ton Clydesdale truck chassis successfully passes a hill-climbing test from the British War Office.

Clydesdale manufactured truck chassis, like the one here. They did not produce entire trucks, as most manufacturers during this time relied on third-party body builders to offer custom bodies for customers. Here, Clydesdale representatives stand with a motor truck chassis outside the factory.

In all, 294 independent manufacturers in the United States exported trucks to armies around the world for war service. And armies bought them. U.S. exports to Europe exploded to $5.6 billion in 1917, compared to $2.2 billion just four years earlier.[27] By the end of 1918, American manufacturers produced and exported 227,000 trucks, exceeding Pershing's order by more than four times.[28]

Bill Hudgins, columnist for *Land Line* magazine, noted "The vehicles — and their drivers — performed heroically."[29] The government of France even awarded the White Truck Company's Model A truck, made in Cleveland, Ohio, the French Croix de Guerre for its wartime performance.

In addition to the benefits that trucks provided armies with regard to versatility and economy, motor trucks were viewed by many as an efficient use of resources, or responsible stewardship, as part of the war effort. Clydesdale vice-president and director of sales A.C. Burch insisted that trucks conserved steel for munitions. Compared to a railroad freight car, which was the dominant hauling vehicle at the time, trucks were far more steel-efficient. A railroad freight car could haul 800 tons per day, but required an estimated 25 tons of steel for construction; four motor trucks could offer the same hauling capacity, and required just five tons of steel, he reasoned.

Burch calculated:

The average freight car mileage is only twenty miles per day carrying an average load of forty tons. Therefore, the daily average per car is eight hundred ton miles. It follows, from this, that four two-ton trucks will have a daily carrying capacity of one freight car. But it takes only a ton and a half of steel to build the truck, and twenty-five tons to build a freight car. Therefore, the four two-ton trucks will save twenty tons of steel. This equals five tons to each truck.

But we must also take into consideration the motive power used to pull the freight car. It takes a hundred and fifty tons of steel to build a locomotive and its tender.... Figure for yourself what a tremendous saving of steel this would amount to if 200,000 trucks were put into service. It would run way over the million ton mark.[30]

Clydesdale employees are at work in the factory machine shop. Many of the employees were former engineers with the Elmore Manufacturing Company or Krebs Commercial Car Company. They brought decades of experience to the new company.

Clydesdale chassis were built inside an open shop in the factory. Assembly lines, while increasingly common at the time, were not used by the Clydesdale Motor Truck Company to assemble trucks (*courtesy Clyde Heritage League, Clyde, Ohio*).

Such steel conservation with just 200,000 trucks, he implored, would accumulate into massive amounts of additional steel across the market.

It is important to remember that the Clydesdale factory manufactured truck *chassis*, or the truck frame and parts — everything but the cab and body. Clydesdale workers assembled chassis from beginning to end. Many parts were manufactured onsite, while certain parts, like engines, axles, tires, and brakes, were ordered from suppliers. "The factory is modern and up to date in every respect and production and inspection methods are of the highest order," boasted company officials.[31] The Clydesdale Motor Truck Company facility was modern and expansive with 50,000 square feet. The company facility included an office, wood shop, machine shop, machine room, assembly room, chassis assembly room, engine test center, paint shop, shipping area, and storage warehouses. The shipping and storage areas, as noted, were adjacent to a railroad line for convenient access to markets.

With so many of Clydesdale's initial orders going overseas for war service, shipping access was crucial to the early success of the company. Even then, transporting trucks halfway around the world for war service was no easy task. Manufactured Clydesdale chassis were packed in crates for overseas shipment to designated yards, where they were assembled

No. 3 Part of the automatic screw machine equipment.
The Clyde Cars Company, Clyde, Ohio.

Clydesdale employees operating the factory's "automatic screw machine equipment."

onsite. Packing a truck chassis in a wooden create took coordination and skill. Clydesdale technicians, like all American truck exporters, understood "how to pack [trucks] so scientifically and make the boxes so small that the freight, which for this kind of merchandise, is quoted per cubic measurement would not make the biggest item in the invoice."[32] In fact, the Clydesdale company gained a reputation in the auto industry for their efficient packaging, as one international exports expert noted: "I will not give away details of this packing method, only state the fact that the manufacturers of the well-known 'Clydesdale' truck pack their five ton model in boxes much smaller than those of Ford cars."[33]

　　Once overseas, Clydesdale truck chassis were assembled in shops by trained mechanics, often recruited by armies for this purpose, as well as to perform general repairs and ongoing maintenance. After assembly, Clydesdale chassis could be customized for a variety of war

Top: Each Clydesdale chassis was assigned a serial number, which was engraved on an identifying plaque like this one, then attached to the chassis. Note this plaque came from a Clydesdale Model 65, serial number 5771. *Bottom:* Clydesdale employee Hugh Dicken sits on top of a crated chassis. The company gained a reputation for its efficient packaging of chassis that needed to be shipped overseas.

service capacities. Clydesdales were used for direct war service in countries such as England, France, Greece, and Java, moving everything from healthy and wounded soldiers, to supplies, ammunition, and mail. As the truck earned a reputation for reliability, the Clydesdale Motor Truck Company continued to fill orders. The American Red Cross, headquartered in Paris, ordered 52 Clydesdale trucks, which were used primarily as ambulances. By the end

Top: Employees load crated Clydesdale chassis onto a rail car outside the factory. One crate is stamped "Sydney," so the shipment was likely headed to Australia. *Bottom:* Crated Clydesdale chassis on its way to Durban, South Africa. Note the chassis number on the side of the crate, number 9799.

No. 1 One of the stock rooms with a few trucks crated for export shipment in the foreground.
The Clyde Cars Company, Clyde, Ohio.

One of the Clydesdale factory stockrooms, with crated chassis ready for shipment in the foreground. Note stacks of wheels and crated fuel tanks.

of the war, Clydesdale trucks were approximately 20 percent of the Red Cross's entire fleet.

World War I was, in fact, the first war that involved extensive use of motorized battlefield ambulances, primarily because of their widespread use by the Red Cross. Reliable and safe trucks, like the Clydesdale, became extremely important to all soldiers, but especially ambulance drivers. One ambulance driver explained:

It is difficult for one who had not led the life to appreciate just what his [truck] means to the ambulancier. For periods of weeks, mayhap, it is his only home. He drives it through rain, hail, mud and dust, at high noon on sunshiny days, and through nights so dark that the radiator cap before him is invisible. Its interior serves him as a bedroom. Its engine furnishes him with hot shaving water, its guards act as a dresser. He works over, under and upon it. He paints it and

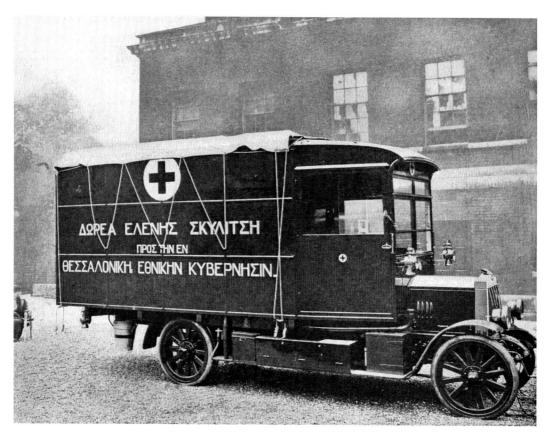

World War I was the first major war to make use of trucks as ambulances. The Greek War Department equipped this Clydesdale chassis with a full field hospital body for use on the battlefield.

oils it and knows its every bolt and nut, its every whim and fancy. When shrapnel and shell fall, he dives under it for protection. Not only his own life, but the lives of the helpless wounded entrusted to his care depend on its smooth and efficient functioning. Small wonder then that his [truck] is his pride. You may reflect on an ambulancier's mechanical knowledge, his appearance, morals, religion, or politics, but if you be wise, reflect not on his [truck]. To him, regardless of its vintage or imperfections, it is not only a good [truck], it is the best [truck].[34]

To many, Clydesdale trucks were indeed the *best* trucks. They earned the nickname "Liberty Truck of Europe." A French officer who had knowledge of the Clydesdale's performance visited the United States and told company officials, "They have all been in continuous service close behind the line in one of the most active sectors — they have gone through the battle of the Marne and scores of other battles. Up to the time [I] left [they] were still in operation and giving a good account of themselves. It takes more than a few German shells to stop a Clydesdale. More than a year of the hardest service the world has ever known."[35]

Success on the battlefield was exactly what the Clydesdale engineers hoped for as they plotted the future of their company. The war provided an unprecedented proving ground for new technologies. "The ultimate motor truck will be the car with all the best features that survive[s] this war," predicted W.P. Dodge, Clydesdale sales manager in 1918. "Motor truck users have been patiently waiting for the war to evolve a car that will answer all the

This photograph appeared in the local newspaper, the *Clyde Enterprise*, on October 24, 1918, with the headline "Clydesdale Trucks in Red Cross Service in France." By this time, the American Red Cross had ordered at least 52 Clydesdale trucks, supplying approximately one fifth of the organization's entire fleet. The article provided a glimpse into the Clydesdale trucks in war service for the American Red Cross and reassured Clyde residents that "it takes more than a few German shells to stop a Clydesdale" (*courtesy Clyde Heritage League, Clyde, Ohio*).

purposes of commercial needs and be strong enough to stand the test of battle."[36] In fact, by the war's end, motor truck performance was rivaling that of other common transportation — railroads — with development in a fraction of the time. "The motor truck of today is more highly developed in its mechanism than the finest locomotive and greatly superior in performance," declared editors at *Dun's Review* in 1918.[37]

The success of the "Liberty Truck of Europe" on the battlefield provided Clydesdale officials with plenty of marketing opportunities. The company showcased its war service record in much of its advertising. Using taglines like "A World-Proven Motor Truck," "The Proof of a Truck's Worth," and "Tested in the Crucible of War — and Found Fit," Clydesdale officials hoped to capitalize on overseas success in domestic markets.[38]

> The Clydesdale motor truck has met the harshest tests of all time — the tests of the great European war — *and has conquered....* It has been tested in the crucible of war — *and found fit.* It has satisfied the most critical group of men in the world — the army truck drivers of the Allies.
>
> But traffic managers in this country are *equally enthusiastic* over its performance in *peaceful commerce.* The Clydesdale embodies important and exclusive features — features that have proved their value in both war and peace.[39]

Clydesdale
MOTOR  TRUCKS

Tested in the Crucible of War—and Found Fit

The Clydesdale motor truck has met the harshest tests of all time—the tests of the great European war—*and has conquered.* Nearly three years ago this truck, which was efficiently performing its peaceful duties here, was selected for war service in Europe.

The keenest engineering minds of France, England and America met and in joint conference made certain changes in its construction to enable it to meet better the super strains of war service. As a result it now embodies the best practices of these three nations—combining the refinements of European design with the advantages of American manufacturing methods.

Production was rushed and hundreds of trucks have been sent abroad. Continuous repeat orders are eloquent evidence of the service the Clydesdale is rendering. It has been tested in the crucible of war—*and found fit.* It has satisfied the most critical group of men in the world—the army truck drivers of the Allies.

But traffic managers in this country are *equally enthusiastic* over its performance in *peaceful commerce.* The Clydesdale embodies important and exclusive features—features that have proved their value in both war and peace.

Prominent among them is the Krebs Patented Automatic Controller. This device is not an ordinary *governor,* but an *exclusive patented attachment that practically acts as a second driver.*

It *maintains any speed*—up hill or down, and positively *prevents engine racing.* This feature alone effects a tremendous saving in the life of your entire truck. It also enables a comparatively inexperienced man to handle the Clydesdale efficiently.

Another exclusive feature is the Clydesdale radiator, patterned after the famous London General Omnibus radiator—with a tremendous cooling surface of plain standard copper tubing. It is mounted on the chassis frame on double acting springs, eliminating all excessive jarring and vibration.

Clydesdale transmission has four speeds, giving greater power and flexibility. Final drive is through worm-gear.

The Clydesdale deep pressed steel frame is heavily cross braced, giving ample strength for any emergency. A rugged four cylinder L head motor supplies an abundance of power with a minimum expenditure of fuel. The drive is taken through substantial radius rods. Long chrome vanadium springs give perfect suspension, and all suspension pins are ground accurately to size and operate in bronze bushings.

Each detail of construction is an index to the strength of the entire truck—a strength that has enabled the Clydesdale to win its spurs under conditions far harsher than you will ever impose upon it.

The Clydesdale line is *complete*, ranging in capacity up to five tons. Ask our dealer to call and demonstrate.

The Clyde Cars Co., Clyde, Ohio

Above and Opposite: "Tested in the Crucible of War — and Found Fit": Clydesdale truck advertisement, which appeared in *Literary Digest*, December 29, 1917. Most of the Clydesdale Motor Truck Company's early inventory was shipped overseas for service in World War I. The truck's wartime success became the subject of subsequent marketing campaigns.

The Literary Digest for December 29, 1917

Opposite top and bottom: Clydesdale trucks as parade floats for the Lake Shore Tire Company, San-dusky, Ohio. The "big gun" is made of tires (*courtesy of the Sandusky Library Follett House Museum Archives, Sandusky, Ohio*). *Above:* Early model Clydesdale customized as a beverage truck. Some of the earliest Clydesdale trucks, like this one, actually had steering wheels on the right side of the cab. Clydesdale engineers worked closely with engineers from the London General Omnibus Company, and may have designed their first chassis after European examples (*courtesy of the Clyde Public Library, Clyde, Ohio*).

Likewise, a January 27, 1918, advertisement that appeared in the *Chicago Tribune* described the truck's wartime reputation as proven and worthy of envy:

> Three years ago the Clydesdale truck was selected by Allied engineers for special war service in Europe. It was chosen because the basic principles of its design were closely akin to those already approved by the Allies, and because it had such an impressive record service here.
>
> The keenest commercial car designers of France and England, in joint conference with our own engineers, made certain changes in the Clydesdale specifications — changes made necessary by the extreme conditions of the war zone — changes that would better enable the Clydesdale to meet the tests of the battlefield.
>
> The perfected trucks were sent to the front, and how well they served is now a matter of his-tory. Repeat order after repeat order is eloquent testimony to their effectiveness. Clydesdale motor trucks are upholding an enviable reputation.[40]

Sometimes the owners of Clydesdale trucks indirectly helped to evoke memories of the truck's wartime success. One Clydesdale truck owned by the Lake Shore Tire Company in Sandusky, Ohio, was used repeatedly in parades to memorialize deceased local servicemen.

Clydesdale trucks gained a reputation for durability and reliability. Here, an unidentified man uses a Clydesdale truck to transport materials. Note the brackets on both sides of the radiator to help with the hauling of long length of pipe or lumber.

"The Big Gun" float featured a Clydesdale truck with World War I soldiers during a July 4, 1918, parade. The "big gun" was constructed from tires sold by the company, but the connection between their Clydesdale truck and the battlefront could not be overlooked.

By the end of World War I, the Clydesdale Motor Truck Company needed more space to complete orders. In 1918, the company acquired land and buildings from a neighboring factory. The factory land grew to approximately three and one half acres, and total factory floor space to 151,000 square feet. The expansion not only tripled the amount of building space, but also doubled the length of access to the adjacent railroad tracks. The company "found it vitally necessary to secure this property on account of its rapidly increasing business. It now has a railroad frontage of nearly 1,000 feet."[41]

The Clydesdale brand emerged from World War I with a proven record of success and reputation for reliability. With state-of-the-art expanded facilities, the company was poised for the future. Wartime success essentially propelled the company from a new-on-the-scene brand to an international player. In a letter from the company to Clydesdale truck dealers, new company vice-president, and former Signal Motor Truck Company engineer A.C. Burch noted, "Four years of war have done more for the motor truck business than could

Success on World War I battlefields left the Clydesdale Motor Truck Company poised for sales at home. Early model Clydesdale truck with an open box body owned by E. Weiler & Sons of Boston (*courtesy of the Clyde Public Library*).

have been accomplished in ten years of peace."[42] The war overseas had indeed provided unprecedented challenges and opportunities, and the Clydesdale Motor Truck Company was ready to prove that it could be successful in domestic markets.

The Sixteenth Annual Boston Automobile Show

In the spring of 1918, the still relatively new Clydesdale Motor Truck Company exhibited at the Sixteenth Annual Boston Automobile Show. This appears to be one of the earliest, if not the first, such show in which Clydesdale motor trucks appeared. The show took place in the Mechanics Building, near the Hotel Lenox, and lasted for one week, March 2–9. Sponsored by the Boston Automobile Dealers Association and the Boston Commercial Motor Vehicle Association, the wartime show was open daily, 10:00 A.M.–10:30 P.M., and the price of admission was 50 cents.

Organizers viewed the show as an important, if not supportive, part of the war effort, and a direct response to the success of American trucks on the battlefront. Boston Automobile Dealers Association president J.H. MacAlman explained:

The uppermost thought in the mind of every American must be to win the war. As American business men, we are more interested in having democracy as usual after the war than we are in

Cover from the 1918 Boston Automobile show program, which was one of the first national automobile shows in which the Clydesdale Motor Truck Company participated.

having "business as usual" during the war. It is necessary, however, that the industries of this country be kept going at as high speed as possible, so that our people may be employed at good wages and so that the proper basic structure for the Government's war program may be had.... We should, therefore, be glad and proud to be contributing to the transportation facilities of the country at this time.

The show featured over 300 exhibitors, including passenger cars, commercial trucks, tractors, and automobile accessories. Of those, 62 vendors, including Clydesdale, were commercial truck representatives. There were also trade magazine representatives, as well as vendors selling accessories such as garages and "automobile apparel." The Clydesdale Motor Truck Company occupied two exhibition booths, numbers 324 and 325. Two Clydesdale truck models, the 1½-ton and 3½-ton chassis, were on display. Live music filled the exhibition hall each day, courtesy of the Boston Philharmonic Orchestra, Bostonia Orchestra, and the Adele Nininger Orchestra.[43]

2

What Makes a Clydesdale?

The Clydesdale truck was truly an international collaboration between engineers at the company, and British and French engineers. The Clydesdale Motor Truck Company seemed to explode onto the manufacturing scene not only with a vehicle design suitable for wartime use, but also a reliable product for peacetime commercial purposes. But upon further examination, it becomes clear that the development of the Clydesdale truck was much more strategic, and ultimately a model of exceptional idea-sharing partnerships. Company officials described its development as a process of trial and error. Engineers experimented with many kinds of models until they perfected one "fundamentally correct" design.[1] Early trade journals discussed the efforts of its makers:

> The Clydesdale commercial chassis were designed at the beginning of the European war when the French and English Governments needed a large number of trucks for Army transport purposes, the design being worked out by the engineers of the Clyde Cars Company ... in consultation with the European engineers who were in America at that time endeavoring to purchase cars to suit the rigorous requirements of the European conditions.[2]

The Clydesdale model, company officials advertised, embodied "the best practices of three nations — combining the refinements of European design with the advantages of American manufacturing methods."[3]

Initially, Clydesdale engineers developed six different truck models capable of carrying a variety of loads. The smallest truck model was called the ¾, designed to carry three quarters of a ton, or 1,500 pounds. The largest model was the 5-ton truck, designed to carry loads weighing up to 10,000 pounds. Additional models increased in hauling capacities between these extremes. They included: the "1-tonner" (2,000 pounds), which was followed by the 1½-ton truck (3,000 pounds), 2-ton truck (4,000 pounds), and 3½-ton truck (7,000 pounds).[4] The 2-ton and 3½-ton truck models were frequently exported to France and England for wartime use. Prices started at $1,650 for the 1-ton model, and increased to $4,750 for the 5-ton model.

Specific models were named with numbers and letters, with each changing according to periodic redesigns or upgrades. For example, initially, the 5-ton truck model was labeled as the Model 120. A subsequent catalog, however, labeled the 5-ton model as the Model 120B. While this pattern was not consistent throughout the life of the Clydesdale Motor Truck Company, it does offer an idea of how all Clydesdale models were named, and would have been referred to in catalogs. Every chassis received an individual serial number, which was imprinted on a metal plate, mounted on the frame of the chassis. All models were under

A Model-12 Clydesdale truck chassis in front of the Clyde Public Library. Note the absence of a bunk seat on this chassis (*courtesy Clyde Heritage League, Clyde, Ohio*).

warranty—parts and construction, provided no significant alterations had been made to the truck that would affect stability, parts, or original chassis construction—for 90 days under the standard Clydesdale Motor Truck Company guarantee.[5]

Each Clydesdale truck chassis featured numerous components, which together produced what company officials described in *Motor Age* as "a scientifically right assembly."[6] In a post-war reference to President Woodrow Wilson's Fourteen Points plan, one advertisement that appeared in the *Chicago Tribune* on May 25, 1919, lists "Fourteen Points of Clydesdale superiority," which were key to "putting the Clydesdale to service in every civilized country on the globe."[7] They provide a window not only into the unique characteristics of a Clydesdale truck, but also the distinguished craftsmanship poured into every chassis:

Point 1—The Clydesdale controller, an exclusive Clydesdale feature, keeps the truck's speed constant regardless of condition of road or load. It practically forces even an inexperienced driver to handle a truck with all the care and judgment of a thoroughly trained operator.
Point 2—Clydesdale radiator is made up of seamless copper tubing with cast aluminum tanks and sides. No soldered seams to spring a leak. It is protected by heavy aluminum guard bars.
Point 3—Heavy pressed radius rods are used, swiveled at the rear end to prevent all possibility of straining or breaking.
Point 4—All springs and pins are bushed with bronze. Every part and feature of the truck down to the most minute detail is given extra long life.

Clydesdale
MOTOR TRUCKS

The Most Practical Truck Design in Existence

Developed from twenty years' actual operating experience by the London General Omnibus Company, London, England. Taken as a basis four years ago by Clydesdale and adapted to universal service conditions—now featuring valuable Clydesdale improvements of an exclusive character, among which is the famous Clydesdale Automatic Controller. The fitness of Clydesdale for the most strenuous and gruelling service is shown by the fact that upwards of one thousand Clydesdale trucks have been purchased by France and England, largely for army transportation work.

Six Clydesdale Superiorities

Clydesdale Automatic Controller
Worm gear drive rear axle
Straight copper tube radiator
Separate unit four speed gear box
Massive pressed steel frame
Right hand drive and control

Established Dealers

Deliveries are now being made of all Clydesdale models. Our specially condensed method of boxing enables us to land Clydesdales at much less than others. We have several territories still open and are desirous of making reliable connections. We will gladly mail you our catalogs and other interesting literature. Cable inquiries are invited.

"Cromotor New York"

Five Models: 30, 45, 65, 90 and 120 c.w.t.

Clyde Cars Company
44 WHITEHALL ST., NEW YORK CITY
U. S. A.

"The Most Practical Truck Design in Existence": This early Clydesdale advertisement appeared in the August 1918 issue of *Dun's International Review* and highlighted the truck's relationship with the London General Omnibus Company. The left side of the page features "Six Clydesdale Superiorities," with the first being the Clydesdale Automatic Controller, followed by the "Worm gear drive rear axle, Straight copper tube radiator, Separate unit four speed gear box, Massive pressed steel frame," and "Right hand drive and control." In the foreground of the advertisement, a New York distributor of Clydesdale trucks is prominently featured (*courtesy of Google Books*).

Point 5 — A heavy channel steel frame is used of much greater strength and depth than is found on the ordinary truck. It is deeper in the center where the greatest load comes. Thus all units are kept in true alignment.

Point 6 — The Clydesdale is accessible to a surprising degree. Every motional part can be withdrawn and is get-at-able without disturbing the main structure.

Point 7 — Silico manganese steel springs with long, wide, flat plates and large bushed eyes are used in the Clydesdale. Spring breakage is almost unknown.

Point 8 — A four-speed transmission is used, located amidships with large Timken Roller Bearings and wide gear faces.

Point 9 — Large bearing surfaces and fine workmanship insure [sic] long life and ample power to Clydesdale motors.

Point 10 — An extra heavy, irreversible gear steering mechanism is used with large sized steering arms that reduces danger of accidents to a minimum.

Point 11 — A multiple disc dry plate clutch is used, the finest clutch mechanism found in any truck.

Point 12 — Four large universal joints are used on the drive shaft.

Point 13 — An extra capacity 30-gallon gasoline tank is provided, thus fitting the Clydesdale ideally for long, cross-country hauling.

Point 14 — The design of the Clydesdale follows very closely that of the London General Omnibus Truck — the most famous make of truck in the world. Into Clydesdale construction is put the greatest fund of definite data on truck operation ever compiled by any truck manufacturer.[8]

In addition, general advertisements for the 2½-3-ton Model 6-X highlight over 20 different features of the Clydesdale truck, including not only the previously listed "fourteen points," but also the steel-covered and optimally tilted veneer dashboard, high pressure lubricating system, double-acting brakes, cam and lever steering gear, extra large filler cap, and an extra large and "convenient" foot step, compared to a more traditional running board. Many of the Clydesdale's distinctive transmissions and clutches were custom-manufactured for the company by the Brown-Lipe Gear Company of Syracuse, New York. Each Clydesdale transmission featured four speeds, or four forward gears, plus one reverse gear. In addition, the full floating front and rear axles were manufactured by the Timken Roller Bearing Axle Company of St. Louis, and later Canton, Ohio.

According to company brochures, all of the Clydesdale chassis were painted a standard gray color. They all featured distinctive pyramidal headlamps with an octagon-shaped front. Almost all early Clydesdale trucks featured steel spoke wheels, except for models with hauling capacities less than 3½ tons, which included wood spoke wheels. By 1922, however, all Clydesdale truck wheels had been upgraded to steel discs or metal hollow spokes. Also by 1922, all of the chassis placed the driver on the left side of the truck. Prior to 1922, Clydesdale models could be ordered to seat the driver on the right side of the truck, in what was perhaps a homage to the London General Omnibus model.[9]

A Scientifically Right Assembly

Five distinctive components of the Clydesdale trucks were featured prominently in much of the company's advertising, and become closely associated with the Clydesdale brand. They included the chassis itself — Clydesdale's custom-designed pressed steel frame. They also included the automatic controller, copper tubing radiator, and engine. In addition, many of the Clydesdale parts were made with cast aluminum, which was innovative, even cutting-edge, for the time.

Here is a Good Looking Truck

When you see a spirited, trim limbed horse come prancing down the street with neck arched and tail and glossy mane floating in the breeze, you know inherently that it is a thoroughbred.

Perfection speaks for itself. The same is true of perfection in a manufactured product. One glance at the trim, clean cut lines of the Clydesdale and you recognize that same thoroughbred look.

The sturdy appearance; the absence of surplus weight; the balance; the look of brutish power; make you realize immediately that the truck will stand up under the most trying service.

That Clydesdales do stand up is a matter of history. And that they are particularly well adapted for the Telephone Business is borne out by the experience of Western Electric Company and other Clydesdale users.

Interesting literature will be mailed upon request.

No Other Truck Has It
"The Driver Under the Hood"

One to Five Tons Net Load

THE CLYDESDALE MOTOR TRUCK COMPANY, CLYDE, OHIO

CLYDESDALE

A WORLD PROVEN MOTOR TRUCK

"Here is a Good Looking Truck": This Clydesdale advertisement appeared in the March 20, 1920, issue of *Telephony* magazine, and compared the truck to a prize-winning horse: "When you see a spirited, trim limbed horse come prancing down the street with neck arched and tail and glossy mane floating in the breeze, you know inherently that it is a thoroughbred.... One glance at the trim, clean cut lines of the Clydesdale and you recognize that same thoroughbred look." The Clydesdale Automatic Controller is also featured prominently in the foreground.

Top: A finished Clydesdale chassis. Often, customers would custom order cabs and bodies from third-party body builders, which allowed every Clydesdale chassis to be designed according to the owner's needs. *Bottom:* A fleet of several Clydesdale trucks, with enclosed cabs, photographed with their drivers.

An early Clydesdale standard chassis dashboard and controls.

Finally, it is important to remember that, as chassis manufacturers, the Clydesdale company produced only the frame and working parts of the truck. Initially, the Clydesdale Motor Truck Company did not manufacture truck bodies, but rather, provided specifications for bodies, which could be followed by third-party body builders. By not having their bodies mounted in the factory, Clydesdale trucks were completely customizable according to customer needs. This also meant that Clydesdale was part of a professional ecosystem that included manufacturers, dealers, and third party body builders. It is worth examining the five most prominent Clydesdale features, and the variety of ways in which customers tailored trucks for both professional and everyday tasks.

The Car Foundation — A Massive Frame

Clydesdale frames have very deep center sections giving exceptional strength. The frame members are perfectly straight, having no insweeps and having an equal web the full length, but properly tapered toward front and rear so as to avoid excessive weight of material where the frame stresses are considerably less. Heavy cross members with large gusset plates are used throughout the length, and special care is taken to have the springs mounted so as to minimize the driving shocks to the frame and reduce frame distortion to a minimum. All cross members and brackets are hot riveted to the frame.[10]

The foundation of the Clydesdale chassis, and one of its most prominently marketed features, was the pressed steel frame. It was an exclusive design, as detailed above. Its center depth

Top: A later model Clydesdale standard chassis dashboard and controls, with an enclosed cab and windshield. *Bottom:* Timken worm gears drove the axles of all early Clydesdale trucks. This cutout view of the rear axle offers a closer look at how the Clydesdale truck was powered and assembled.

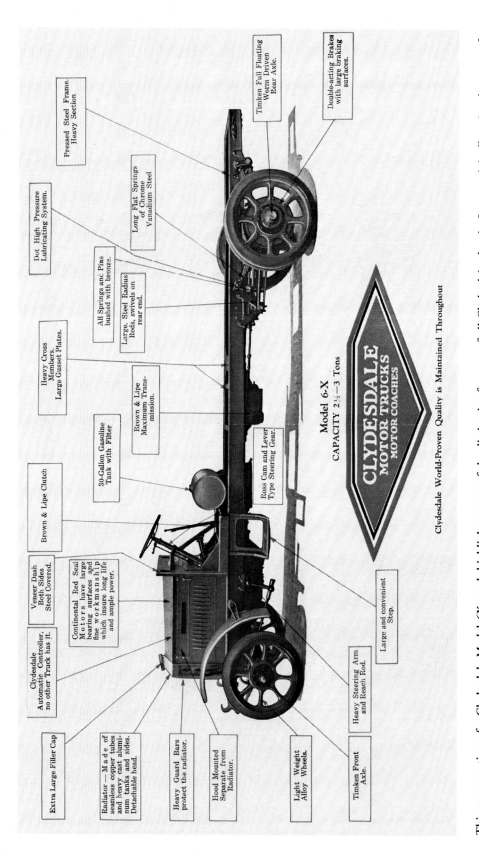

Pressed Steel Frame.
Heavy Section

Timken Full Floating
Worm Driven
Rear Axle.

Double-acting Brakes
with large braking
surfaces.

Dot High Pressure
Lubricating System.

Long Flat Springs
of Chrome
Vanadium Steel

All Springs and Pins
bushed with bronze.

Large, Steel Radius
Rods, swivels on
rear end.

Heavy Cross
Members.
Large Gusset Plates.

Brown & Lipe
Maximum Trans-
mission.

Brown & Lipe Clutch

30-Gallon Gasoline
Tank with Filter

Ross Cam and Lever
Type Steering Gear.

Model 6-X
CAPACITY 2½—3 Tons

CLYDESDALE
MOTOR TRUCKS
MOTOR COACHES

Clydesdale World-Proven Quality is Maintained Throughout

Veneer Dash
Both Sides
Steel Covered.

Clydesdale
Automatic Controller,
no other Truck has it.

Continental Red Seal
M o t o r s have large
bearing surfaces and
heavy cast alumi-
num tanks and sides.
Detachable head.

Large and convenient
Step.

Extra Large Filler Cap

Radiator — M a d e of
seamless copper tubes
and heavy cast alumi-
num tanks and sides.
Detachable head.

Heavy Guard Bars
protect the radiator.

Hood Mounted
Separate from
Radiator.

Heavy Steering Arm
and Reach Rod.

Light Weight
Alloy Wheels.

Timken Front
Axle.

This cross section of a Clydesdale Model-6X truck highlights many of the distinctive features of all Clydesdale chassis. It was originally printed as part of a fold-out brochure. The company produced similar brochures for each of their models.

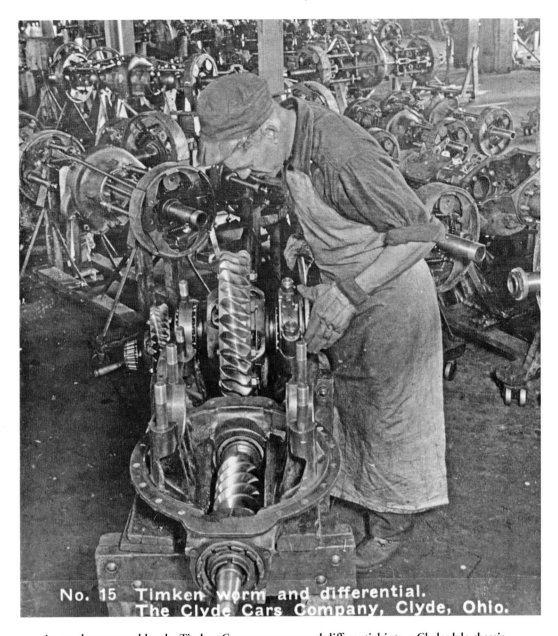

No. 15 Timken worm and differential.
The Clyde Cars Company, Clyde, Ohio.

An employee assembles the Timken Company worm and differential into a Clydesdale chassis.

of 10 inches was unusual within the truck manufacturing industry. The frame was developed not only for strength and durability, but also flexibility. One brochure described the frame as providing one "big safety factor for every possible contingency of service."[11]

Other chassis on the market sometimes used a rolled channel steel frame, which Clydesdale officials described as "rigid," and prone to getting out of alignment "after a short period of service," or "after being subjected to stress."[12]

The Clydesdale frame, according to engineers, was "stronger than usual in American practice."[13] The design was modeled after frames used by the London General Omnibus

Top: The Clydesdale's pressed steel frame included deep center sections to create a stronger, more stable chassis foundation, as seen in this front view of a finished Clydesdale chassis. *Bottom:* Clydesdale truck with winch equipment mounted behind the cab offers a clear view of the chassis's pressed steel frame.

Company. Engineers maintained that the deep center and lighter weight tapered ends increased the strength of the frame without increasing its overall weight. In addition, the center section, with an increased surface area compared to thinner frames, allowed for the use of more rivets to fasten brackets and additional parts as the truck was completed. This, claimed company officials, contributed to a more stable, secure chassis product.

The Driver Under the Hood

The automatic controller, nicknamed "The Driver Under the Hood," was a standard feature, and *the* most prominent selling point, of every Clydesdale truck chassis. Company officials boasted: "No other truck has it."[14] Patented by Krebs Commercial Car Company engineers Frank Bachle and Walter Wells in 1914, the Clydesdale controller was an enhanced variable speed governor. It was called the "controller" because it did more than simply control the maximum truck speed. Unlike other standard governors, it controlled the truck at *all* speeds.[15]

Company officials described the Clydes-

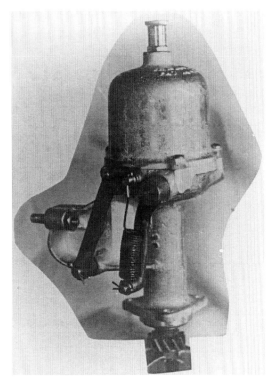

Clydesdale's patented Automatic Controller, or "Driver Under the Hood," was a multispeed engine governor that not only reduced speed, but also increased speed, making it function like modern cruise control.

dale automatic controller as the "most ingenious and most practical speed governing device ever employed on motor trucks." From the driver's perspective, it acted similarly to modern cruise control technology.[16] The Clydesdale driver could set the throttle at a desired speed, and the automatic controller would maintain that speed, accelerating or decelerating as conditions required. A Clydesdale advertisement explained:

> It automatically controls the operation of the motor, opening the throttle when the truck strikes mud, snow, an upgrade, or when the clutch is thrown in, accelerating the motor smoothly and evenly to take care of the increased pull, keeping the truck moving at a constant rate of speed.... Then when the truck strikes smooth going, or when the clutch is thrown out, "The Driver Under the Hood" closes up the throttle, preventing useless, destructive "racing."[17]

All the driver had to do, according to Clydesdale engineers, was watch traffic, steer, and operate the foot pedals.

In September 1919, the Clydesdale Motor Truck Company conducted a public test of the controller, and published the results in newspapers around the country. A four-mile course was plotted near the factory in Clyde. The first two miles included various hills and "a number of grades of various pitches," while the other two miles were almost completely flat. Louis Krebs, in the presence of witnesses, started the truck, and set the throttle at approximately 20 miles per hour. Time was recorded at the start; at the two-mile mark,

Top: Underneath the hood of a Clydesdale truck. The automatic controller, or "Driver Under the Hood," is clearly visible in the foreground, while the cooling fan and copper tubing radiator are seen at the right. *Bottom:* Front of a pamphlet advertisement for the Clydesdale Automatic Controller. Clydesdale marketed the automatic controller prominently, including producing special brochures, like this one.

The CLYDESDALE
AUTOMATIC CONTROLLER
(The Driver under the Hood)

A remarkable device, *found only on Clydesdale Trucks,* which makes any driver an expert driver.

It automatically controls the operation of the motor, opening the throttle when the truck strikes mud, snow, an upgrade, or when the clutch is thrown in, accelerating the motor smoothly and evenly to take care of the increased pull, keeping the truck moving at a constant rate of speed, just as the most experienced driver would do if he had nothing else to do but watch the motor. It absolutely protects every moving part of the truck from the unnecessary wear and strains which sudden accelerating by an inexperienced or careless driver always causes.

Then when the truck strikes smooth "going" or when the clutch is thrown out, "The Driver Under the Hood" closes up the throttle, preventing useless, destructive "racing."

Driving a Clydesdale Truck for the first time is a novel experience. It is so easy. All the driver has to do is to set the throttle lever for the speed he wishes to maintain—then watch the road, handle the wheel and work the clutch and brake pedals.

"The Driver Under the Hood" does the rest.

It saves gas.

It saves motor parts—bearings, universals, rear axles and tires.

It does away with the most serious difficulty which confronts motor truck operators—securing careful, experienced drivers. It is literally saving thousands of dollars in upkeep and repair bills for Clydesdale owners.

And drivers like the Clydesdale Controller.

It makes driving so easy. Gives them all their time and attention for watching the road. Helps them avoid accidents. Helps them show low operating costs and big haulage records and thus put them into line for promotions and better pay.

The Clydesdale Controller is *found only on Clydesdale Trucks.* It is only one of a number of important improvements on the Clydesdale which has made it famous throughout the world.

There are five Clydesdale models, varying from one to five tons capacity.

The Driver Under the Hood

Built by
The Clyde Cars Company
Clyde, Ohio

This is one of many Clydesdales operating in Pittsburgh

Inside pamphlet advertisement for the Clydesdale Automatic Controller. The controller is featured prominently in the center, while an illustration of a Clydesdale truck dominates the foreground.

The "Driver Under the Hood"

The "Driver Under the Hood" is not an ordinary governor. It automatically and skillfully regulates the flow of power to immediately meet every changing road or load condition. It keeps the speed constant, prevents racing of the motor and clashing of gears.

NO OTHER TRUCK HAS IT

How the "Driver Under the Hood" Saves Effort

About all the driver of a Clydesdale truck has to do is watch the road and steer. There is a "Driver Under the Hood", an automatic controller, which performs most of his work.

When once the truck is set for a desired speed, the "Driver Under the Hood" automatically maintains that speed no matter if the road leads up hill, down hill or through mud or sand.

This little instrument makes it impossible to race the motor even when the clutch is jammed out suddenly; and by preventing clashing of gears, makes shifting speeds an easy operation.

It is impossible to appreciate, without actually seeing a Clydesdale in operation, the amazing way in which this "Driver Under the Hood" saves effort. But ask the driver of any Clydesdale truck to tell you what *he* thinks of it.

The Clydesdale dealer proposition is a particularly alluring one.

1 to 5 Ton Capacities

THE CLYDESDALE MOTOR TRUCK CO.
CLYDE, OHIO

CLYDESDALE

Please Mention "Motor West" When Writing to the Advertiser

"How the Driver Under the Hood Saves Effort": This advertisement appeared in the January 1, 1920 issue of *Motor West.* It featured the "Driver Under the Hood," which Clydesdale officials insisted allowed the driver to operate the truck with less "effort" than what might be required for other trucks. The ad also features the "Clydesdale" name with a crosshatched design, rather than the more traditional solid black lettering.

Put your driver behind the wheel and let <u>him</u> tell you

NO OTHER truck has the Clydesdale, "driver under the hood," the automatic controller.

Frankly, a description of this exclusive feature is beyond us.

We've tried to write it. Clydesdale dealers have tried to talk it.

But, when the claim is made that this simple instrument holds the truck to a predetermined speed up hill or down, on paved streets, thru sand and mud; that it is prevention against gear stripping; and that it effects a really great saving in fuel and tires our claims sound presumptuous and are greeted with skepticism.

We have been forced to the decision that, like the first ride in an airplane, the performance of the Clydesdale controller is indescribable, and that an actual demonstration is the only proof to support our claims.

We might go on with an argument that the other features of the Clydesdale are unusually good. But we believe that our showing through eight years of successful manufacture in which we have put trucks into service in 26 countries from Iceland to South Africa under every condition of roads and climate is sufficient evidence of its ability to perform satisfactorily.

When such concerns as the Standard Oil of Cal., Midwest Refining Co., Regal Shoe Company, Western Electric Company, Standard Sanitary Manufacturing Company and others have picked Clydesdale out of a field of good trucks in vigorous competitive tests there should be no question in your mind as to their service qualities.

But, we want you to know why Clydesdale "driver under the hood" goes a step farther in the perfection of truck performance. Get into the cab of one of our trucks and find out for yourself. Put your driver behind the wheel and *let him tell you.*

No Other Truck Has It

Clydesdale's Automatic Controller

"The Driver Under the Hood"

One to Five Tons Net Load

THE CLYDESDALE MOTOR TRUCK COMPANY
CLYDE, OHIO

CLYDESDALE

"Put your driver behind the wheel and let <u>him</u> tell you": This Clydesdale advertisement from the November 29, 1919, issue of *Literary Digest* was part of a continuing series that appeared in the popular magazine, featuring pithy statements, line drawings and the Clydesdale Automatic Controller.

which was the finish of the hills; and at the four-mile mark, which was at the finish of the level two miles of road. The throttle had not been adjusted from start to finish, but similar times were recorded for both halves of the course. "The time for the hilly two miles was 6 minutes and 8 seconds. The time for the level stretch of two miles was 6 minutes and 5 seconds. Just 3 seconds difference in time."[18] This very public experiment helped to prove company claims about the Clydesdale automatic controller.

In addition to controlling speed for the driver, the Clydesdale automatic controller offered several other benefits. According to company officials, such a governing mechanism saved gas. It also cut down on wear and tear on certain parts such as bearings, universals, axles, and tires. Perhaps most importantly, the controller did away with the "most serious difficulty which confronts motor truck operators — securing careful, experienced drivers."[19] A Clydesdale distributor explained, "One of the most serious difficulties in the operation of motor trucks has been the fact that inexperienced or careless drivers are liable to race the motor when declutching or by sudden accelerating, which prematurely shortens the life of the truck."[20] Finally, the controller allowed drivers to focus on the road, which led to all-around safer driving.

What was it like to drive a truck with the Clydesdale automatic controller? Dealers often described the first-time Clydesdale driving experience as "novel," with drivers "amazed at the ease."[21] The same themes appeared in much of Clydesdale's advertising. The automatic controller was featured prominently in almost all Clydesdale advertisements, often with pithy statements about how drivers simply could not live without that other "driver under the hood."

> *"Why didn't you tell me it would do this?"*[22]
> *"Put your driver behind the wheel and let him tell you"*[23]
> *"You Will Believe When You See It"*[24]
> *"Try to induce your driver to run a truck without it"*[25]
> *"I Wish I Could Buy Them to Install on My Other Trucks"*[26]
> *"You probably won't believe it until you see it work"*[27]
> *"Two drivers on your truck are better than one"*[28]
> *"Why drivers swear* by *this truck, not* at *it."*[29]

Such praise for the Clydesdale automatic controller was exceptional within the truck manufacturing industry. Many truck owners questioned the utility of a device that sought to regulate a fundamental feature of trucks — speed. The 1921 *Motor Truck Manual,* which was produced annually by the editorial staff of the *American Automobile Digest,* noted that there is "great difference of opinion as to the value of a governor."[30] While some drivers thought it simply limited the power of an engine, others saw it as protecting the engine from deleterious effects of excessive speeds. For Clydesdale owners, however, the automatic controller was far more than a typical governor, and came to symbolize fundamental function, or the provision of a service, to drivers. At least one company advertisement compared the automatic controller's assistance to a driver to the coal propelling a steam engine: "Just as the locomotive engineer looks to his fireman to see that enough steam is maintained to pull the load, the driver of a Clydesdale truck depends upon the Clydesdale Controller to keep the motor going at whatever speed is necessary to pull the load."[31]

To Clydesdale engineers, the automatic controller was the most significant feature of the truck, and ultimately responsible for sales. A trade journal noted during World War I:

The Literary Digest for December 27, 1919 129

Why didn't you tell me it would do this?

YOU men all say this to Clydesdale dealers after you have had the performance of the truck demonstrated to you.

All of our dealers, and we at the factory, have finally come to the conclusion that "The Driver Under the Hood," Clydesdale's automatic controller, cannot be described in words or writing.

You are hardly expected to believe us when we say that "The Driver Under the Hood", an exclusive, patented Clydesdale feature, really has more to do with the driving of the truck than the operator himself. It eliminates use of the accelerator in gear shifting, driving through crowded traffic, it saves fuel, tires and wear on the entire driving mechanism.

Just go and ride in the truck. Drive it yourself, or let one of your drivers operate it. Find out what an excellent truck has been evolved from our eight years' building experience in which time we have installed trucks in thirty-one countries throughout the world. We have sold fleets of trucks to such big users as the West Penn Power Company, the American Tin and Terne Plate Company, Frick Coke Company and many others.

Watch the effects of "The Driver Under the Hood;" then you will say, "Why didn't you tell me it would do this?"

No Other Truck Has It
"The Driver Under the Hood"

One to Five Tons Net Load

THE CLYDESDALE MOTOR TRUCK COMPANY
CLYDE, OHIO

CLYDESDALE

"Why didn't you tell me it would do this?" This Clydesdale advertisement from the December 27, 1919, issue of *Literary Digest* encouraged customers to try the Clydesdale truck, and assured them that they would be asking that headline question.

The Literary Digest for January 3, 1920   71

I Wish I Could Buy Them to Install on My Other Trucks

BUT there is no truck other than Clydesdale which has, or can have, "The Driver Under the Hood." This Automatic Controller is a patented and exclusive Clydesdale feature.

Can you imagine a truck which will maintain a fixed speed, eight, twelve or fifteen miles per hour, whatever the driver sets the throttle for, and maintain that speed, uphill and down, through sand and mud, on paved streets or any other road condition, without the driver paying any attention to throttle or accelerator.

Here is a device which controls the engine automatically. When shifting gears the engine idles in the shifts, due to the action of the controller, and through the operation of the same instrument picks up the truck speed when the clutch is engaged. It saves countless shocks on the driving mechanism, prolongs the life of tires, cuts down gasoline bills— all done by a simple and fool-proof instrument.

Do these claims sound preposterous? Probably they do. The least we can ask is that you visit the Clydesdale dealer and make him furnish the proof by demonstration.

He will show you many more excellent features in Clydesdale construction. You will watch the performance of a truck which has proved its worth in eight years of successful manufacture; a truck which has won out in competitive tests and been accepted by such concerns as National Gypsum Co., Riverside Storage Co., Detroit; and Langley and Michaels, San Francisco.

One to Five Tons Net Load

THE CLYDESDALE MOTOR TRUCK COMPANY
CLYDE, OHIO

No Other Truck Has It

"The Driver Under the Hood"

CLYDESDALE

"I Wish I Could Buy Them to Install on My Other Trucks": This Clydesdale advertisement is from the January 3, 1920, issue of *Literary Digest*. The illustration in the right lower corner features a line of Clydesdale trucks, while the text asks customers to try the truck at their nearest dealership.

The Literary Digest for January 24, 1920   123

Try to induce your driver to run a truck without it

Take your driver to the establishment of the Clydesdale dealer and arrange for a demonstration.

Let the dealer show the man who handles your trucks how Clydesdale's Automatic Controller, "The Driver Under the Hood", eliminates a racing engine with its consequent tearing strains; permits a fixed speed under practically every driving condition without the use of throttle or accelerator.

Let him have the proof of the savings effected by this simple instrument — how it practically prohibits stripping of gears, saves tires and gasoline and reduces the wear and tear on the truck to a remarkable extent.

He will tell you why Clydesdale is the greatest truck for the driver—why the Automatic Controller, an exclusive patented feature, coupled with a truck which has proved its every unit thru eight years successful building, makes the most profitable investment for you.

Take stock in the proof of others. The Chicágo Artificial Ice Company, W. N. McAbee Power Company, Hawkeye Fuel Company, of Spokane and many others have selected Clydesdale in vigorous competitive tests because Clydesdale outperformed its competitors.

No Other Truck Has It
"The Driver Under the Hood"

One to Five Tons Net Load

THE CLYDESDALE MOTOR TRUCK COMPANY
CLYDE, OHIO

CLYDESDALE

"Try to induce your driver to run a truck without it": This Clydesdale advertisement from the January 24, 1920, issue of *Literary Digest* features an illustration of a crane loading materials into the back of a Clydesdale truck.

You probably won't believe it until you see it work

You have heard so many claims for unusual performance made by different truck manufacturers for their product that we are inclined to hesitate in making the statements we do about the performance of Clydesdales equipped with the Automatic Controller, " The Driver Under the Hood."

Yet, the most convincing proof is the actual performance of the truck itself. In the sketch below is a Clydesdale dropping from a stretch of concrete into a road of deep mud ruts—but the driver of that truck need touch nothing but his steering wheel and clutch.

He pushes out the clutch and the truck speed drops from twelve miles per hour down to a safe pace for entering the ruts. The engine idles down automatically. Once in the mud he lets in the clutch again. The truck speed gradually comes up to twelve miles per hour— the speed at which the truck was travelling on the concrete.

All this is done automatically by Clydesdale's " Driver Under the Hood." Yet, this is only one of the duties of this exclusive Clydesdale feature. We might give scores of reasons why we claim it is the greatest saving feature ever placed on a truck. But you probably would not believe us—so go and see it work. That's the only proof.

There has never been an unsatisfactory Clydesdale in eight years building. Such concerns as Diamond Ice & Fuel Company, Spokane; the Florida Citrus Exchange, and the Sullivan Cartage Company, Milwaukee, have adopted Clydesdales.

No Other Truck Has It
"The Driver Under the Hood"

One to Five Tons Net Load

THE CLYDESDALE MOTOR TRUCK COMPANY
CLYDE, OHIO

CLYDESDALE

"You probably won't believe it until you see it work": This Clydesdale advertisement from the February 28, 1920, issue of *Literary Digest* features a confident claim: "There has never been an unsatisfactory Clydesdale in eight years of building."

"The controller is used exclusively on the Clydesdale truck and is one of the features that made the truck so popular with European engineers that the entire output of the Clyde factory was purchased for use in France."[32] During a subsequent interview in 1920, Clydesdale company vice-president A.C. Burch credited the controller with many truck sales: "To one small piece of mechanism placed under the hood of every Clydesdale truck must go the credit for the larger part of the phenomenal demand for Clydesdale trucks within the past four years."[33]

As part of a clever marketing campaign that took place during the spring of 1919, the Clydesdale company sponsored a national contest, which asked customers to answer one question: "What does the Clydesdale controller do?" The ad appeared in trade magazines for one month. The company offered prize money—$100 for first place, $50 for second place, $25 for third place, and $5 for five runners-up—to anyone who owned a Clydesdale truck and would provide a short statement about what the Clydesdale automatic controller did for their business, or daily truck driving. The three contest judges were A.C. Burch, vice-president of the company; Wallace Blood, member of the Society of Automotive Engineers; and Darwin Hatch, editor from *Motor Age*. Clydesdale company officials hoped to gather personal testimony for use in future marketing materials: "Users of the Clydesdale Truck say we don't do our Controller justice in our advertising, so we ask them to help us."[34] In the end, the company received approximately 100 entries.

THE CLYDESDALE CONTROLLER: Q & A

The Clydesdale automatic controller raised questions among potential customers, who were unfamiliar with it, or may have been used to driving motor trucks with other types of governors. An informative "Question and Answer Book about the Clydesdale Controller," published in 1919, sought to assuage fears of operating challenges and provide customers with practical knowledge about the controller. Fourteen questions were taken directly from customer letters and answered. Read even today, many of the questions help to explain exactly how the controller worked and affected Clydesdale drivers. The questions provide a glimpse into how customers thought about the new technology of the motor truck.

Q: Is the Clydesdale controller simple?
A: It is extremely simple—will last the life of the truck. A centrifugal governor driven by a bevel gear from the pump shaft is attached to the throttle rod through a lever and spring. The pull between the spring and the centrifugal governor is balanced. Changing the throttle lever changes the tension on the spring, thus changing the motor speed and the truck rate. Suppose the truck is moving at 10 miles an hour, with the motor moving at 1000 rpm. Suppose that it comes to a stretch of sand. The motor slows down. The centrifugal governor consequently starts to slow up. The balance between the spring and the governor is destroyed. Instantly, the spring begins to pull the motor up to the fixed speed required to keep the truck moving at 10 miles per hour, and restores the balance between the spring and the governor. When the truck strikes smooth going again, this whole process is reversed. This is all done instantly.

Q: How does the controller act when the truck strikes a down grade?
A: When the truck strikes the top of a hill, the heavy load on the motor is relieved. As it starts down the hill, the motor would have a tendency to race. The Clydesdale controller prevents it. It automatically closes the carburetor throttle, keeping the truck moving at the same speed, unless the grade is so steep that the momentum of the truck itself would carry it faster. Then, of course, it would be necessary to apply the brake.

The Literary Digest for March 27, 1920   59

Is truck driving difficult on the straightaway or in the pinch?

There is minimum of wear and tear on a truck when it is rolling along a smooth stretch of road. The big strains come in the pinch.

Clydesdale's Automatic Controller, "The Driver Under the Hood," positively and automatically relieves the truck of the major portion of these strains.

Below is a sketch of a Clydesdale truck pulling out from under a load of cinders. The driver opens his throttle part way, then with his clutch he does all the rest of the work. With the clutch out the engine automatically idles. With the clutch engaged the engine gradually picks up its load—all automatically, without attention on the part of the driver.

It is impossible to race the engine or drop the clutch in with the engine running too fast. Thus, tires, driving mechanism and the entire truck are relieved of the breaking-down strain which the use of a manually-operated accelerator incurs.

But this is only one thing "The Driver Under the Hood" does. Ask for a demonstration. See for yourself the remarkable performance of Clydesdale.

In our eight years of truck building we have placed Clydesdale in thirty-five countries throughout the world. We have sold trucks to such companies as the Timken-Detroit Axle Company, Goodyear Tire and Rubber Company, and the Edwards Electric Company of New York. This should be evidence to you that the truck is a thoroughly competent performer.

No Other Truck Has It

"The Driver Under the Hood"

One to Five Tons Net Load

THE CLYDESDALE MOTOR TRUCK COMPANY

CLYDE, OHIO

CLYDESDALE
A WORLD PROVEN MOTOR TRUCK

"Is truck driving difficult on the straightaway or in the pinch?" This Clydesdale advertisement from the March 27, 1920, issue of *Literary Digest* features a Clydesdale truck pulling out from under a load of cinders.

Did You Ever Drive One of Your Own Trucks?

IF every truck buyer had risen from the ranks of truck drivers he would make his selection of a truck in a much different way. The man who is behind the wheel of a truck, eight to twelve hours a day, knows the terrific strains of starting and stopping, accelerating and braking, not only on the mechanism but on himself.

Clydesdale drivers soon forget these factors which have worried them on other trucks. "The Driver Under the Hood", the remarkable automatic controlling device on the Clydesdale, has relieved the driver and the machine of the most frequent source of trouble in the usual truck.

When the gears are shifted the engine speed is right for the shift. When the truck is accelerating it does so automatically up to the speed set by the throttle. Regardless of the going the truck maintains this even speed until the throttle is moved. If the driver is forced to throw out his clutch he does not have a racing engine. He has little else to do but steer.

It seems hardly possible that a simple mechanism such as "The Driver Under the Hood" could perform these tasks better than the driver himself. However, we are ready, through any of our distributors, to prove that such is the case.

For the past eight years Clydesdale trucks distributed throughout thirty-five countries of the world have proved themselves to be above the average in service rendered. Such companies as Penn Storage & Van Co., Philadelphia —Perry, Buxton & Doane, Boston—and The American Glue Company, Pittsburg, have proved to their own satisfaction that Clydesdales are right.

One to Five Tons Net Load

THE CLYDESDALE MOTOR TRUCK COMPANY
CLYDE, OHIO

No Other Truck Has It

"The Driver under the Hood"

The Clydesdale
Automatic
Controller

A World Proven Motor Truck

"Did You Ever Drive One of Your Own Trucks?" This Clydesdale advertisement from the May 1, 1920, issue of *Literary Digest* was the last advertisement in a continuing series that appeared in the popular magazine, featuring the Clydesdale Automatic Controller. It appears to be a direct appeal to the everyday truck driver, rather than the commercial fleet owner.

What Does the
CLYDESDALE
Controller Do?

WE offer a First Prize of $100, a Second Prize of $50, a Third Prize of $25 and Five Honor Prizes of $5 each, for the best answers to this question.

In case of a tie between two or more contestants, the full amount of the prize will be awarded to each.

THIS contest is open to anyone who owns or operates a Clydesdale Truck. What we want is practical testimony from practical men. Literary ability cuts no figure one way or the other.

Write a sentence or a short description telling what you have found that the Clydesdale Controller accomplishes in the operation of the Clydesdale Truck—what it does for the driver or what it does for the owner. Use ten words or a hundred as you please.

We want to use the material you send us in getting to the truck-buying public the real importance of this device. Users of the Clydesdale Truck say that we don't do our Controller justice in our advertising, so we ask them to help us.

BOARD OF JUDGES:

A. C. BURCH
Vice-President
The Clyde Cars Company

WALLACE B. BLOOD
Member S. A. E.
The Green, Fulton, Cunningham Co.

DARWIN S. HATCH
Editor
Motor Age

Contest Closes April 1st, 1919   Address all Entries to Contest Department

CLYDESDALE MOTOR TRUCKS, CLYDE, OHIO

The advertisements in MoToR are indexed. See MoToR's Classified Index on pages 24a and 24b.

(10)

In March 1918, the Clydesdale Motor Truck Company sponsored a contest during which customers were asked to answer the question: "What does the Clydesdale Controller do?" The contest was advertised in national trade magazines, like this one, *Motor Age*. The winning entries from the contest were not located in published form, but the company did run follow-up advertisements featuring some of the entrants' comments.

CLYDESDALE

The Final Touch in Truck Efficiency

Dealers

There is no truck that will sell on demonstration like the Clydesdale. Its appearance denotes its strength; its performance, due to the Automatic Controller, is a revelation. Our service co-operation with you rounds out a dealer proposition which is bound to return to you a liberal profit and maintain for you, year after year, an ever-increasing list of not only satisfied, but enthusiastic customers.

On every kind of road or trail, in all varieties of climatic conditions, carrying loads of every description, operated by able drivers and inexperienced ones of almost every nationality—the Clydesdale has proven itself a truck of enduring strength; a truck of balanced worth, the entire assembly as efficient as each individual part.

But the final touch in truck efficiency—exclusive with Clydesdale—is the Automatic Controller, "The Driver Under the Hood," an instrument which eliminates inexpert handling of the throttle by taking the control of the engine very largely out of the driver's hands.

In our last advertisement we offered prizes to drivers and owners of Clydesdale Trucks who would describe most completely and in the most easily understood way the remarkable, almost human, performance of "The Driver Under the Hood." Our board of judges is weighing the merits of hundreds of letters already received—letters written by those who drive and own and therefore know the performance of this truck which may be operated, successfully and economically, by inexperienced drivers.

One driver goes as far as to say that, "If the gear shifting and steering were automatic, the Clydesdale Controller would run the car." Yet, his statement is true, remarkable as it sounds.

THE CLYDE CARS COMPANY, CLYDE, OHIO

"The Final Touch in Truck Efficiency": This Clydesdale advertisement appeared in the April 3, 1919, issue of *Motor Age*. It was a follow-up to the "What does the Clydesdale Controller do?" marketing campaign that had been featured in the previous month. Though the left margin features the distinctive copper tubing radiator, the text refers to "The Driver Under the Hood," and the contest from the past month. "Our board of judges is weighing the merits of hundreds of letters already received," the advertisement explains before featuring one of the contest entries. "One driver goes so far to say that, 'If the gear shifting and steering were automatic, the Clydesdale Controller would run the car.'"

Q: **Does the controller cut down the power of the motor?**

A: No, it doesn't cut down the power because, unlike the ordinary governor, it doesn't require an additional valve in the intake manifold. With the ordinary type of governor, which is required, cuts down the power of the motor as much as 7 to 10 percent. This decrease in power is caused by the added obstruction to the smooth flow of the gases through the manifold known as "gas impingement."

Q: **How does the controller act when the driver shifts gears?**

A: Ordinarily, it is necessary to accelerate after each shift is made and the clutch engaged to provide for the increased pull on the motor. Clydesdale controllers take care of this automatically. All the driver has to do is de-clutch, shift the gears and engage again, without paying any attention to the throttle or accelerator pedal. The Clydesdale controller takes care of this for him.

Q: **How does the Clydesdale controller act in traffic?**

A: One of the greatest advantages of the Clydesdale controller will be found when the truck is operating in traffic. Under ordinary conditions, particularly when the hand throttle is set for a given speed, as the driver de-clutches for a sudden stop in traffic, the motor instantly races. This wears out the motor and causes needless repair and depreciation and a waste of fuel. The Clydesdale controller prevents this. As the clutch is disengaged, as quick as a flash it closes the throttle to an idling speed. As the clutch is engaged again, it opens the throttle and the motor picks up — all done more smoothly and more skillfully than the most experienced driver can do.

Q: **Supposing the driver wants to speed up suddenly to pass another truck in front of him. Does he have to reset the controller speed by the hand lever?**

A: No. The Clydesdale is equipped with an accelerator pedal like every other truck which the driver can use for such occasions. The accelerator acts on the throttle through the controller which has just sufficient dampening effect to prevent "choking the motor" which so frequently happens when one steps on the accelerator on other trucks.

Q: **Is it easy for the driver to learn to operate the Clydesdale truck with the controller?**

A: There is nothing new to learn. All the driver has to do is to set the throttle at the speed he wishes to maintain just as he would do in driving a truck under ordinary conditions. The only difference is that, from that time on, he does not need to ever change the throttle or touch the accelerator pedal unless he wishes to increase the speed beyond this fixed point. The controller does all this automatically.

Q: **How does it differ from the ordinary governor?**

A: The three types of ordinary governors are merely speed limiting devices working on the centrifugal, suction or hydraulic principles which allow the motor to operate up to a certain speed and when it reaches this point they close the butterfly valve in the intake manifold. There is no governing action at lower speeds and no account is taken of the constantly changing road and load conditions. The Clydesdale controller is entirely different. It is connected directly to the throttle of the carburetor and operates the throttle on the carburetor the same as a driver would operate it. It not only performs the one function of the ordinary governor, that of limiting the motor to a maximum speed, but it automatically controls the motor at all speeds.

Q: **What are the actual benefits which the truck owners will derive from the use of the controller?**

A: Big savings in upkeep. Troubles with inexperienced drivers will be almost entirely eliminated. The operation of the truck is greatly simplified by the controller. The driver has nothing to do but shift gears and steer. The greatest trouble with careless, ignorant or inexperienced drivers is their tendency to race the motor or overload it suddenly. This cannot happen with the controller on the job. Within a short time a totally inexperienced man can be driving with all the care and skill of an old experienced driver. The controller protects every moving part of the truck — transmission, universals, clutch, bearings and rear axle, as well as the motor itself.

Q: **Is there any great saving of fuel with use of the controller and why?**

A: Yes. The saving of fuel alone, to say nothing about the other advantages of this controller, will pay more than 10 percent annually on the investment, where the truck is in continuous use ten hours per day. Driving with either hand throttle or foot accelerator, as is necessary with ordinary governors, the speed of the truck is constantly changing as road conditions change, or the throttle or the accelerator is being changed. This results in sudden changes of the speed of the motor which has a tendency to jerk in an excess of fuel, changing the mixture, with resultant waste. One only has to note the black smoke coming from the muffler at such times to

Clydesdale Motor Truck Company promotional brochure that highlighted the Clydesdale Automatic Controller by answering customers' questions.

realize their losses. With the controller there is no change in the speed of motor. The throttle is opened or closed so evenly there is no chance of waste.

Free from Radiator Troubles

The second most prominently advertised feature of the Clydesdale truck, after the automatic controller, was the radiator, which appeared in numerous ads, and even served as a company logo in many advertisements. The radiator featured an exclusive design with separate copper tubes, cast aluminum tanks, and a detachable head. The Clydesdale radiator was modeled after those found on motor buses manufactured by the London General Omnibus Company. The *Automobile Trade Journal* explained, "This English omnibus concern, operating some fourteen hundred omnibuses, made extensive experiments before they determined which type of radiator would best fulfill the hard usage to which the omnibuses in England are put, and they finally decided to use the type which is known as the L.G.O. radiator."[35]

The radiator consisted of seamless copper tubing with cast aluminum tanks and sides. Everything rested on coil springs and was protected by five strong guard bars. There were

Clydesdale trucks carried an exclusive radiator design. The guard bars on the outside offered protection. If one copper tube was broken, it could be easily replaced without disturbing the other tubes.

no soldered seams that could develop leaks. One brochure boasted, "You literally have to smash a Clydesdale's radiator to make it leak."[36] If one of the tubes did develop a leak, it could be individually replaced without disturbing the other tubes, or having to replace the entire radiator. This design, boasted the company, "entirely freed Clydesdale from radiator troubles."[37]

CLYDESDALE

What's In a Truck?

THE CLYDESDALE is one of the world's standard trucks. It has established an international reputation through seven years' service in over twenty countries from America to Japan—from Norway to South Africa.

It has proven its worth under every road condition, in every climate, by drivers of almost every nationality—proven to possess every quality that trade requirements demand.

The Answer Is

Because Clydesdale construction is uniformly good. It is a

scientifically right assembly—right in every unit of assembly.

It is the possessor of exclusive features—features which make trucking by inexperienced drivers a matter of real profit.

In our next advertisement we will describe to you the Clydesdale Automatic Controller, probably the greatest feature ever offered for making the driving of a truck the job of a novice.

Dealers: The Clydesdale truck and the rock-bound organization behind it can prove a real profit-bearing connection for you.

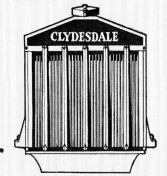

One to Five Ton Capacities

CLYDESDALE MOTOR TRUCKS — BUILT IN CLYDE, OHIO

"What's In a Truck?" This Clydesdale Motor Truck Company advertisement appeared in the December 26, 1918, issue of *Motor Age* magazine. It features the distinctive Clydesdale copper tube radiator, but note that it is part of a series, and the next issue of the magazine will "describe to you the Clydesdale Automatic Controller, probably the greatest feature ever offered for making the driving of a truck the job of a novice."

One Clydesdale customer's testimony regarding the performance of his truck's radiator served as a full-page ad in a 1920 issue of *American Lumberman*:

And the Clydesdale Came Through Smiling
    A corduroy road, eighteen inches of snow, and a six-ton load of frozen cedar posts, with a 10 percent grade for good measure. That was an everyday trip of twelve miles for the Clydesdale truck owned by M.L. Bruce of Sandpoint, Idaho.
    Every lumberman knows that 350 posts is *some* load, and he knows that a snow-covered corduroy road is a regular "washboard." ... The right front wheel of the truck was in one hollow and the left rear wheel in another. The deflection from the upper edge of the radiator to the hood was 4¼ inches, showing the terrible twist of the entire load, and proving beyond doubt that the Clydesdale radiator construction will stand most anything.[38]

The radiator was supplemented in cooling by a cast aluminum fan, which measured approximately 20 inches, depending on the size of the truck. The fan was mounted on annular ball bearings and driven by a wide leather belt, which was held in place by a tight spring. With this construction, the fan did not require regular adjustment.

Power Plants: The Engines

Clydesdale trucks were powered by four-cycle, four-cylinder gasoline engines. According to industry experts, "The four-cycle, four-cylinder was universally employed as the source of power for motor trucks."[39] Comparing the Continental engine inside a Clydesdale truck with those found in other motor trucks at the time, a company brochure detailed how the engine choice differentiated the brand from others on the market, and solved "the motor problem." "High-speed motors used by some motor truck builders were found to be utterly lacking in the stamina necessary for truck service," the brochure explained. "The slower speed motor with the big bore and stroke ratio — with increased bearing surfaces, and light reciprocating parts — which is now used in the Clydesdale truck, was the solution of the motor problem."[40]

Clydesdale engines, nicknamed "power plants" in marketing materials, were rated anywhere from 25 to 45 horsepower, depending on the model. A company catalog described the "power plant:"

Clydesdale engines possess to an unusual degree, the qualities of power, reliability, and economy which are so important to the satisfaction of the motor truck user. In the details of design and construction the Clydesdale power plant exhibits the most practical features of advanced engineering practice and possesses the ability to operate indefinitely under high duty service as well as having a large reserve stamina to stand up under possible abuse and mishandling.
    The general massiveness of Clydesdale motor construction is carried throughout the power plant even to the smallest internal detail. The dimensions of all moving and wearable parts such as the crank shaft, cam shaft, pistons, connecting rods, valve mechanism, and so on, are very generous in order to obviate the possibility of excessive wear and to ensure long endurance under most operating conditions.[41]

The Clydesdale company ordered engines almost exclusively from Continental Motors, located in Detroit, Michigan. Founded in 1905, Continental Motors produced engines for at least 100 independent auto, truck, farm equipment, and aircraft manufacturers until the 1960s. The company's 1929 offshoot, the Continental Aircraft Engine Company, is still in business today.

CLYDESDALE

"The Driver Under the Hood"

What's in a Truck Controller?

THERE is only one truck that "drives itself"— the Clydesdale.

Under the hood of this good-all-over truck is a small, simple and trouble proof controlling instrument which answers, undeniably, the question, "Can an inexperienced driver handle a truck profitably?"

What Does This Controller Do?

It controls the maximum speed of the truck—just like ordinary governors do.

It automatically accelerates the engine when the driver is shifting gears. It is impossible to strip Clydesdale gears. It is impossible to drop the clutch in while the motor is racing—because the motor cannot race.

It maintains through any conditions, uphill or down, in sand or mud, on pavement or dirt road, the speed at which the throttle is set. In easy going the engine will idle the truck along at 8 or 10 or 12 miles per hour, wherever the throttle is. In hard going the engine will work just as much harder as it is necessary in order to maintain the speed at which the throttle is set.

Anybody can drive a Clydesdale without danger of injuring its mechanism by inexpert handling.

Dealers

This controller is but one of the points which makes Clydesdale the most practical truck for the average buyer. If your territory is open you would do mighty well to get in line.

One to Five Ton Capacities

THE CLYDESDALE TRUCK
Built in Clyde, Ohio

(4)

"What's in a Truck Controller?" This Clydesdale Motor Truck Company advertisement appeared in the January 23, 1919, issue of *Motor Age* magazine. It was the second in a series of advertisements that spotlighted the Clydesdale copper tubing radiator and the automatic controller. The "Driver Under the Hood" controller is featured prominently at the top of the advertisement, while the radiator is featured in the right foreground.

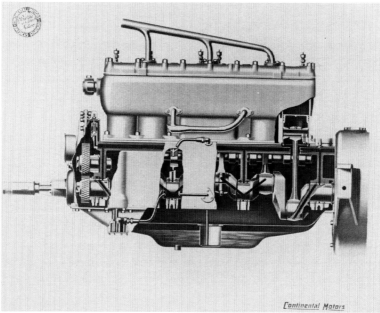

Right (top) and left (bottom) sides of the gasoline engine manufactured by Continental Motors for use in Clydesdale trucks.

The four-cylinder Continental engine under the Clydesdale hood was known as the "Hercules" model. *Motor Truck* magazine offered additional details about the Hercules engine's construction:

Hercules models are used in all [Clydesdale] models, this having proved more satisfactory to the company engineers. The crank shaft is fitted with five journals instead of the conventional three, and the engine is constructed unusually heavy throughout for hard, consistent service. The engine is of the four-cycle, four-cylinder, vertical type, L-head, having the base cast in two sections, and the cylinders cast en bloc and separate from the upper half of the crank case.[42]

Engines on the 3½- and 5-ton models, by contrast, included four cylinders in pairs, rather than "en bloc," with the cylinders "cast from a special grade of reverberatory air furnace iron."[43]

A Clydesdale company catalog explained how the engine construction, and specific testing, contributed to the overall quality of the truck. The description serves as a window into the craftsmanship of the Continental engine, and precision and quality standards of the Clydesdale brand:

A rigid test under water pressure is given each cylinder before and after it is machined. It is then finish-bored and carefully ground to a mirror finish and to standard size. The water jacket heads are cast separately on all motors, being retained by screws, and can be easily removed. This construction permits greater uniformity in the cylinder core, and ensures a better casting.

Crank case and oil pan are separate, both being aluminum castings. All bearings are carried in the crank case and are quite accessible by removing the oil pan.

The enclosed valves, which are of generous size, are mechanically operated on one side of the motor by a single cam shaft. Inlet and exhaust valves are interchangeable and have nickel steel heads electrically welded to carbon steel stems, seats and stems being accurately ground to size. The clearance around the valves is of ample size so as to maintain the highest possible efficiency.

The pistons are cast in the same grade of metal as the cylinders. They are accurately ground to correct size so as to ensure a perfect fit into the cylinders. Each piston is fitted with three diagonally concentric expansion rings. These rings, having gone through a special machining process which relieves all strains, are carefully ground on both face and sides.

The piston pin is made of No. 3 annealed special steel tubing, hardened and accurately ground to size. It is held stationary in the piston bosses by means of a simple locking device, and has its bearing in a large bronze bushing which is pressed into the connecting rod. Ample lubrication is obtained through an opening in the upper end of the connecting rod in which oil from the splash is trapped.

Connecting rods are of "I" beam construction, and made of .35 carbon steel, deep-forged and heat treated, which ensures great stiffness.

The cam shaft is drop-forged from a single piece of low carbon steel, the cams being integral with the shaft. This shaft runs in long nickel babbitt bearings and is lubricated by the oil that collects in the oil pockets, which are cast in the crank case for this purpose....

The crank shaft of this motor is of the three-bearing type with well-proportioned and liberal sized bearings. It is made up of a special crank shaft steel, deep-forged and heat-treated, giving a tensile strength of 100,000 pounds per square inch.

Flanges are provided on both ends of the center crank shaft bearings to take any end thrust which may be imparted from the clutch or some outside mechanism.

All timing gears are helically cut on automatic hobbing machines.

The crank, cam and connecting rod bearings are made of the highest grade of nickel babbitt. Connecting rod and crack shaft bearings are backed with bronze, which being a good conductor aids materially in keeping the bearings cool and are held in place by brass retaining screws. All bearings, after being carefully fitted, are expanded on special expansion arbors, reamed and finished with a slow-running spiral-cut power "burnisher" to a flawless perfection which gives over 98 percent of actual bearing surface.

A well proportioned centrifugal pump is fitted on the motor and ensures ample water circulation at all speeds. The pump is provided with two extra large bearings fitted with stuffing boxes and equipped with a drain cock so that the water can be drawn off during the freezing weather.

The motor has a combination force feed and splash system of lubrication. A vertical double plunger pump, driven by eccentrics on the cam shaft, forces oil through copper tubes direct to the timing gears and over the rear main bearing. From these points the oil drains back into the oil pan, thus maintaining a proper level for the splash lubrication of pistons, connecting rods, cam shaft bearings and middle crank shaft bearing. Provision is made for proper draining of the oil and removal of the strainer for cleaning.[44]

As intricately as the Clydesdale truck's engine and supplemental parts may have been assembled, all of the moving parts underneath the hood of the Clydesdale truck could be easily removed for repairs. The entire setup was an intricate, but solvable puzzle designed to serve the customer, driver, or mechanic who would encounter the setup.

Use of Cast Aluminum Parts

All of the Clydesdale trucks made use of cast aluminum for certain internal components such as the radiator, cooling fan, crank case, and oil pan. While the company did not advertise this as frequently as other features like the automatic controller, it was a distinctive and innovative feature in auto production at this time. Aluminum was a relatively new metal on the refining and mass manufacturing scene in the early twentieth century, and was becoming increasingly viable as a commercial building material. It was malleable, comparable to lead, so could be shaped and molded for parts. It was lightweight — one third the density of steel. Because fuel economy is a direct result of vehicle weight, aluminum became a desirable alternative to heavier materials. It also rusted at slower rates than iron and steel. It conducted heat more efficiently, which helped to maintain a cooler surface. Aluminum was, however, expensive, compared to steel. It was easy to incorporate into automobiles, including trucks, and by 1922, the ratio of aluminum to other metals in auto production was approximately 1:5, with 20 percent of all manufactured aluminum being incorporated into auto parts.[45]

The Mobile Platform: Customized Bodies

The Clydesdale Motor Truck Company manufactured *chassis*, or the frame and working parts of the truck. Standard models included everything under the hood, front and rear axles, tires, the driver's seat, foot controls, dashboard and mounted controls, manual gear shifter, fenders, and head and tail lights — essentially everything but the truck body, and sometimes the cab. By today's standards, this might seem incomplete. For the early trucking industry, however, this was customary, and actually preferable to many buyers. The motor truck was quite customizable, so manufacturers worked to ensure that customers had plenty of opportunities to develop individual truck bodies:

> The adaptability of the power wagon to a great variety of uses in many different lines of business has called for very wide limitations in the matter of body design. In fact the sale of commercial vehicles often depends upon the ability of the dealer to supply, either through the truck manufacturer or a body builder, a body which will meet individual requirements. That this fact has long been recognized by the most successful dealers and makers is shown by the fact that most motor wagon manufacturers have adopted the policy of selling their product in chassis form....[46]

Clydesdale officials recognized this industry custom and adopted this policy:

> Owing to the large variety of body types required for different uses of commercial vehicles, the [Clydesdale Motor Truck Company] does not manufacture nor furnish any truck bodies, but

After Clydesdale customers bought a chassis, they had the option of adding a custom body from a third party builder. The Van Dorn Iron Works, of nearby Cleveland, Ohio, manufactured several bodies for Clydesdale trucks as a third party body builder, including this dump body. "It never fails," the dump body boasts.

> devotes its entire production facilities to the manufacture of Clydesdale chassis. Special bodies to suit the particular requirements of Clydesdale users may be procured in most cases from local body builders with promptness and at reasonable cost.[47]

Customers could, and often would, order custom truck cabs and bodies from third-party builders. Clydesdale sales representatives could also refer customers to particular builders.

One of the body builders that worked closely with the Clydesdale company was the Van Dorn Iron Works Company, in nearby Cleveland.[48] Established in 1872 as a small fence business, Van Dorn expanded by 1878 to manufacture a variety of ornamental iron works, and for many years was the nation's largest producer of jail cells. The company also developed a structural steel business, and by the turn of the twentieth century was able to supply frames, fenders, and bodies to local auto manufacturers. The firm pioneered the development of the mechanical dump truck hoist, which was added to several Clydesdale models.[49]

The design and construction of the truck body were extremely important. The editorial staff of *American Automobile Digest* explained in 1921: "The motor truck earns money by transporting loads, and the axiom, 'keep the truck moving,' certainly applies in the selection of the body, for it can be readily understood that this has a direct effect upon the economic operation of the vehicle."[50]

Depending upon how the truck would be used, there were many considerations. There

Clydesdale "The All Purpose" Truck

No. 1 "Omnibus"

No. 2 "Sightseeing"

No. 3 "Delivery Van"

No. 4 "Open Bus"

No. 5 "War Transport"

No. 6 "Ambulance"

Standard Body Designs

See Also Page 40

Prices Upon Application.   When Applying for Prices Specify Which Chassis Model Desired.

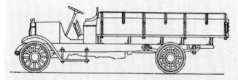

No. 7 Standard Transport Body.   Used also for General
Carting Purposes.

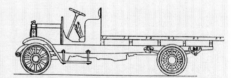

No. 9 Platform Body Used by Contractors
for Building Material

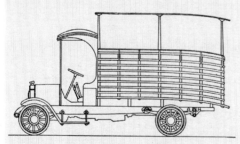

No. 8 Produce Body with Arched Platform and Upper
Rails on Each Side for Canopy

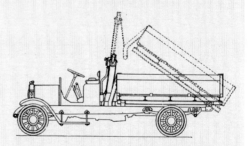

No. 10 Contractor's Steel Dump Body with
Power Operated Hydraulic Hoist

were basic weight and size proportion concerns. There were construction concerns. Most truck bodies were made of wood or steel. They were fastened to the chassis frame, and rested on the frame's crossbars. In addition, bodies might need to dump or open in certain directions, include particular design elements to accommodate their loads, or be removed from the truck entirely. One editor cautioned, "Numerous instances could be quoted to show the need of a careful study of hauling proportions before a type of body has been decided upon."[51] To preserve the integrity of their trucks, the Clydesdale company provided customers and third-party builders with specifications for 14 different body options.[52]

Generally, truck bodies could be organized into four types, depending upon their construction or hauling purposes: (1) stationary bodies; (2) elevating and dumping bodies; (3) demountable bodies; and (4) special bodies.[53]

Stationary bodies were the most common among truck owners, and included all bodies completely and permanently attached to the chassis. Clydesdale engineers detailed specifications for eight stationary bodies. They included the "Delivery Van" and the "Ambulance" bodies. Both offered closed box bodies suitable for transporting materials or people. There was also a "Moving Van" design, which could be customized with wood or cloth sides. The "Standard Transport Body" was similar to a modern pickup truck design, featuring a flat bed with sides that could be used for "general carting purposes."[54] The "Platform Body"

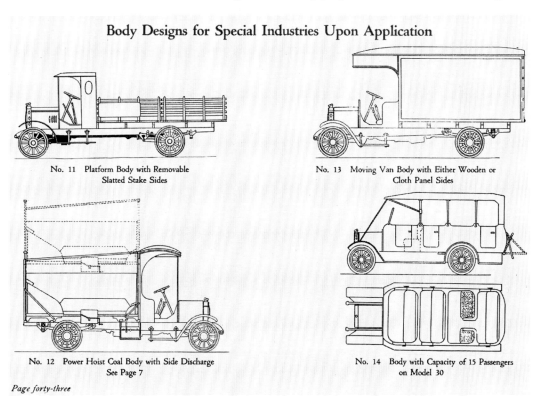

Body Designs for Special Industries Upon Application

No. 11   Platform Body with Removable Slatted Stake Sides

No. 13   Moving Van Body with Either Wooden or Cloth Panel Sides

No. 12   Power Hoist Coal Body with Side Discharge See Page 7

No. 14   Body with Capacity of 15 Passengers on Model 30

Page forty-three

Above, Opposite Top and Opposite Bottom: Even though the Clydesdale Motor Truck Company did not manufacture bodies for their chassis, company engineers developed specifications that customers could provide to third party body builders. The company offered approximately fourteen different sets of specifications for bodies upon customer request.

Top: This Clydesdale truck owned by the Albert Pick Company, Chicago, Illinois, features a stationary body. On this particular truck, the wheels are spring-loaded, an idea that was not successful. *Bottom:* Clydesdale truck with a stationary body in use by the Garden City Oil Company, Chicago, Illinois.

Winching a frame, this Clydesdale flatbed truck included equipment for contractors. There is a possibility that this image was mailed to the factory from a customer or distributor to showcase it at work — it was marked "received" by factory officials June 16, 1920.

was a standard flatbed truck, minus sides, described as suitable for use by building contractors to haul materials. For building contractors, in particular, these bodies could be additionally customized to include special tools. One 1920 Clydesdale with a "Platform Body" was outfitted with a windlass and hoist at the back of the platform for moving materials and razing buildings.

Customers could also provide body builders with plans for the "Platform Body with Removable Slatted Stake Sides." Clydesdale engineers also outlined the "Produce Body," which was an arched platform bed surrounded by open rails, including upper rails for securing a canopy; and the "War Transport" body, which was similar to many modern trucks with a flat open truck bed, but included an overhead frame suitable for hanging canvas.

There are many examples of Clydesdale owners customizing their trucks with stationary bodies. The Fred Muth Company of Cincinnati used a "War Transport" body on their Clydesdale model. The "Open Box" design was added to a Clydesdale truck, which was used by the Carson Pirie Scott Company to deliver goods to their Chicago department stores. Similar Clydesdale trucks made deliveries from warehouses to retail merchants for the George W. Travers Company in Hoboken, New Jersey. Clydesdale trucks were also used

Top: Clydesdale truck with a "delivery van" body in use by the American Glue Company, Boston, Massachusetts. *Bottom:* Clydesdale truck owned by the Fred W. Muth Company, Cincinnati, Ohio. The truck features a "war transport" body.

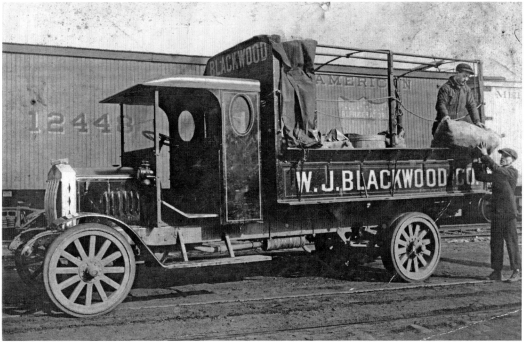

Top: Clydesdale truck with a "delivery van" body in use by the Goodyear Tire & Rubber Company, Akron, Ohio (*courtesy Clyde Heritage League, Clyde, Ohio*). *Bottom:* Clydesdale truck with an open box body owned by the W.J. Blackwood Company, Pittsburgh, Pennsylvania (*courtesy of the Clyde Public Library, Clyde, Ohio*).

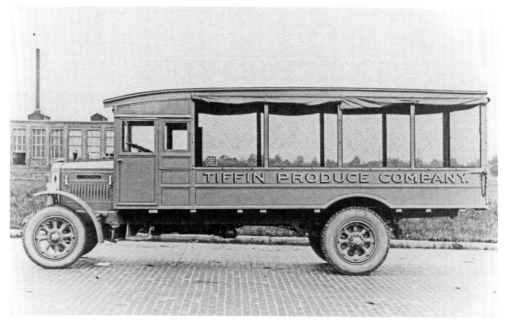

Top: An open box body on a Clydesdale delivery truck owned by the Carson Pirie Scott department store, Chicago, Illinois. *Bottom:* Clydesdale Model-65 truck chassis with an open box body, owned by the Tiffin Produce Company, in Tiffin, Ohio (*courtesy Clyde Heritage League, Clyde, Ohio*).

Top: Clydesdale truck owned by the G.B. Tussing Company features a "moving van" style body. *Bottom:* Clydesdale truck with "moving van" body owned by the A.H. Jackson Manufacturing Company of Sandusky, Ohio.

by the W.J. Blackwood Company of Pittsburgh. The Goodyear Tire and Rubber Company of Akron, Ohio, included a Clydesdale "Delivery Van" body among their fleet. The American Glue Company of Boston also included a Clydesdale model with a steel dump body in their hauling equipment.

The A.H. Jackson Manufacturing Company of Sandusky, Ohio, customized a Clydesdale "Moving Van" body with an additional door and billboard advertising. The Waverly Auto Express Company of New York used the same body on their fleet of Clydesdale delivery trucks, which were used for "intercity haulage in the metropolitan district."[55] The moving van style of body quickly became popular among delivery contractors, who were looking to offer additional services. "It is part of the business of professional movers to haul [loads] of goods by motor truck between all of the Eastern cities," explained one trade journal of the burgeoning "move for hire" model.[56] A distance of 250 miles could be covered in just two days. This was quicker than shipping by rail, and cheaper, as cargo did not need to be crated, and was only handled twice — loading and unloading — with the truck.

Lay Brothers Fish Company of Sandusky, Ohio, customized a Clydesdale truck with a "Platform Body" to haul materials to and from their fishery. The Altemus Hibble Company of Washington, D.C., also used a Clydesdale truck, transformed to carry beverage crates, to transport their Reif's "pure liquid food" product.

Clydesdale with a "moving van" body in use by the A. Werner Storage Warehouse, Camden, New Jersey.

Top: Clydesdale truck with a platform body and removable sides owned by Lay Brothers Fishery, Sandusky, Ohio (*courtesy of the Sandusky Library Follett House Museum Archives, Sandusky, Ohio*). *Bottom:* Clydesdale truck customized as a beverage truck for the Altemus Hibble Company, which distributed Reif's Special, a "near beer" product marketed during Prohibition. Advertisements for the drink warned customers, "Don't let Old Man Thirst ruin your good times. There is one way to eject him. Give him the cold shoulder over a cold bottle of Reif's Special. By golly it's good" (*courtesy of Shorpy.com*).

Top: Clydesdale 1½-ton chassis owned by Falls City Ice and Beverage Company, Louisville, Kentucky. Originally the Falls City Brewing Company, the company began delivering ice and nonalcoholic beverages following Prohibition in 1920. All of the delivery trucks, including this Clydesdale, had to be reconfigured to haul ice. *Bottom:* Clydesdale truck, Model 90, with dumping body. This truck was owned by the Buckland Milling Company in Celina, Ohio.

Delivered to Wm. B. Whiting Coal Co.
Dunbar-Laporte by Motor Co. Holyoke.

Top: Clydesdale truck with the "power hoist coal body" in use by the William B. Whiting Company, in Holyoke, Massachusetts. Just a decade before, according to records, the company hauled coal using horses. *Bottom:* Clydesdale truck with a dump body in use by the L. Stapp Company florists, a large rose grower in Rock Island, Illinois. The sides of the back could lift open to allow for swift dumping of materials, such as soil or fertilizer.

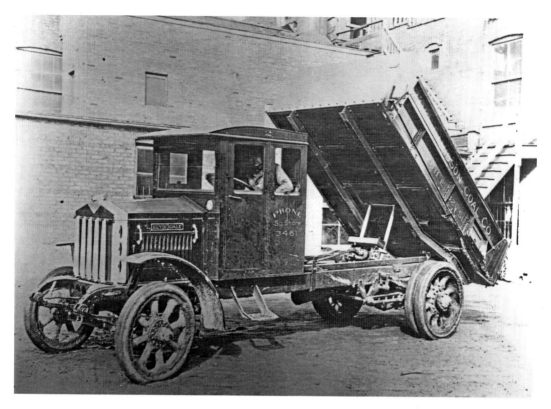

Top: Clydesdale truck with a "steel dump" body in use with the Davidson Coal Company, Chicago, Illinois. *Bottom:* Dump body on a Clydesdale truck owned by C.L. Gates in Hamburg, New York.

Clydesdale "steel dump body" coal delivery truck owned by the Vander Wagen Brothers, Chicago, Illinois.

Many Clydesdale customers found the stationary body, despite being permanently attached, adjustable for significant modifications. The Falls City Brewing Company of Louisville, Kentucky, for example, customized a Clydesdale 1½-ton truck for deliveries in 1919. When Prohibition became law in the United States the following year, the company quickly changed its name to the Falls City Ice and Beverage Company, and began selling ice, soda, and nonalcoholic beer. All of the trucks in the fleet had to be reconfigured to haul, and in the case of ice, chill, the new cargo.

After stationary bodies, elevating and dumping bodies were the most common among motor truck owners. Elevating and dumping bodies were used extensively in hauling, and could save time by discharging a load quickly — usually 30 seconds per ton. These bodies were typically nine to twelve feet long, and pivoted at the rear end, or to one side, which allowed for an inclined surface. Hoists installed at the front, or on the opposite side, raised the body into an incline. Hoists could also be installed to raise the truck bed straight up, for alternative discharge options. Clydesdale engineers developed plans for the "Steel Dump Body," which was a flat dump truck with a power-operated hydraulic hoist. They also developed the "Power Hoist Body," which was a standard truck bed that raised straight up, and opened on the sides, for particular discharge needs. Finally, they also developed the "Sand Dump Body," which featured sides that flipped open to allow for dumping.

Top: Close-up of the rear view of a Clydesdale truck with a wood and metal custom dumping body. Note the Clydesdale nameplate on the back of the truck. *Bottom:* 2½-ton Clydesdale truck owned by Platoff & Bush Contractors, Louisville, Kentucky. Note the pinstripe painted along the bottom of the truck frame.

3½-ton Clydesdale truck with a dump body, owned by Edward Torstrick, Louisville, Kentucky.

Examples of Clydesdale trucks with dumping bodies included the "Steel Dump Body" used by the Vander Wagen Coal Company in Chicago. Platoff and Bush General Contractors of Louisville also used a similar truck for their work. The Buckland Milling Company in Celina, Ohio, owned a Clydesdale truck with the "Sand Dump Body." The William B. Whiting Coal Company of Holyoke, Massachusetts, selected the "Power Hoist Coal Body" for the Clydesdale truck in their fleet. The L. Stapp Company, a large rose grower in Rock Island, Illinois, also selected the "Power Hoist Coal Body" model for transporting soil and fertilizer. The F.W. Menke Stone and Lime Company in Quincy, Illinois, wrote to a stone worker's trade magazine to let readers know that the "use of two Clydesdale [trucks] enables us to make deliveries of crushed stone and building material. We consider the motor truck a paying investment."[57] With the ability to dump materials from the side panels, the truck most certainly allowed more flexibility with delivery positioning.

The third type of popular truck body was the "demountable body," which was designed to be quickly transferred from one truck chassis to another. These bodies' were far less common than stationary and dumping or elevating types. Demountable bodies were ideal for situations when the running time of one truck could optimized by not waiting for the discharge of its body contents, and truck bodies could be rotated among an entire fleet. They were most commonly installed on trucks used by large department stores, warehouses, or hauling companies with timed deliveries. Demountable bodies could be organized into two groups, based on how the body was removed from the chassis. One type used a hoist mounted on trolley rails, and the body could be removed with or without its load. The second type was similar to the first, but did not use a hoist. The body was simply rolled off the chassis without being lifted. Clydesdale engineers did not develop specifications for any demountable bodies. These were typically more expensive, and designed by the customers and body builders planning to use them.

5 ton Clydesdale which travels 75 miles every day and has never been in the shop in 18 months.

No other truck has it —"The Driver Under the Hood"

Quicker Deliveries—
Happier Drivers

WITH customers on one side, clamoring for coal, and drivers on the other asking for more money and less work, the coal dealer is between two fires. He wants to please his customers, but he doesn't want to lose his drivers.

The easiest way out of such a problem is to improve transportation equipment so that the customer can be served promptly and the drivers' work made easier. And the Clydesdale truck is especially well suited to the coal business because of its controller.

This automatic device is not a governor, for it controls the motor at all speeds. If the distance to be covered is 15 miles and the throttle is set at this speed according to speedometer, the trip will be made in one hour, except for possible traffic holdups and gear shifts. The driver does not need to use the accelerator unless he wants to spurt ahead of another truck, for the Clydesdale will maintain an even speed up or down hill, on rough or smooth road.

Such a feature not only makes the Clydesdale easy to operate. It saves gas, oil and tires. It makes a smoother running and longer-lived truck. It enables the owner to be sure of deliveries on time, and it keeps drivers on the job because they like to drive the Clydesdale.

Your dealer will show how this remarkable controller operates. Write us for his name.

THE CLYDESDALE MOTOR TRUCK COMPANY
CLYDE, OHIO

CLYDESDALE
MOTOR TRUCKS

Stocking High Priced Coal Is Expensive. Keep the Coal Moving.

"Quicker Deliveries—Happier Drivers": This Clydesdale advertisement appeared in the October 1920 issue of the *Retail Coalman.* The Clydesdale Motor Truck Company marketed heavily to coal companies, as the trucks, particularly those with dump bodies, could quickly and efficiently serve their needs.

Customized Clydesdale spray truck owned by the city of Spartansburg, Pennsylvania. The city mounted the 1,200 gallon tank on the 5-ton truck. Spartansburg, along with the cities of Janesville, Wisconsin, and Chikopee, Massachusetts, were featured in Clydesdale advertising to municipalities looking to purchase motor trucks.

The fourth body type, "special bodies," included the *very* customized trucks that did not fit into the other three categories. These were not common among commercial fleets or individual truck owners. Even though Clydesdale Motor Truck Company engineers developed specifications for four special bodies, there is no evidence of any of these bodies' ever being added to any Clydesdale truck. They included the "Omnibus" Body, which was a compact double decker bus body with steps tracing up a back corner of the truck to the second level; and a "Sightseeing" coach with six rows of open bench seating. The third special design was the "Open Bus" body, which offered closed seating rows with an open roof, similar to a streetcar. The fourth design was unnamed, but described as "Body with Capacity of 15 Passengers." It was an open air motor coach resembling an elongated modern golf cart, with a canopy top and side doors accessing two front rows and one back row of seating. The back of the body flipped open, much like the ends of modern pickup truck beds. These special bodies, regardless of whether they were ever manufactured, were most certainly the result of Clydesdale's relationship with the London General Omnibus Company.

Other custom bodies were developed entirely by Clydesdale customers and their body builders. As one trade journal noted, "Considering the motor truck chassis simply as a foundation or mobile platform, it is apparent that an endless variety of structures and devices for special purposes can be mounted on it."[58] The engineers in the cities of Spartansburg,

JANESVILLE
WISCONSIN

Illustration
shows Flusher
in Action

A Studebaker Power Pressure Sprinkling-Flushing Unit

on the

CLYDESDALE

A WORLD-PROVEN MOTOR TRUCK

The Clydesdale is a truck built for American haulage requirements, which by its record in world-wide service—more comprehensive in the aggregate than any national usage alone could be—has established a "Factor of Safety" unique in American motor truck building.

One to Five Ton Capacities

CLYDESDALE MOTOR TRUCKS *built in* CLYDE, OHIO

By Truck Builders Among the Oldest in America

(7)

"A Studebaker Power Pressure Sprinkling-Flushing Unit": This Clydesdale Motor Truck Company advertisement appeared in *American City* magazine, and featured the true story of a Clydesdale customer — the city of Janesville, Wisconsin. At the bottom of the advertisement, the description reads "Clydesdale Motor Trucks *built in* Clyde, Ohio, by truck builders among the oldest in America."

Top: Clydesdale trucks were used as fuel trucks by several oil companies. This truck features a customized tank mounted on a Clydesdale truck, and was owned by the Manhattan Oil Company. *Bottom:* Customized Clydesdale truck owned by the Agni Fuel Company, Baltimore, Maryland. The company used the truck to distribute their fuel, "Alcogas," around the Washington, D.C., metro area.

Top: Clydesdale truck used to transport Zerolene, a popular motor oil distributed by Standard Oil. Note that the truck is missing a front fender, and is carrying a spare tire. *Bottom:* Clydesdale truck with wrecker body, owned by Akins Wrecked and Ditched Car Service, Louisville, Kentucky.

Detailed rear view of a Clydesdale truck with a wrecker body owned by the Pennsylvania Indemnity Exchange.

Top: Heavy Clydesdale truck used to switch freight cars for the Bowser Railroad, Fort Wayne, Indiana. The photograph was taken in 1941, but features a decades-old Clydesdale truck still at work. *Bottom:* Clydesdale fire truck ordered directly from the factory by the city of Clyde in 1920. It was custom made for the Clyde Fire Department, and included unique octagonal headlights. The body was later shortened because the weight of the equipment in the back caused the front wheels to lift off the ground.

Top: Members of the Clyde Volunteer Fire Department toast their 5-ton Clydesdale truck in Clyde, Ohio. *Bottom:* Members of the Sandusky Fire Department with their Clydesdale truck, customized as a fire truck, in Sandusky, Ohio. Note the unique headlamps (*courtesy of the Sandusky Library Follett House Museum Archives, Sandusky, Ohio*).

This Clydesdale truck features a customized cab encouraging customers to "Build a Home" with the Riverside Lumber Company, New Orleans, Louisiana.

Pennsylvania, and Janesville, Wisconsin, for example, each mounted a flusher tank on the back of a 5-ton Clydesdale to assist with spraying projects. At least two companies adapted their Clydesdale trucks to be some of the first modern fuel trucks. The Agni Motor Fuel Company of Baltimore, developed a fuel known as "Alcogas," which was distributed around Washington, D.C.; while the Manhattan Oil Company used a Clydesdale truck to transport its "Race-O-High" gasoline.[59] The Akins Wrecked and Ditched Car Service of Louisville, Kentucky, as well as the Pennsylvania Indemnity Exchange, each installed a wrecker body on the back of their Clydesdale trucks.

At least three Clydesdales were used as fire trucks. One served the factory's home town of Clyde, Ohio. The fire department financed the truck through subscriptions, and city officials purchased it directly from the factory in 1920. It was known as the "Pride of Clyde" for several years, and, to date, the Clyde Fire Department is the only fire department in Ohio to have a fire truck that was manufactured in its own town.[60] Another Clydesdale fire truck served the nearby city of Sandusky, while a third fire truck served the city of West Springfield, Massachusetts. Fire trucks were particularly complicated bodies, as the firefighting equipment was often quite heavy, typically weighing approximately 1,600 pounds. Fire truck bodies were often custom built to carry the specific equipment used within their department. The Clydesdale fire truck used by the Clyde Fire Department, for example,

Clydesdale employees assembling chassis in the "light and airy" factory assembly room. Company officials prided themselves on the dedicated professional staff of the Clydesdale company. The factory was, they boasted, "free from labor troubles."

featured a shortened body, as the fire equipment behind the rear wheels was quite heavy and initially made the front of the truck rather unstable.

In addition to bodies, truck cabs were also customizable. Clydesdale sometimes built cabs on chassis, but most of the time did not. Cabs were often added later with the body. Many truck owners opted for weatherproof cabs that would allow the truck to be driven comfortably all year. One example of a unique Clydesdale truck cab was from the Riverside Lumber Company, of New Orleans, which transformed the front of a truck into a house to showcase building materials.

To be sure, the Clydesdale truck offered seemingly endless opportunities for customiza-

(Left to Right)
Maude Crockett Friedley, Marie Leonard Doebel
Bess Gallagher Clapp, Fern Thurstin Bacon
Naomi Taylor Jarke, Marie Krebs
Frances Crockett Lewis, Wilda Sherloh

1921 OFFICE STAFF
CLYDESDALE FACTORY

Clydesdale truck was smallest ever built, called PONY EXPRESS

The office staff of the Clydesdale Motor Truck Company, 1921. The women in the photograph were identified as, from left, Maude Crockett Friedley, Marie Leonard Doebel, Bess Gallagher Clapp, Fern Thurstin Bacon, Naomi Taylor Jarke, Marie Krebs, Frances Crockett Lewis, and Wilda Sherloh (*courtesy Clyde Heritage League, Clyde, Ohio*).

tion, making it a versatile machine for companies and drivers across the country. Yet there were similarities among each model, most notably Clydesdale's reliable pressed steel frame and patented automatic controller. These characteristics defined the Clydesdale Motor Truck Company's market success, and would distinguish them among the industry for years to come.

Clydesdale Employees

Part of the quality of a Clydesdale truck could no doubt be attributed to the company's employees. Many of the company engineers had been with the company since its beginning, and others even longer, working for Krebs Commercial Cars and the Elmore Manufacturing Companies. Clydesdale publicly attributed much of its success to its employees in advertisements.

The Clydesdale factory employees did not work in an assembly line, but in an open shop with skilled engineers performing specific tasks. A company brochure painted an almost utopian scenario:

The Clydesdale factory is located in Clyde, Ohio, away from the hustle of the large city, away from the restless labor conditions. There are no such things as strikes and labor troubles found here for each man is interested in his job and the product he is building.

... [You] would be immediately struck by the type of workmen. Each is an expert and many of them have been with the Clydesdale company for years. Most of them own their own homes and will remain as long as they live.... Every workman takes pride in doing his work as nearly perfect as humanly possible. Naturally such conditions are bound to be productive of a finer product than could be expected from less pleasant surroundings.

M.R.Pence

SPECIAL REPRESENTATIVE
The Clydesdale Motor Truck Co.
CLYDE, OHIO

Business card of M.R. Pence, sales representative for the Clydesdale Motor Truck Company.

Information about particular Clydesdale workers, or their day to day activities, is limited. One employee, M.R. Pence, who was the Clydesdale Motor Truck Company direct sales representative, reported earning a salary of $350 per month, plus one percent commission on all of the trucks of which he facilitated sale. He conducted demonstrations for prospective truck buyers, and even used trucks to perform work on family farms in an attempt to showcase the utility of the truck. "Some men don't demonstrate at all, but I believe you get better results if you demonstrate," he advised.

Historic photographs show that working women also played a role in Clydesdale's operations. This was not that unusual for the time, as World War I helped many women enter workplaces traditionally reserved for male laborers. According to the 1920 U.S. Census, women made up approximately one quarter of the national workforce as workers outside the home. Clydesdale's bookkeeping staff in 1921 included several women from Clyde.

3

Business Is Booming (1919–1922)

In the years following World War I, the Clydesdale Motor Truck Company continued to prosper. More broadly, by 1919, American automobile manufacturing had become the third largest industry in the country, employing 800,000 workers, affiliating with 30,000 dealers and 25,000 garages, and contracting with over 1,000 third-party producers of bodies, tires, and other parts and accessories.[1] Clydesdale trucks were sold by sales representatives across the country, and in over 30 countries around the world. The company also expanded production to Canada, participated in national auto shows, traveled national promotional truck tour circuits, and participated in an industry-wide lobby for better roads and the use of trucks for shipping, all within a few years. In other words, business truly was booming.

The Clydesdale Motor Truck Company's success was bolstered by the same "Roaring '20s" phenomenon that was affecting the rest of the United States following World War I. With wartime production at an end and soldiers returning home looking for work, the nation actually experienced an economic recession. At the same time, however, increased immigration, technological advances, and the growth of the automobile industry allowed companies like Clydesdale to generate profits. Prices stayed the same or increased, when many Americans predicted a postwar decline to prewar conditions. In addition, labor organizations were making significant inroads into many industries, particularly manufacturing. Such conditions highlighted a very interconnected relationship between labor and production. Clydesdale's vice president, A.C. Burch, compared the postwar manufacturing economy to the "eternal triangle" of modern fiction:

> There are three angles of the present material and labor situation which remind me of the "eternal triangle" of modern fiction. The three angles are the high cost of living, the cost of labor, and the cost of material.
>
> First, the workmen find the cost of living so high that they demand higher wages which they get by some means or other. The manufacturers of various materials are then forced to increase their prices on the finished product to make up for the extra cost of labor. Then it works back around so that it costs more to produce food products and up again goes the cost of living.
>
> After wrangling among themselves, the three factions find themselves in exactly the same situation as before, and go through the whole process again, with the result that prices of everything from a toothpick to a locomotive are going up.
>
> It was anticipated by many that after the war, prices of motor trucks would decline, but much to their surprise there was no drop, nor do I believe there will be. If there is any change at all it will go up rather than down....
>
> But, as in the movies, it must turn out all right, for never was there as much money in circu-

Top: The Clydesdale Motor Truck Company continued to prosper in the years following World War I. Their truck chassis were completely customizable. This truck features a mounted tank. Notice the driver and children posing for the photographer. *Bottom:* Finished Clydesdale chassis underwent extensive testing at the factory prior to final sale.

Clydesdale Motor Truck Company official band and baseball team in Clyde, circa 1917 (originally a single photograph). Company-sponsored baseball clubs were very common around Ohio and the Midwest during this time, and the team would have likely played other company clubs from around the region (*courtesy of Randy Dick, Clyde, Ohio*).

lation, never such great prosperity in every line of business, or in every social strata, and it is certain that this prosperity will continue until conditions gradually adjust themselves and we arrive at the proper balance between the various factions of the triangle.[2]

Clydesdale's prosperous place within the "triangle" was bolstered by the fact that trucks, in particular, were in high demand following the war. Thousands of American-made trucks had been shipped overseas for wartime service.

Some experts predicted that a postwar influx of decommissioned trucks would saturate the American market and decrease demands for production. This would turn out not to be the case:

Military use has proved to the world that the motor truck is without a rival as an economical means of transportation for all short hauling operations and also for cross-country carrying.... Probably none of the immense number of American trucks now in Europe will be returned. America will have thousands of trucks at work hauling on regularly established freight lines to every part of the country and every manufacturer will be called on to turn out trucks, and then more trucks, and then more trucks to meet the huge demand at home and abroad.[3]

American trucks were so reliable during war that they enjoyed an immediate market for postwar peacetime activities. Clydesdale officials recognized the international market for motor trucks, and expanded their overseas sales. They also capitalized on domestic demands, particularly on American farms. According to U.S. Census records, motor truck ownership on American farms increased nearly 6½ times between 1920 and 1930. This was due in large part to the innovative marketing techniques of truck manufacturers, including Clydesdale.

Reaching a Global Market

The greatest possible proof of the correctness of the Clydesdale design and construction is found on the highways of the world. Every hour of the day Clydesdale trucks are giving super transportation service in 31 different countries under conditions which vary from the extreme cold of Siberia to the intense heat of the Tropics.[4]

After World War I, the Clydesdale Motor Truck Company managed what trade journals and newspapers at the time recognized as one of the most sophisticated overseas marketing campaigns of any American truck maker. "Clydesdale has one of the most highly developed foreign sales organizations of any American built truck and is today used in practically every country on the globe."[5] The company had established its reputation for reliable trucks, and was, as a local newspaper proclaimed, a "notable" industry: "Wherever motor transportation is used in the civilized world, the Clydesdale Truck ... has helped to make Ohio known to many races of people."[6]

The Clydesdale Motor Truck Company's global network allowed the company to become one of a few American truck makers to successfully break into the relatively new Japanese truck market. On February 9, 1919, the *New York Times* reported that 260 Clydesdale trucks had been shipped to Tokyo.[7] This was part of a massive influx of automobiles, particularly trucks, into the Japanese empire following World War I. In 1917, there were just 3,000 automobiles, including only 21 trucks, inside Japan. By 1921, however, there were over 10,000 vehicles, including a large representation of Clydesdale trucks.[8] This was the result of a concerted effort among American truck manufacturers to court Japanese customers. Trade journals printed articles that explained "Why Japan Needs Trucks," and truck

THE SATURDAY EVENING POST   47

CLYDESDALE
A WORLD-PROVEN MOTOR TRUCK

ONE of the world's standard trucks, used for seven years in over twenty countries—from America to Japan, from Norway to South Africa.

Proven under every road condition, in every climate, by drivers of almost every nationality—proven to possess every quality that your own truck requirements demand.

The international position so firmly established through the years-long and worldwide proof of its worth should lead every prospective truck buyer to consider the Clydesdale.

One to Five Ton Capacities

CLYDESDALE MOTOR TRUCKS
BUILT IN CLYDE, OHIO

This Clydesdale Motor Truck Company advertisement from the January 4, 1919, issue of the *Saturday Evening Post* maps all of the countries where Clydesdale trucks were in use. There are over 30 countries around the world highlighted.

Top: Following World War I, Japan experienced enormous demand for trucks. American manufacturers like Clydesdale were quick to respond. In 1919, an order of 260 Clydesdale trucks was shipped to Tokyo. Here are Clydesdale trucks with company representatives in Japan. *Bottom:* Flotilla of Clydesdale trucks on the island of Java. The trucks were sold to the Dutch army and postal service by Verwey en Lugard Automobile Company, the largest vehicle seller on the island (*courtesy Clyde Heritage League, Clyde, Ohio*).

No other truck has it —"The Driver under the Hood"

As They Do It in Sweden

THE absence of good logging roads does not hinder this lumberman in Sweden from getting his timber to the mill. He simply puts chains on his 3½-ton Clydesdale, hitches on a few sleds, loads up to capacity, and makes a boulevard of the frozen lake.

Of course it looks easy enough, but conditions like this demand two big requirements of a truck: plenty of power and absolute dependability. When a truck is away out in the woods, far from a service expert and a supply of extra parts, it must "deliver the goods" without falling down in the hard places.

The day-after-day reliability of the Clydesdale has built for it a reputation in foreign countries just as it has at home, and the preference for Clydesdale is shown by its use in 35 countries, in almost every kind of business where unfailing performance is essential.

Nothing about the Clydesdale is taken for granted. The lumberman can prove for himself by any test he may suggest that this truck is fully able to do the average work of logging, without any more than reasonable care, under any conditions where the wheels can get traction.

Go to your nearest Clydesdale dealer and see this truck. Have it work for you. Watch the Clydesdale Controller and learn how it lengthens the life of a truck. Your dealer's name may be had for the asking.

THE CLYDESDALE MOTOR TRUCK COMPANY
CLYDE, OHIO

"As They Do It in Sweden": This Clydesdale Motor Truck Company advertisement appeared in the November 6, 1920, issue of *American Lumberman.* It is similar to many other Clydesdale ads with its distinctive call-out to the Clydesdale Automatic Controller. Yet, it is unique in that it features an international customer from Sweden.

Clydesdale

MOTOR TRUCKS

MADE IN CANADA

¶THE compared prices of two makes of trucks means but little. What a truck costs is what it costs *per year of service.*

¶CLYDESDALE Trucks are consistently maintaining the records earned all over the world of low operating and up-keep costs. This is entirely due to the inbuilt goodness and the perfection of design of the Clydesdale.

¶CLYDESDALE is built by a Canadian manufacturer who established here to better serve Canadian manufacturers. The manufacturers of Clydesdales can give the best service in Canada to users of motor transportation units.

CLYDESDALE TRUCKS ARE PRODUCED
IN 1, 1½, 2½, 3½ AND 5-TON CAPACITIES

The Clyde Cars Company Canada Limited

Factory and General Offices - - 73-81 Pearl Street, Toronto, Canada

In 1919, the Clydesdale Motor Truck Company opened a second factory in Toronto. This Clydesdale Motor Trucks "made in Canada" newspaper advertisement is dated Wednesday, April 9, 1919.

Representatives from Montreal Motor Sales stand by a platform Clydesdale truck, made in Canada, 1920 (*courtesy of the McCord Museum, Montreal, Quebec, Canada*).

sales representatives traveled frequently to share new products.[9] At least one American Clydesdale distributor, P.W. Gaylor of New York, made an extensive sales trip not only to Japan, but also to China, Siam, and India, leading up to the final contract.[10] Taking this into consideration, one might assume that the 1919 purchase was not simply a coincidental order, but the product of strategic marketing.

At approximately the same time in 1919, the Clydesdale Motor Truck Company went beyond exporting to other countries and opened a second production facility, an assembly plant, in Toronto, Canada. Not much is known about Clydesdale's Canadian production facility, but it seemed a sensible move for the company at that time. One year before, in 1918, the Canadian government had instituted a steep tariff of 35 percent on all imported automobiles. Many successful American manufacturers, like Clydesdale, were compelled to establish production facilities, rather than ship finished products, across the border. Clydesdale trucks were customized for work with several Canadian companies, including the Montreal Quarry and E. Benoit Fils (Sons) general store, also in Montreal.

This success allowed the Clydesdale Motor Truck Company to increase its capitalization from $500,000 to $1.5 million in December of 1919.[11] By the end of that year, Clydesdale trucks were sold in approximately thirty countries outside of the United States, including:

Top: Clydesdale truck in use by the Montreal Quarry, Ltd., in Montreal, Quebec, 1920. *Bottom:* Montreal Quarry, Ltd. Clydesdale truck tows another disabled truck out of the quarry (*courtesy of the McCord Museum, Montreal, Quebec, Canada*).

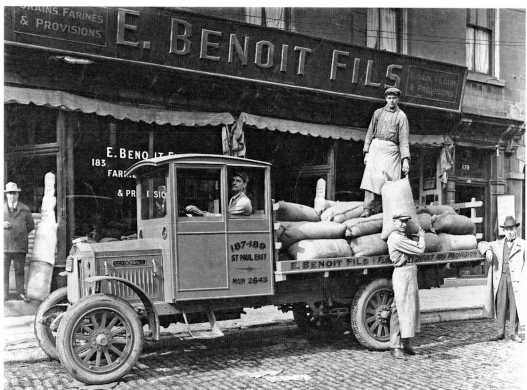

Top: Clydesdale flatbed truck hauls steel rods at a railroad yard in Montreal, Quebec, 1925. *Bottom:* Clydesdale truck with flatbed body owned by E. Benoit Fils (Sons) of Montreal, Quebec, 1920 (*courtesy of the McCord Museum, Montreal, Quebec, Canada*).

Top: Clydesdale dump truck owned by the H.A. Charlebois Carter in Montreal, Quebec, 1920. *Bottom:* An early model Clydesdale truck with flatbed body hauls materials for National Electro Products, in Canada (*courtesy of the McCord Museum, Montreal, Quebec, Canada*).

Clydesdale Trucks Travel Steadily Uphill or Downhill Without Attention to the Throttle

The practical advantage of the Clydesdale Controller to the driver of a Clydesdale truck is in making it unnecessary for him to pay constant attention to the hand throttle or foot accelerator in order to keep his truck running at a uniform rate of speed. The value of this relief can really be understood and appreciated only after the driver has operated a Clydesdale truck and has actually experienced the difference between its operation and that of other trucks equipped only with governors.

The man who starts out with a Clydesdale truck for the first time is amazed at the ease with which it is controlled in going through the different gears up to the high speed gear. It is an entirely new and very pleasing experience to get away from a standstill without having to step on the accelerator whenever the gears are changed and the clutch let in again. With the Clydesdale truck the Controller makes the motor automatically pick up the extra load when the gears are changed to a higher speed and the driver after getting in high need only set the hand throttle lever to give the speed he wishes.

In regular driving the same condition is true. As charted above, the Clydesdale truck negotiates all kinds of roads at a uniform speed (when this is desired by the driver) without any necessity for the driver giving the engine more gas for hill climbs of heavy going, or less gas for down grades when the truck runs partly or wholly of its own momentum. In each case, the demand of the truck for more power or less power from the engine is automatically and instantly taken care of by the action of the Controller in opening or closing the carburetor throttle the proper amount.

One of the only promotional advertisements from the Clydesdale company in Canada for the Clydesdale Automatic Controller. It illustrates dramatically how the controller governs speed like modern cruise control technology.

Every User Is a Satisfied User

CLYDESDALE Motor Trucks are built in 1—1½—2—3½ and 5-ton capacity. They are Made in Canada in our Toronto plant, and are maintaining their record, earned all over the world, for continuous uninterrupted operation, low operating and upkeep costs. This is due to the perfection of design found in Clydesdale Trucks and the high quality of materials used.

AT THE EXHIBITION

The space allotted to us permits only the display of one model, a Clydesdale 5-ton truck equipped with a Hydraulic Hoist and Steel Dumping Body,—of especial interest on account of its adaptability in connection with the Provincial activity in the building of good roads.

An invitation is extended to all interested in motor truck transportation to inspect our full line of five models at our plant.

CLYDE CARS COMPANY CANADA LIMITED
General Office and Plant — 73 PEARL STREET
TORONTO, CAN.

"Every User Is a Satisfied User": This advertisement featured the Clydesdale Motor Truck Company's Canada factory. It is one of few such advertisements that provide the factory's Toronto address and emphasize that, at least as far as this market is concerned, the trucks are made in Canada.

Argentina, Australia, Canada, Cape Colony, China, Cuba, Denmark, England, France, Gold Coast, India, Japan, Java, Manchuria, Martinique, Mexico, New Zealand, Norway, Peru, Philippines, Portugal, Puerto Rico, Russia, Siam, Sumatra, and Sweden. This allowed Clydesdale officials to market test trucks all over the world in a variety of terrains and climates beyond the battlefield. This led one advertisement to proclaim, "Proven under every road condition, in every climate, by drivers of almost every nationality — proven to possess every quality that your own truck requirements demand. The international position so firmly established through the years-long and worldwide proof of its worth should lead every prospective truck buyer to consider the Clydesdale."[12]

Clydesdale vice-president A.C. Burch attributed the company's overseas success to the ability of engineers to respond to the needs of customers, even in countries outside the United States:

> American manufacturers of trucks, as well as practically every other commodity, have one serious handicap in selling in foreign markets. But they also have a decided advantage, which more than offsets it. The handicap is the inability or the unwillingness of the American manufacturer to get the foreign viewpoint and make his goods to suit the foreign buyer. He has always seemed to take the attitude of "my goods are good enough for the home market and the foreign buyer can take them or leave them." And it usually happens that the foreign buyer leaves them. We attribute our success in selling Clydesdale trucks in foreign markets to the fact that we have studied the foreign buyers' requirements very closely.[13]

It seemed that Clydesdale Motor Truck Company engineers also paid attention to American buyers' requirements. While exact numbers are not available from historical records, numerous photographs, articles, and advertisements provide clues relevant to Clydesdale's domestic sales. Many American companies owned entire fleets of Clydesdale trucks. For example, the West Pennsylvania Power Company owned 13 Clydesdale trucks. In New York, Borden Dairy owned 18 trucks; Robinson & Lewis, 10 trucks; Union Freight and Express Company, 5 trucks; Waverly Auto Express, 5 trucks; George Travers, 3 trucks; and the Interstate Forwarding Company, 2 trucks.[14] In Baltimore, a fleet of Clydesdale

"A Representative Fleet": Seven of the thirteen Clydesdale trucks owned by the West Pennsylvania Power Company, Connellsville, Pennsylvania. The same fleet would be featured in a subsequent advertisement describing the "years of experience" of the Clydesdale Motor Truck Company.

Top: Fleet of Clydesdale trucks with open box bodies owned by Primalt Products of Chicago, Illinois. *Bottom:* Small fleet of Model 120-B Clydesdale trucks owned by the Wasson Pocahontas Coal Company, Chicago, Illinois. The company ordered one truck in 1919, and then ordered two more in the spring and summer of 1920.

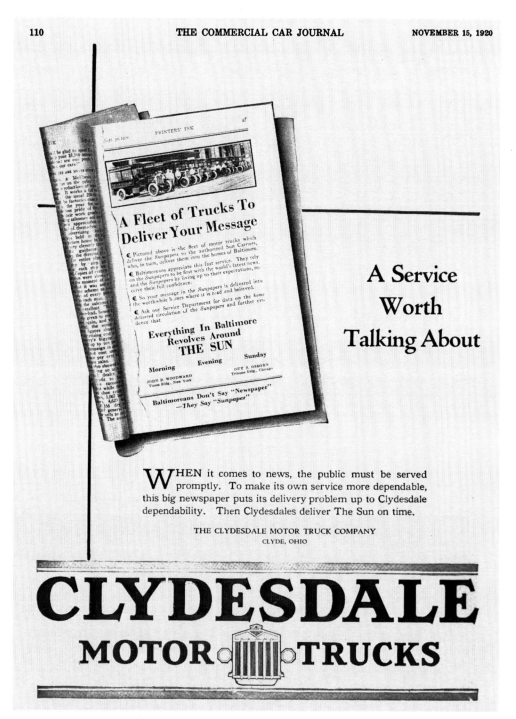

A Service
Worth
Talking About

WHEN it comes to news, the public must be served promptly. To make its own service more dependable, this big newspaper puts its delivery problem up to Clydesdale dependability. Then Clydesdales deliver The Sun on time.

THE CLYDESDALE MOTOR TRUCK COMPANY
CLYDE, OHIO

CLYDESDALE
MOTOR TRUCKS

"A Service Worth Talking About": This advertisement from the November 15, 1920, issue of the *Commercial Car Journal* described how a fleet of Clydesdale trucks were used to deliver the *Baltimore Sun* newspaper each morning: "When it comes to news, the public must be served promptly. To make its own service more dependable, the big newspaper puts its delivery problem up to Clydesdale dependability. Then Clydesdales deliver *The Sun* on time."

Movers with the Hans Lochen & Sons industrial moving company in Milwaukee, Wisconsin, with their custom Clydesdale Model 120 truck on a "winch job." The truck hauled the 6-ton tank two miles from a factory to Goldman's Department Store, then assisted with its secure placement. The whole move took approximately three hours, according to notations on the reverse of the photo. When Hans Lochen & Sons bought their Clydesdale truck directly from the factory in 1917, they became the first such company in Wisconsin to use a motor truck.

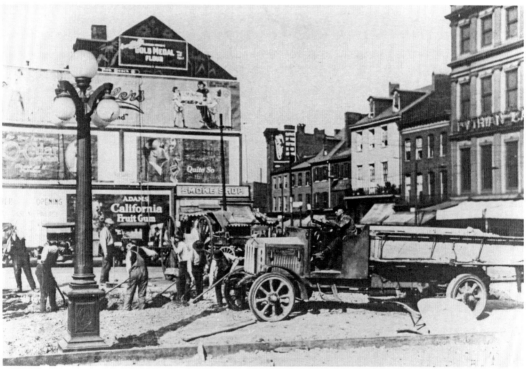

Top: Customized street cleaning spray truck in action in Spartansburg, Pennsylvania. *Bottom:* 2½-ton Clydesdale truck with a dump body helps to excavate City Hall Plaza in Baltimore, Maryland. The truck was owned by E.L. Parrish & Son. Clydesdale trucks were used extensively in municipal work around the United States.

Top: Clydesdale truck with overhead line work platform used by the Lake Shore Electric Railroad, Lorain, Ohio *Bottom:* One of the twenty Clydesdale trucks owed by the City of Philadelphia Police Patrol, Philadelphia, Pennsylvania. The body is an "open bus" style, with canvas covering the roof with fold-down sides.

trucks helped to deliver the *Baltimore Sun* newspaper each day: "When it comes to news, the public must be served promptly. To make its own service more dependable, this big newspaper puts its delivery problem up to Clydesdale dependability. Then Clydesdales deliver *The Sun* on time."[15] Chicago's Wasson-Pocahontas Coal Company and Primalt Products also owned fleets of Clydesdale trucks.

There is also evidence that Hans Lochen & Son, a longtime industrial moving company in Milwaukee, Wisconsin, established their fleet with a Clydesdale truck. According to local newspapers, in 1917, company founder Hans Lochen bought the truck directly from the factory, then drove it from Clyde back to Milwaukee. With it, Hans Lochen & Son became the first industrial mover in the state of Wisconsin to use a motor truck.[16]

By 1920, Clydesdale trucks were in widespread use by many local governments for city maintenance activities. In addition to the customized Clydesdale fire trucks mentioned in the previous chapters, cities used Clydesdale trucks for a variety of municipal projects. Trade journal advertisements featured testimonies from city officials in both Chicopee, Massachusetts, and Janesville, Wisconsin, who had selected their Clydesdale trucks.[17] In both cities, flushers were mounted on the Clydesdale chassis for use with spraying and street cleaning activities. The city of Philadelphia owned a fleet of Clydesdale trucks for its police patrol. Historic records also show that the city of Baltimore owned at least one additional Clydesdale truck that assisted with excavation projects.

Truck Dealers and Sales

While large orders of Clydesdale motor trucks shipped directly from the factory, individual truck sales took place primarily through authorized dealers and sales representatives. Clydesdale truck dealerships and authorized sales distributors were located across the United States. The largest and most successful Clydesdale dealerships appear to have been those in New York, Philadelphia, Chicago, and San Francisco. Historical records show that the Clydesdale Motor Truck Company also maintained relationships with authorized sales representatives such as the Arlington Motors Company and Hoffman Motor Company, both in New York; Holland System Trading Company in Boston; Gawthrop and Wister in Philadelphia; Schmidt Motor Company in Milwaukee; Lagerquist Carriage Company in Des Moines; Hausman Motor Company, in Louisville, Kentucky; R.N. Vansant in Casper, Wyoming; Puget Sound Motors Company, in Tacoma, Washington; Rochester Motors Company in Spokane, Washington; and Pacific Motor Truck Company in Los Angeles.

In the western United States, the Spokane-based Rochester Motors served as Clydesdale distributors to several markets in Washington, Oregon, Montana, and Idaho. In particular, they supplied Clydesdale dealers in Seattle, Washington; Portland, Oregon; Helena and Great Falls, Montana; and Boise, Idaho.[18]

It was not exactly easy to become a Clydesdale truck agent. Prospective dealers and sales representatives were reviewed extensively by the company before any contract could be finalized. This helps to explain why, when Fred Henderson was named the New England Clydesdale truck agent, he became the subject of a feature article in the June 1918 issue of *The Motor Truck*. "Obtaining representation by an established organization that intensively operates what is recognized as one of the best truck markets of the country is not usually quickly accomplished. Often this requires long periods of time and patient endeavor...."[19]

Top: Fleet of Clydesdale trucks used by the City of Philadelphia Police Patrol. Notice the gleaming whitewall tires. *Bottom:* The Clydesdale Motor Truck Company dealership in San Francisco was one of the largest in the company's distribution network, and the only showroom owned by the company itself.

CLYDESDALE
A World-Proven Motor Truck

The superstandard construction of the Clydesdale, with its oversize and overstrength parts, and its excess power has made it famous in thirty countries, from Iceland to Africa, in all climates, on all varieties of roads, with all sorts of drivers.

Cne to Five Ton Capacities.

Clydesdale Motor Trucks
Built in Clyde, Ohio

Puget Sound Motors Co.,
Tacoma, Washington.
Rochester Motors Co.,
Spokane, Washington.
Pacific Motor Truck Co.,
Los Angeles, Cal.   (11)

Clyde Cars Co. Factory Branch: 1217 Market St., San Francisco

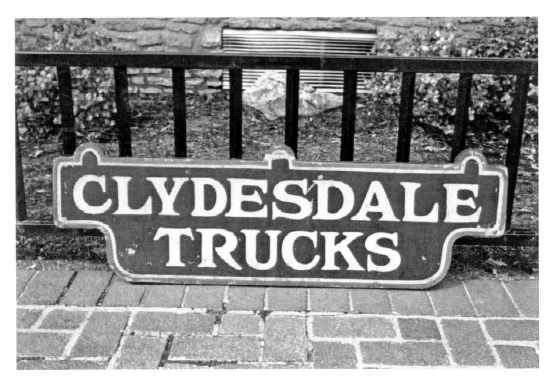

Opposite top: The Clydesdale sales network extended across the country. This advertisement, which ran regularly in *Motor West* magazine, lists dealers and distributors in the western United States. *Opposite bottom:* 3½-ton Clydesdale truck hauling wooden barrels, parked in front of Hausman Motor Company, the Clydesdale Motor Truck dealer in Louisville, Kentucky. *Above:* "Clydesdale Trucks" display sign from the Hausman Motor Trucks dealership in Louisville, Kentucky.

At the same time, Clydesdale actively solicited new representatives, particularly through the Motor Truck Dealers of America Association. They promised new representatives would be "backed up by a good organization, well financed, whose policies are sound and whose merchandising plans are of such a nature that you, as a dealer, will be quick to appreciate their help to you in your territory."[20]

The "back-up" often materialized in the form of building local connections. Dealers and distributors often ran customized advertisements on behalf of the Clydesdale Motor Truck Company in local newspapers in an effort to appeal to local potential buyers. In Philadelphia, for example, the Gawthrop and Wister Company customized several Clydesdale advertisements around true stories from their customers, including a man named Ed:

> One of our men called on a Clydesdale owner the other day to see how things were going and reported this incident, which shows more plainly the sort of service Clydesdale owners are getting than anything we could say.
> "How is your Clydesdale Truck behaving?" he asked the owner.
> "Don't know about it," was the reply. "Haven't heard of any trouble. I'll see if Ed's around. He drives it."
> He pushed button, and in a couple of minutes, in comes Ed.
> "How is the Clydesdale working?" asked the owner.
> "Well," said Ed, "since you've asked me I'll say it's the best ever. And I've driven a lot of them in the past five years. Seven different makes if I remember right. Burns less gas, pulls better, and

Locust 838, *Quick!*

That's the number Clydesdale owners and drivers call when they need help. And they get it quickly.

Accidents don't keep the Clydesdale out of service any longer than it takes us to get on the job. And we make it our business to keep your trucks running.

It's a fine thing to know that you have service actually within reach of your hand.

Our work is not half finished when we have sold a man a Clydesdale Truck. We know when a business house purchases a Clydesdale they are not just buying so many pounds of metal and rubber. They are buying quicker, safer, more economical transportation for their goods.

The Clydesdale factory has done all in their power to build a good truck, and have, we believe, built the most reliable truck on the market today.

Now it is up to us to see that buyers in this territory get out of the truck all of the good quality and improved transportation which the factory has built into it.

We must see to it that the truck is operated in the most efficient manner possible.

We must see to it that it is kept on the job day and night if required, and that even accidents don't delay it one moment longer than is absolutely necessary.

This is our ideal of service—an ideal which we are living up to—an ideal which we are carrying out by maintaining a service station that is second to none.

It will certainly pay you to investigate the Clydesdale Truck and our Clydesdale service.

Let us tell you about our service and just how we take care of our customers.

GAWTHROP & WISTER CO., Inc.
Dealer and Distributor

2218 MARKET ST. Locust 838

CLYDESDALE
MOTOR TRUCKS

This Clydesdale advertisement featured the company's large Philadelphia dealer, Gawthrop & Wister. This ad, and others like it, appeared regularly in the *Evening Public Ledger* newspaper. This advertisement is dated March 5, 1919.

Top: A motor truck chassis for sale from R.N. Vansant, the Clydesdale distributor in Casper, Wyoming. *Bottom:* Three different models of Clydesdale trucks on display at the R.N. Vansant distributorship in Casper, Wyoming. Note the different headlamps and cowl lamps.

GETTING THE MOST
OUT OF
EVERY ACRE

with the aid of a
Motor Truck

Clydesdale Motor Truck Company promotional brochure from 1919, which explained to farmers how motor trucks might be used on a farm, and in particular, how trucks were more efficient than horses. The decision to transition from horse to motorized transportation, in particular, use of a truck, was an important consideration for farmers.

makes less fuss about it than anything I've ever driven. She hasn't seen the inside of a service station or shop since we had 'er. Haven't found anything that would stop 'er yet. I've nick-named her 'the tank.'"[21]

By the same token, when Clydesdale representatives opened new service facilities, they told the public. When the Gawthrop and Wister Company opened a new four-story deal-ership and service center for Clydesdale shoppers and owners, they issued a press release that appeared in trade journals.[22] In New York, Edward Hoffman of the Hoffman Motor Company issued a press release explaining that Clydesdale trucks have a "Fine Record." The release described his style as supervisor: "Being a mechanical expert he is more interested in supervising the service given his customers and working with his sleeves rolled up than he is in fine office furniture and fine words. He is a practical truck man and his Clydesdales keep running...."[23]

Clydesdale dealers and distributors took long-term customer service seriously. In Chicago, in 1920, for example, the Clydesdale dealership announced the opening of a 24-hour service garage for all Clydesdale truck owners.[24] According to one company represen-tative, Clydesdale dealers honored an "unwritten obligation" when managing service stations, to provide exceptional, even supremely optimistic, service across all aspects of customer interactions:

> When a dealer opens up a service station, he takes on an unwritten obligation to serve the pub-lic agreeably and pleasantly. If he is going to give service, it should be given graciously, or not at all.... It is not enough to simply render service — this service must be gladly, freely, even joyfully given, it must be service which accommodates and does not aggravate the customer.[25]

The Most Successful Truck Saleswoman in the Country

One extraordinary Clydesdale salesperson was a young woman named Anna Baumwald, of New York. In 1919, she earned the distinction of being "the most successful truck sales-woman in the country." She sold an average of six trucks per month for the Arlington Motors Company, the New York distributor of Clydesdale trucks.

Baumwald started her career working at an automobile factory, then attended night school, and eventually became a bookkeeper for the same company. She continued to take accounting classes, and explained: "One day, while attending a lecture at the college, I became thoroughly disgusted at the thought of being an office machine." So, as the press explained, "she decided to cut loose from office work," and sought a position in truck sales.

Customers called her the "nerviest woman in the world" for entering a profession dom-inated by men. Baumwald, however, attributed much of her self-confidence to the Clydesdale Motor Truck Company, which was symbolic as an "organization that backs up any promises" she made to customers.[26]

Appealing to the Horse Mind

The Clydesdale Motor Truck Company prospered at a time when the truck industry was relatively new, and many Americans, particularly farmers, were transitioning from horses to motorized transportation. The *New York Times*, in 1918, estimated that 350 million tons of farm products had been hauled to market in trucks during the previous year.[27] The 1920 U.S. Census, which, incidentally, tracked the growth of the automobile during this time period, counted 139,000 motor trucks in use on American farms. By 1930, the count had exploded to 900,000 trucks. Automobile production, in general, soared from 2.2 million cars and trucks in 1920 to 5.3 million in 1929.

If someone was counting the increasing numbers of trucks in use across America, then someone else was counting the decreasing numbers of horses. In New York City alone, the number of horses declined by 41 percent between 1910 and 1919. This led the Wheeling, West Virginia, *Register* to report that "the motor truck is rapidly emptying the stables of the nation."[28]

The U.S. Department of Agriculture was also quick to recognize the role of the truck in the decline of the horse. While the general growth of automobiles contributed to the declining use of horses, trucks were particularly effective at displacing their four-legged antecedents. "Apparently, the most effective foe of the horse has appeared in the last ten years in the motor vehicle, although its importance in this respect is popularly exaggerated. With motor trucks and commercial vehicles the case is different. Here is clearly a complete substitution of fuel power for horse power."[29] More precisely, auto experts estimated that one motor truck could replace approximately three horses. Despite this, the decision to purchase a motor truck was not easy for American farmers. One magazine described the "slow and difficult matter to move from the horse habit to the engine habit."[30] Trucks were often twice the cost of horses, and carried similar loads, but in much less time. To move a 2-ton load 120 miles by horse, for example, it would require one team plus four men, approximately four days. A 2-ton truck, by contrast, could move the same load the same distance in approximately ten hours, and required just two men, a driver and a helper. Trucks also required new and different types of care and maintenance procedures from horses, which intimidated many prospective owners.

Truck builders like Clydesdale tried to assist, and capitalize on, decision-making by farmers. The company produced a brochure, *Getting the Most Out of Every Acre with the Aid of a Motor Truck,* which advised every farmer to "decide for himself" if, and when, to purchase a truck:

> When considering the purchase of any high priced piece of machinery, a farmer must study his own business and determine *whether or not the investment will carry itself and pay him a profit besides.* The farmers who have bought motor trucks based on such careful study are satisfied that their money has been well spent. Others have made the mistake of guessing at their requirements or have bought trucks simply to be "in style."
> The size of farm, the distance to market, the kind of roads to be traveled, the number of horses now owned and the cost of keeping them — all of these are factors which determine the value of a truck. But it must be remembered above all that the *true* value of a motor truck is in keeping it busy most of the time.[31]

In an attempt to reach farmers, the company also began marketing the Clydesdale 1½-ton model as the Clydesdale Farm Special. "Experience has taught that a ton-and-a-half truck is best fitted for farm work, because the average farm load is from one to two tons," officials determined.[32] Clydesdale engineers also outlined how the 1½-ton chassis could be customized with special bodies to meet several different types of farm needs. As before, the Clydesdale Motor Truck Company did not offer these bodies to buyers, but suggested specifications for customized body options. One farm-friendly option included the hay rack, for example. It was a low box body with flare boards adjusted at right angles, for carrying

Farmers inspect a Clydesdale truck during one of the several motor truck tours in which Clydesdale participated. The company participated in at least three such tours around the American Midwest between 1919 and 1920.

loose hay or bundles of grain. The basket rack body extended the flare boards vertically to accommodate the hauling of crates or baskets of produce. The grain tight body was a deeper box, with boards positioned at 30-degree angles to accommodate the hauling of loose or sacked grains, cement, manure, and other loads. Finally, the stock rack body included slatted sides suitable for weaving and tying rope in order to corral livestock. Marketers also claimed that it made hog washing easy with its "smooth inside finish."[33]

To interact with and directly influence decision-making farmers, the Clydesdale Motor Truck Company participated in a number of industry-sponsored "truck development tours" between 1919 and 1920. These were organized, high-profile caravans of motor trucks that traveled through portions of the country, and along the way, stopped in towns to meet with farmers and demonstrate the work of a motor truck by doing work on actual farms. "There is no question as to the benefit to be derived by the farmer from a farm motor tour.... It not only gives him a chance to look the trucks over and see them at work on his own jobs without expense to him, but it enables him to get an accumulation of cost records."[34]

The first, and largest, such tour that involved the Clydesdale Motor Truck Company took place during the summer of 1919. It left St. Louis, Missouri on Monday, June 9, 1919.

Thirty-three 2-ton trucks traveled 400 miles across Missouri and Illinois in five days "to demonstrate to the farmer, the small city dweller … that motor truck transportation is entirely feasible…, and to awaken local interest in the use of motor trucks for every transportation need."[35] The tour was organized by the St. Louis Automobile Manufacturers' and Dealers' Association at the suggestion of the National Automobile Dealers' Association. It was commanded by former U.S. Army Captain Robert "Bob" E. Lee.

A small army of automotive engineers and press corps traveled with the tour. Marketing for the tour started weeks in advance:

> The widest possible publicity campaign was carried on for several weeks before the tour started, so that not only in the towns and cities were the trucks seen by thousands, but along the highways, at every crossroads and at every farmhouse, people were gathering to see the trucks go by, to receive literature relative to highway transportation, and to get an actual personal idea of what the motor truck will mean to them in future transportation matters.[36]

The tour visited approximately 35 locations along the route. From St. Louis, it traveled northwest to St. Charles and Hannibal, Missouri; then northeast across the Mississippi River into Quincy, Clayton, Rushville, and Beardstown, Illinois. Finally, the tour headed

Clydesdale 1½-ton "Farm Special" on the National Motor Truck Development Tour in August 1919. The tour traveled 3,000 miles around the Midwestern United States demonstrating for farmers how trucks could be more powerful and more efficient than horses.

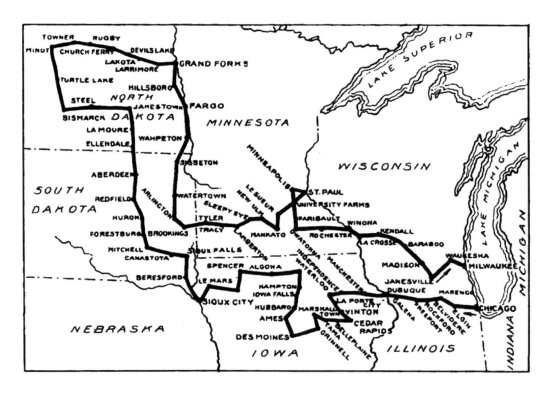

Map of the route traveled by the 1919 National Motor Truck Development Tour. The entire trip was 3,000 miles long and stopped at 72 cities, demonstrating for farmers the power and efficiencies of motor trucks over horses.

south, back to St. Louis, passing through Whitehall, Jerseyville, and Alton, Illinois, before crossing back over the river.

Each night along the tour, a special program would be planned for the townspeople in that location. A speaker would appear, who would then be followed by a display of moving pictures. "Each evening, as soon as darkness came, trainmaster Duffy unlimbered the moving picture machine mounted on the Maxwell truck, flashing moving pictures of motor trucks in all manner of rural service on the outdoor screen usually stretched across a prominent street or against the side of a building where all could see."[37]

During the trip, the Clydesdale truck, which was driven by H.W. Leigh of the Midwest Motor Car Company, was involved in a crash with another truck. The copper tubing radiator made the national press when it continued to function. The copper tubes had done exactly what they were designed to do.

Two months after the St. Louis tour, the Clydesdale Motor Truck Company participated in what would be its longest and most prestigious tour, the National Motor Truck Development Tour, which took place in the late summer and fall of 1919. By all accounts, it was an incredibly successful tour and became the standard-bearer for other, smaller motor truck tours that followed. The National Motor Truck Development Tour was organized by the National Association of Motor Truck Sales Managers. A fleet of twenty trucks, including one Clydesdale 1½-ton "Farm Special," traveled 3,000 miles throughout the American Midwest. The tour stopped in 72 towns along the way to demonstrate how trucks could reliably

A flatbed Clydesdale truck hauls bags of feed for a local farmer. During tours, Clydesdale trucks would do demonstrations by doing actual farm work for people in the community.

simplify work and increase productivity on farms. "In addition to this there was a desire on the part of the manufacturers to study more closely the hauling problems of the farmer, to go into his fields and actually perform for him various jobs and find out if there are any possible improvements which can be made that will increase the efficiency and usefulness of the motor truck for farm hauling."[38]

The tour was grand. It left Chicago on August 4, 1919. The sendoff from the city's Grant Park was a busy scene, with a "crowd of a thousand or more spectators." Clydesdale vice-president A.C. Burch was among the attendees. Colonel Humphries, the keynote speaker, outlined the importance of the truck in the recent world war, bade the caravan Godspeed, and assured the sponsors that the U.S. Army would be watching with interest during the coming months. The tour was staffed by 80 men, including an accountant, press secretary, courier, and the 25-piece sailor band from the nearby Great Lakes Naval Training Station, which would furnish music for events in each stop on the itinerary. In addition, a Goodyear service man would monitor tire pressure and provide each driver with written reports about the condition of his truck's tires, while a Vacuum Oil Company representative would take care of all of the trucks' lubrication needs. A representative from the Atlas Film Company was also on the tour, and took photographs and motion picture films during stops in towns as part of a plan to share footage with the U.S. Department of Agriculture for use in educating the public about trucks. As the caravan left Chicago, the trucks were escorted out of the city by police, and the "epoch making tour was under way in real earnest."[39]

There were no direct sales representatives on the tour, but manufacturers instead relied on local dealers and distributors to create marking opportunities along the route. According to planners, "this emphasized the fact that it really was a cooperative and educational effort rather than purely a selfish sales effort."[40]

Each stop on the itinerary varied in length from one hour to several days, depending on the population in each destination. Each of the trucks on the tour carried signs that shared statistics related to the performance of a truck compared to a horse. The Clydesdale truck, for example, carried a sign that read: "A motor truck makes three round trips to each one of a horse drawn vehicle." In addition, two men were dispatched ahead of the tour to stop in every city along the route, make local arrangements, visit newspapers, and generate as much publicity ahead of the caravan as possible.

The first stop on the tour was Elgin, Illinois, outside of Chicago. Demonstrations were scheduled, and several trucks were dispatched to farms to haul wheat and grain. Records were kept of costs to illustrate for farmers the comparison between the truck and the horse. It was even reported that one dealer made a sale immediately following one of the demonstrations. One driver on the tour explained how one stop was a success:

One incident that happened during the first few days of the tour stands out very clearly in my memory. It happened not far from Lena, Illinois. We had left Freeport early that morning and had been rolling along the road very smoothly for a couple of hours when we were suddenly

Clydesdale truck hauls baskets of potatoes for a farm family. Notice the woman in the driver's seat, which is on the right side of the cab.

flagged by a hayrack load of farmers. These men were on their way to haul oats to a threshing machine. When we stopped they asked if we wanted a real job. It seemed that the threshing rig was set in the cow yard, the oat field was about a quarter of a mile away, and the crew was short of wagons. In a few minutes the ... trucks were on their way to the field. While the trucks were in the field the moving picture men got busy and recorded the whole business, from the loading of the oats to the hauling away of the grain from the grain thresher, and next fall or winter these same farmers will have an opportunity to see themselves in the "movies."[41]

The Clydesdale Motor Truck Company played an active role throughout the National Motor Truck Development Tour. Clydesdale representative Mr. Hannon became a featured speaker at many of the stops along the tour route. In addition, the Clydesdale truck was frequently dispatched to perform work as part of daily demonstrations.

In addition to educating spectators about trucks and their functionality, the tour also raised awareness about then new automobile technology and accessories. For example, all of the trucks along the tour rode on pneumatic tires in a show of raising public awareness about the economy of air-filled tires for truck hauling. Early Clydesdales and other trucks featured hard rubber tires, which vibrated violently at speeds greater than 15 miles per hour. Pneumatic tires, however, alleviated these riding conditions. Many drivers were skeptical that an air-filled tire could provide a more reliable and efficient base for a truck than the solid and sturdy hard rubber tire. After all, it was *air*. There was also concern that air-filled tires on a road surface could be easily punctured. On the National Tour, Goodyear Tire and Rubber provided pneumatic tires for all of the trucks, along with men who checked tire pressures each day. The manufacturers hoped to demonstrate the efficiency and economy of pneumatic tires, as well as their general performance on roads.

The tour made a 3,000-mile loop through six Midwestern and Western states — it traveled west through Iowa, then north across South Dakota and North Dakota, then southeast into Minnesota and Wisconsin. Reports from along the tour were numerous. On August 14, 1919, the tour stopped in Iowa City. The Clydesdale truck on the tour attended to threshing operations at a farm that belonged to Mr. Frank Gilbert. The truck continued hauling operations until 8:00 in the evening. Again, on September 10, the Clydesdale assisted with threshing duties on a farm in Grand Fork, North Dakota. Then, on September 21, just outside of Sleepy Eye, Minnesota, the Clydesdale truck hauled two loads, two tons each, for a local farmer.

The trucks completed the National Motor Truck Development Tour two months after it began, on October 4, 1919, in Milwaukee. It was the largest and longest tour of its kind at the time, and organizers marketed its success as evidence of the reliability and efficiency of the motor truck. They hoped that such a tour — completed on schedule, with such a variety of successful demonstrations — would be "prima facie evidence of the dependability of the motor truck."[42] The Clydesdale company followed the tour with a special advertisement depicting townspeople crowded around the Farm Special, featuring the headline, "They are interested in Clydesdale."[43]

Inspired by the success of the National Motor Truck Development Tour, smaller tours immediately began taking place across the United States. Significant tours left from Los Angeles, California; Omaha, Nebraska; and Columbus, Ohio. Taking advantage of the success of the early national tour, and the opportunity to reach an even wider audience, the Clydesdale company participated in several other activities targeting the American farmer.

To demonstrate just how useful a truck could be a on a farm, this Clydesdale is winching a barn to a new location.

Many of these events were within weeks of one another. It is worth noting that only a company with a national network of personnel could manage such rigorous schedules. Not long after completing the Development Tour, for example, Clydesdale trucks appeared at the National Dairy Show in Chicago. Held at the International Amphitheater at the Union Stockyards, October 6–12, 1919, the Dairy Show included a special motor trucks exhibit. Clydesdale appeared, along with fourteen other truck makers.[44]

During the following week, October 13–18, 1919, the Clydesdale Motor Truck Company was one of thirty truck makers that participated in a 500-mile tour around the state of Iowa. The Des Moines Motor Truck Dealers Association sponsored the trip. As they had done during the national tour, the trucks carried farm implements and other merchandise, and participated in demonstrations along the way. The tour left Des Moines on October 13, then traveled north to Nevada, Iowa; then east to Kellogg, Iowa; and then south to Eddyville and Albia. On October 16, 1919, the tour then headed back west, stopping in Creston, Iowa, before heading north to Winterset and Adel, and finally, east back to Des Moines. A.R. Kroh, who had been in charge of the National Development Tour, joined the Des Moines tour as the keynote speaker.[45] A Delco lighting apparatus was also carried on the tour, so that 100 20-watt lamps could illuminate the trucks at night.

A few months later, during the next year, the Clydesdale company participated in one more truck tour, this time in Wisconsin. The tour left Milwaukee on June 28, 1920. It was sponsored by the *Milwaukee Sentinel* newspaper, and included twenty different trucks. Clydesdale again showcased the 1½-ton Farm Special model. "Free demonstrations were given at every stop and at times the line was halted while a truck or two went out into a

They Are Interested in Clydesdale

This is an illustration of the immense amount of interest displayed in Clydesdale's exclusive feature, "The Driver Under the Hood."

The truck shown is the one which went on the National Truck Development Tour, and the men are prospective truck purchasers in one of the towns at which the truck train stopped. These men had heard of the "Driver Under the Hood" and were so engrossed in an examination of it that they failed to see the camera man.

This intense interest which is always shown in "The Driver Under the Hood" is one of the secrets of the success of Clydesdale dealers. And back of this are engineering principles and manufacturing practices which have made the Clydesdale a leader among motor trucks for more than eight years.

Increased production facilities will enable us to offer the Clydesdale franchise to a few more dealers who have facilities for handling a "world proven" motor truck.

No Other Truck Has It
" The Driver Under the Hood "

One to Five Tons Net Load

THE CLYDESDALE MOTOR TRUCK COMPANY, CLYDE, OHIO

Please Mention "Motor West" When Writing to the Advertiser

"They Are Interested in Clydesdale": This advertisement appeared in the February 1, 1920, issue of *Motor West* magazine, and depicted a scene from the recently completed National Motor Truck Development Tour. It described the men as so engrossed in the "Driver Under the Hood" that "they failed to see the camera man." The Clydesdale automatic controller is also featured in the foreground.

farmer's field at a psychological moment to do some hauling." The entire tour covered 350 miles and returned to Milwaukee on July 3, 1920. Like the other tours, the purpose of this trip was to "educate the farmer to the utility of the motor vehicle in agricultural haulage," and "to demonstrate the only feasible means of efficient and economical transportation."[46]

Once a farmer bought a Clydesdale truck, there was the need for regular maintenance. Perhaps the most personal and lasting way that the Clydesdale company supported farmers who were transitioning from horse to truck was through the truck's 24-page owner's manual. The standard manual offered basic dos and don'ts of truck operation, lubrication charts, and troubleshooting advice. Notably, it compared the care of a truck to the care of a horse and other livestock in very accessible ways. "Take a horse and keep him fed well, well groomed, well shod, and treat him kindly and he will do twice the amount of work and remain in good condition. Treat your truck with the same consideration — don't overload it, for it cannot complain."[47]

The Art of Clydesdale Advertising

Many of the advertisements for Clydesdale trucks feature beautiful line drawings and sketches. Most of the drawings and sketches are unsigned, but several advertisements were signed by Herbert Bohnert. Having signed advertisements provides a glimpse into the artistry that went into company advertisements during this time.

Born in 1888 in Cleveland, Ohio, Herbert Bohnert had a lucrative career as a commercial advertising artist. He studied at the Cleveland School of Art, and was compared during his career to his contemporary, Norman Rockwell. Bohnert drew advertisements for other companies such as Dutch Boy Paints, Royal Electric Vacuum Cleaners, Art Selz Footwear, and Gulf Gas.

There are also Clydesdale Motor Truck Company advertisements signed by another commercial artist named Ben Rino. Less is known about Ben Rino, but he did do advertisements for Royal Typewriters and Atlas Portland Cement, in addition to Clydesdale.

Visit Us at the Show

In addition to truck tours, the Clydesdale Motor Truck Company participated in some of the nation's earliest automobile shows. Much like today, both national and local auto shows were meant to highlight the latest automobile and truck technology available to both individuals and businesses. Unlike today, however, auto shows were one of the primary ways that manufacturers and dealers interacted with members of the general public. Outside of print advertising, walking into a dealership, or a truck tour passing through the community, auto shows were the most accessible places to see new trucks and learn about their capabilities.

Auto shows happened frequently in cities across the country, most prominently in New York, Detroit, Chicago, and Los Angeles, and showcased the most advanced technology related to cars, trucks, and accessories. As trucks grew in popularity, however, it became increasingly difficult for show organizers to accommodate both cars and trucks, in addition to the crowds that each type of vehicle attracted. As one trade journal author noted: "From insignificant beginnings a comparatively few years ago," the truck manufacturing industry

CLYDESDALE
A WORLD-PROVEN MOTOR TRUCK

T HE *"Factor of Safety,"* as it is called by engineers—*strength in reserve*—is determined by putting a structure to tests more exacting than likely to be encountered in its contemplated usage.

The Clydesdale is a truck built for American haulage requirements, which by its record in world-wide service—more comprehensive in the aggregate than any national usage alone could be—has established a "Factor of Safety" unique in American motor truck building.

The superstandard construction of the Clydesdale, with its oversize and over-strength parts, and its excess power has made it famous for its draft work in thirty countries, from Iceland to Africa, in all climates, on all varieties of roads, with all sorts of drivers.

In America, Clydesdale Trucks are in use by such concerns as:

Standard Sanitary Mfg. Co.
Regal Shoe Co.
Frick Coke Company
American Red Cross
U. S. Government

One to Five Ton Capacities

CLYDESDALE MOTOR TRUCKS *built in* CLYDE, OHIO
By Truck Builders Among the Oldest in America

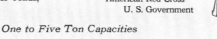

Good Roads and Motor Trucks Will Reduce the Cost of Living

This Clydesdale Motor Truck Company advertisement appeared in the February 15, 1919, issue of the *Saturday Evening Post*, and features a sketch by commercial artist Herbert Bohnert. The inset reads "Clydesdales in Java," the Clydesdale radiator is featured prominently.

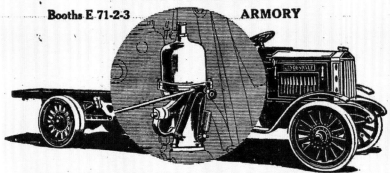

This advertisement, which appeared in the *New York Sun*, invited readers to "See the Driver Under the Hood" at the 1919 New York Auto Show. The Clydesdale automatic controller is featured prominently as the centerpiece of the motor truck. There is also notice that the Clydesdale Motor Truck Company will have three booths, E 71, 72, and 73, and representative available from the company's New York distributor, Arlington Motors Company.

"set a pace that requires 'seven league boots' to follow."[48] As a result, many major auto shows held separate "motor truck" shows, or maintained "motor truck departments." Thus, the Clydesdale Motor Truck Company participated in many motor truck shows in connection with larger automobile shows.

Following success at the automobile show in Boston in 1918, Clydesdale representatives attended a variety of shows the following year. While it is impossible to know exactly how many shows the company participated in, records show that the Clydesdale Motor Truck Company managed exhibits at no fewer than 15 national motor truck and automobile shows between 1919 and 1921.

The first show that the Clydesdale company attended in 1919 was the 19th Annual New York Automobile Show, which took place January 3–10 of that year. As one of the first cities to host a large annual show, New York made sure its show was quite significant. Like the Chicago show, it was typically managed by the National Automobile Chamber of Commerce, a national organization of manufacturers, dealers, and other industry players. Most industry leaders sought membership, which offered not only a ticket to exhibit at shows, but also endorsement from industry peers. Members were elected, with membership based on the standing of the manufacturer, permanency of business, and their importance to the trade. Many times, national auto show exhibit space was distributed among Chamber members through a lottery system. The Clydesdale Motor Truck Company was an active member of the Chamber by 1918.

During the 1919 New York show, passenger cars were exhibited at Madison Square Garden, and trucks were across the street at the Sixty-Ninth Regiment Armory. Clydesdale representatives exhibited all six of the available models across Booths 71, 72, and 73 in the truck show hall. They were one of 63 truck makers from across the country to attend the show. Local Clydesdale dealer A.E. Hoffman, from the Arlington Motor Company, explained to the *Sun* why he agreed to be available at the show to talk to attendees about the exhibited trucks:

> In the Clydesdale trucks, which we have been handling for quite a few years now, we claim to have one of the most perfect running trucks built in America and one of the most lasting. But if anything should go wrong, which in 89 out of a 100 instances is due to the incompetency of their drivers, as our statistics show, we are here to make good in a manner that can leave no question of dissatisfaction. Hundreds of Clydesdale users in this city know this, and it is one of the reasons for the truck's big success in this territory, wholly irrespective of the well known merits of the Clydesdales.[49]

Throughout the week, in addition to the expanse of exhibits, there were meetings to share information about motor haulage and transportation issues. According to trade journals, "Viewed from any angle, [the show] was a success."[50]

Just a couple of weeks later, January 24–31, 1919, Clydesdale trucks appeared again at the Chicago Auto Show with 60 other truck makers. The show at the Coliseum also included 87 passenger car manufacturers and 134 accessory exhibitors. This was the first national truck show to take place in the city since 1913, and it was "pronounced a success from the very start until its close."[51]

The Clydesdale trucks received attention at the Chicago show thanks to the patented automatic controller. "A simple and effective engine governor was brought to the attention of truck men, as part of the equipment of the Clydesdale truck," reported *Automobile Topics*, a trade journal. By the end of the show, it was realized that "order blanks had to be produced soon after the doors were opened, and many a dotted line was smeared with ink." The Clydesdale Motor Truck Company added another successful show exhibit to its record.

Two months after the Chicago show, in March of 1919, the Clydesdale Motor Truck Company attended *three* more shows. The Detroit Auto Show, which took place March 1–8, seems to have been the grandest of the spring shows. At least one trade journal described the show as "Detroit's greatest."[52] It was staged in the new Crosstown Corporation building, which was a mammoth — occupying approximately five acres — showroom that had been opened by Detroit's King Motor Car Company that year. "In past years, Detroit's shows have been so crowded that many exhibitors have been forced to show only half of their models. This year's show will find them with a complete line of cars on exhibition, with many new features which the show management has never before dared to attempt."[53] In fact, the exhibition was complete, even surprising. Alone, the row of trucks at the show was 400 feet long. Attendees also had opportunities to purchase airplanes. One manufacturer attended the show "to offer the public an opportunity to purchase airships for personal use." This mode of transport, predicted trade journals, "is undoubtedly going to be extremely popular in the near future."

On the heels of the Detroit show, Clydesdale Motor Truck Company representatives also appeared in the Dayton Auto Trades Association exposition, which opened on March 8, 1919. This event, like the one in Detroit, also featured airplanes for sale within the 86,000-square-feet exhibition hall. Clydesdale was one of 46 truck manufacturers to appear at the show, along with 115 passenger car makers, and 2 tank manufacturers. According to trade magazines, the show opened majestically, with one of the airplanes flying low over the show building and dropping free admission passes down to the crowd waiting outside. Inside the hall, there was a 40-piece band entertaining show attendees. One Clydesdale truck wowed attendees with its demonstrated hauling ability, even while significantly overloaded. "One of the most interesting exhibits of the show was a 7½-ton tank mounted on a 3½-ton Clydesdale truck. The tank was placed on the truck at the plant of the manufacturers, the Platt Iron Works, and hauled for more than three miles."[54]

After Dayton, Clydesdale representatives headed back to Boston by the end of March 1919. The auto show that year was held around the city in individual company and dealership showrooms, as the large venues in the city were all in use by the federal government for post-war operations. The Clydesdale showroom, located at 949 Commonwealth Avenue, was "especially decorated for the occasion," and the automatic controller again stole the show.[55]

In the summer of 1919, late August to early September, the Clydesdale Motor Truck Company appeared in an automobile show in Des Moines, as part of festivities taking place at the Iowa State Fair. This was apparently the last auto show in which Clydesdale trucks appeared that year. It was significant, as a follow-up to the National Motor Truck Development Tour, which had passed through the city earlier in the year. The show was held in Machinery Hall, and featured 43 passenger car makers, 38 truck manufacturers, including Clydesdale, and 19 truck accessory firms. Each exhibitor was allotted 600 square feet of exhibit space, making the entire show one of the largest in Iowa history. The show was open for ten days, was free to the public, and attracted an estimated 250,000 visitors. When it was all over, officials declared that the show "has drawn the biggest crowd that any motor show ever attracted in Iowa."[56]

By 1920, organizers of the 20th National Auto Show in New York were predicting record numbers of exhibitors, especially truck manufacturers. Clydesdale, too, prepared for additional profits and increased marketing. During that year, the Clydesdale Motor Truck Company exhibited at no fewer than seven auto shows, or one more than they attended during the previous year, and expanded to new locations. The New York show was an industry first for the year, and celebrated the growth of the motor truck:

> The motor truck has grown from a tolerated experiment as an industrial utility at the beginning of the century to a medium of transportation indispensible to the business world of the year 1920. It is now found bearing the burden of traffic in every quarter of the globe, cutting paths for commerce where highways do not exist and railroads are but a dream of the future. No region seems too remote, no country too forbidding, to deter the motor truck from becoming the pathfinder of commerce.[57]

The New York show, which took place January 3–10, 1920, was the largest show that the Clydesdale Motor Truck Company had attended up to that date. It included 77 truck companies, along with 86 car manufacturers, and 234 accessories manufacturers. Passenger cars filled the Grand Central Palace, so the trucks and accessories were stationed at the 8th Coast Artillery Armory, which, as trade journals reported, proved to be a distance away from the rest of the show. Despite the separated exhibit halls, all of the halls were checked out for one show. The bunting to decorate the ceiling in both halls of the show, reported *Motor West*, weighed 8½ tons.[58] Programs during the New York 1920 show also included a Motor Transport Conference and a Motor Truck Reliability Contest. While it is not certain if any Clydesdale trucks participated in the contest, or even which models the Clydesdale company exhibited at the general show, it was estimated that most of the motor trucks on display were of the 1½- and 2-ton capacities.

One week after the New York show, Clydesdale appeared in Philadelphia, at the city's 19th annual show. Like New York's, Philadelphia's show was bigger than ever before, and attracted approximately 60,000 visitors. The Clydesdale truck's patented automatic controller piqued attendees' interest, as it had as other shows and on earlier tours. "Creating more than passing interest was the exclusive Clydesdale truck feature, the automatic speed controller, which because of the manner in which it operates to assist the driver, has been aptly described as "The Driver Under the Hood.""[59]

From Philadelphia, the Clydesdale Motor Truck Company exhibition traveled to Hartford, Connecticut, where the Automobile Trades Association opened its first show on January 17, 1920. The show was open for one week, and exhibited all of the truck makers with showrooms in the region.

At the end of January 1920, Clydesdale appeared at the Chicago Motor Truck Show, in conjunction with the annual Chicago Auto Show. Reviewers of the Chicago Auto Show, in particular, were optimistic about truck production for the coming year, and declared 1920 would be "the most successful year in the automotive business."[60] The Chicago show, staged at the International Amphitheater, by one account, was "the world's greatest exhibit of automobiles and trucks ever staged."[61] Four different truck parades throughout the city preceded the show's opening. And Mr. Ed Spooner painted a chaotic scene in *Motor West*:

> Every train on Monday brought people into town in swarms. Trade men packed hotel lobbies, looking for kind Samaritans who would let cots be placed in their rooms. Outside of every hotel checking room, grips were piled high. "What Will I Do For a Bed Tonight?" was the prevailing

Motor Truck and Accessories Exhibitors at the 20th National Automobile Show in the 8th Coast Artillery Armory, New York City

MOTOR TRUCKS.

Acason Motor Truck Co.
Acme Motor Truck Co.
American Motor Truck Co.
Armleder Sales & Service Co.
Atterbury Motor Car Co.
Autocar Co.
Bethlehem Motors Corp.
Brockway Motor Truck Co.
Clydesdale Motor Truck Co.
Commerce Motor Car Co.
Corbitt Motor Truck Co.
Commercial Car Unit Co.
Commercial Truck Co. of Amer.
Denby Motor Truck Co.
Diamond T Motor Car Co.

Maxwell Motor Co.
Nash Motors Co.
Olds Motor Works
Oneida Motor Truck Co.
Packard Motor Car Co.
Paige-Detroit Motor Car Co.
Pierce-Arrow Motor Car Co.
Rainier Motor Corp.
Reo Motor Car Co.
Republic Motor Truck Co.
Rowe Motor Mfg. Co.
Sandow Motor Truck Co.
Sanford Motor Truck Co.
Schact Motor Truck Co., G. A.
Schwartz Motor Truck Co.
Selden Truck Corp.
Standard Motor Truck Co.

TRAILERS.

Hayes-Diefenderfer Co., Inc.
Warner Mfg. Co.

BODIES.

Metropolitan Body Co., Inc.
Parry Mfg. Co.

ACCESSORIES.

Af-Ford-Able Sales Co. of N. Y., Inc.
Aluminum Brazing Solder Co.
Aluminum Castings Co.
American Bosch Magneto Corp.
American Chain Co., Inc.

Flint Motor Axle Co.
Franklin Machine & Tool Co.
Gray & Davis, Inc.
Hercules Motor Mfg. Co.
Hero Mfg. Co.
Horizontal Hydraulic Hoist Co.
Houpert Machine Co.
Hudson Motor Specialties Co.
Humil Corp.
Jaxon Steel Products Co.
Lauraine Magneto Co.
Lobee Body Co., Inc.
Mead-Morrison Mfg. Co.
Merchant & Evans Co.
Minneapolis Steel & Mach. Co.
Motor Compressor Co.
Pantasote Co.

8th COAST ARTILLERY ARMORY, NEW YORK CITY, WHERE NATIONAL MOTOR TRUCK SHOW WILL BE HELD.

Dodge Brothers
Dorris Motor Car Co.
Federal Motor Truck Co.
Four-Wheel-Drive Motor Truck Co.
Garford Motor Truck Co.
Gramm-Bernstein Motor Truck Co.
Huffman Bros. Motor Co.
Indiana Truck Corp.
International Harvester Corp.
Jackson Automobile Co.
Nelson Motor Truck Co.
Kelly-Springfield Motor Truck Co.
Kissel Motor Car Co.
Koehler Motors Corp., H. J.
Master Trucks, Inc.

Sterling Motor Truck Co.
Stewart Motor Corp.
Sullivan Motor Truck Corp.
Trailmobile Co.
Transport Truck Co.
Three-Point Truck Co.
Triangle Motor Truck Sales Co.
Turnbull Mot. Truck & Wag. Co.
Union Motor Truck Co.
Velie Motors Corp.
Vim Motor Truck Co.
Maccar Truck Co.
Walker Vehicle Co.
Walter Motor Truck Co.
Ward Motor Vehicle Co.
Ward-La France Truck Co.
Wilson Co., J. C.
Winther Motor Truck Co.

American Machine Co.
American Taximeter Co.
Apollo Magneto Corp.
Arrow-Grip Mfg. Co.
Baush Machine Tool Co.
Bendus, J. V.
Buda Co.
Byrne, Kingston & Co.
Challoner Co.
Clark Equipment Co.
Commercial Investment Trust
Continental Motors Corp.
Dayton Steel Foundry Co.
Dixon Crucible Co., Jos.
Duplex Engine Governor Co.
Eastern Machine Co.
Eisemann Magneto Co.
Empire Axle Co.

Parker Axle & Products Corp.
Parry Mfg. Co.
Robertson Cradlelock Wheel Co.
Russell Motor Axle Co.
Schrader's Son, Inc., A.
Service Engineering Co.
Sewell Cushion Wheel Co.
Splitdorf Electrical Co.
Standard Motor Castings Co.
Stromberg Motor Devices Co.
Torbensen Axle Co.
U. S. Specialty Co.
Vacuum Oil Co.
Vaporizer Utilities Sales Corp.
Wellman-Seaver-Morgan Co.
West Steel Casting Co.
Wheeler-Schebler Carburetor Co.
Wisconsin Motor Mfg. Co.

Advertisement for the 1920 New York Auto Show that appeared in the January 1, 1920, issue of *Motor West* magazine. Clydesdale Motor Truck Company is listed among 77 other truck companies, along with 86 car manufacturers, and 234 accessories manufacturers. It was the largest show that the company participated in that year.

song. The hotels had asked ordinary travelers not to "make" Chicago during automobile show week, and otherwise did their best to serve automobile and motor truck men.[62]

The Clydesdale Motor Truck Company appeared with 64 other motor truck exhibitors, along with 84 passenger car exhibitors, and 230 accessories manufacturers and dealers. More people than expected attended the show, and "it was a buying crowd."[63] Special events "drew larger attendances than in any previous year and the participants represented a far greater area of America and more foreign countries than ever before."[64]

Perhaps the successful appearances at several national auto shows and exhibitions that inspired Clydesdale executives to boldly announce in February 1920 that the "Clydesdale Truck sells on appearance":

> It has come to the point, in the experience of the Clydesdale Motor Truck [Company], where shrewd business men are as much influenced by the appearance of a motor truck they contemplate buying, as of a passenger car. In the case of the Clydesdale, appearance symbolizes ruggedness and sureness, qualities which, it is believed, account for its cumulative success.[65]

After four shows in January alone, there were still three more shows scheduled for that year. One month later, February 21–28, Clydesdale participated in the Fourth Annual Pacific Auto Show, in San Francisco. Clydesdale's presence at this West Coast show was especially significant. Not all American truck manufacturers had the resources to travel across the country to attend both East and West Coast auto shows. Other manufacturers lacked a national market infrastructure to fulfill demands for trucks so far away from their manufacturing headquarters, or to ship large numbers of ordered trucks. The Clydesdale Company, however, operated a very successful dealership in San Francisco, which facilitated sales on the West Coast.

In all, 54 passenger car manufacturers, 55 motor truck makers, and more than 60 accessories representatives crowded San Francisco's Exposition Auditorium for the 1920 show. Themed around a theme of exploring the outdoors via car and truck, the show was elaborately decorated with scenery of West Coast mountains, large colonnades and fountains, and special lighting meant to mimic natural sun. Willis Polk, architectural critic, described the scene as "deserving perpetuation in enduring marble. The panoramas of California's scenic wonders alone are worth countless thousands of dollars to the state's enterprises and industries."[66] In addition, three different jazz ensembles helped to create a carnival atmosphere. "Unparalleled in every detail, this year's motor exposition — the first big post-war gathering of automobile dealers, distributors, and enthusiasts on the Coast — gives promise of rolling up a record of public commendation which will echo in all the big cities of the East."[67]

After San Francisco, still in the spring of 1920, Clydesdale attended two more national auto shows, one in the East, and another also on the West Coast. The 18th Annual Auto Show in Boston took place March 13–20, 1920, sponsored by the Boston Automobile Dealers Association and the Boston Commercial Vehicles Association. The Clydesdale Motor Truck Company was one of 75 truck exhibitors. The truck show, in particular, gained press for attracting a record number of 2,000 dealers as attendees.[68]

Two weeks later, the Los Angeles Motor Truck Show, which followed the Los Angeles Auto Show, opened on March 27, 1920. The show took place mostly outdoors, in the city's Praeger Park, with a large canvas tent covering all of the trucks. "Practically every type of motor transport, from the light delivery car to the ponderous highway freight carrier and all types of farm tractors and a wide variety of accessories which increase the efficiency of the motor truck are to be found under the great canvas tent housing the show."[69] The Clydesdale Motor Truck Company again participated in the show, along with 23 other truck manufacturers and 21 accessories manufacturers. The show closed on April 3.

By the end of 1920, automobile show planners were beginning to question whether or not the "still" truck show model, or the exhibition of stationary trucks, was successful. While Clydesdale officials were satisfied with overall attendance at shows, many of the 1920 show crowds simply had not matched industry predictions. The market was shifting. This was, in large part, due to the success of so many motor truck tours. Members of the public enjoyed seeing trucks in motion. According to experts, "still" truck shows were no longer the most logical way to exhibit trucks. "Laboring appliances in evening clothes," suggested at least one trade journal, were not going to induce sales. "The only way to show transportation, highway or other kind, is to show it. And the only place to show it is out in the open where there is room to transport something."[70]

Later that year, in September, Clydesdale trucks participated in just such an exhibit at the Wisconsin State Fair called "Truck Town." Organizers created a miniature city within the fairgrounds and used trucks to perform a variety of functions within the small town. They "demonstrated to the thousands of visitors the many ways in which modern motor trucks accomplish big transportation economics." Each of the approximately 50 exhibitors, including the Clydesdale Motor Truck Company, had a "house" in the city, along with a place to park their trucks. Trade journals declared the demonstrations within "Truck Town" a success, and the town itself "a novel setting."[71]

In an immediate effort to promote confidence in the Clydesdale brand for new customers, the company agreed in October 1920 to lock all Clydesdale truck prices until April 1921. In addition to the price guarantee, the company offered to refund every customer any difference if prices ended up decreasing after purchase.[72]

Throughout 1921, Clydesdale representatives exhibited trucks at fewer automobile shows than in previous years; they attended just three. However, the shows they attended were significant as industry standouts. In the new year, January 3–8, 1921, another "still" truck show opened in New York, despite concerns from industry leaders. The traditional event organizers, the National Automobile Chamber of Commerce and the Automobile Dealers Association of New York, both voted not to organize a show after slumping attendance by the end of 1920. Truck owners, however, maintained that the truck audience still valued a national show, and set out to prove industry experts wrong. The 1921 New York show was significant because it was the first national auto show organized by an owners' organization, the Motor Truck Association of America. They billed the show as a "highway transportation show," which included not only the usual fare of car, truck, and accessories manufacturers, but also education programs, films, and family-friendly events meant to attract the public. Organizers distributed free tickets and offered contests and door prizes, and manufacturers unveiled nearly a dozen new models throughout the week. There were also special promotions, including "Army Day" and "Motor Accident Prevention Day," which were meant to attract attendees. By week's end, however, organizers were thoroughly disappointed. One trade magazine reported, "The men in charge of this year's show found it difficult to induce even a small percentage of the small crowds to climb the stairs to the lecture hall, and finally resorted to presenting speakers at the edge of the armory balcony, where they shouted down to small and ever-changing groups of people, half of them exhibitors, gathered on the [floor] below."[73]

The Clydesdale Motor Truck Company participated in the show, along with just 24 other truck manufacturers. By the end of the show, some exhibitors had declared it a waste of time and money, and there was uncertainty about whether or not such shows would continue. "New York may have another 'still' truck show, and other cities may hold them for another year or so, but among thinking men in the business the trend is away from this sort of promotion and toward something more in harmony with the truck's place in the scheme of things. And the 'working' show is the most logical suggestion yet brought forward."[74]

The working truck show was not an entirely new concept to Clydesdale representatives. As a veteran national tour and show participant, they were familiar with the format, especially after their participation in the Milwaukee show the previous year. Industry leaders recognized the Milwaukee show as a model: "The truck dealers of Milwaukee did it last fall, where they exhibited trucks in booths out of doors and put trucks at work, with loads, on paved and unpaved highways, open fields and plowed ground and sold the motor transportation idea to thousands of farmers, merchants, manufacturers and transportation men who responded instantly to an invitation to see working appliances at work."[75]

With the working show format in mind, the Clydesdale company participated in just two more still shows that year. Representatives went to Boston, March 12–19, for the 1921 National Automobile Show. Organizers declared it a success, despite industry trends: "But the show — it did the job. It just threw all the conservatism and pessimism of old New England to the winds — it fairly shrieked its words of optimism and the enthusiasm and interest which resulted will go on for time indefinite."[76] One trade journal declared the spirit of optimism "very much alive," as thousands of industry experts and potential customers attended the show. Clydesdale's Boston distributor, Ralph Calef, was impressed with the success of the notably "still" show:

> Never before have we seen public interest centered to such an extent in trucks as during the Boston show. Aside from closing several spot cash sales during the week for heavy duty trucks, we obtained a wonderful list of prospects, with the result that our salesmen are now cashing in and each day are closing sales with prospects obtained at the show.... Never before have we received so many direct inquiries from prospects in outlying territory and from Maine, New Hampshire, and Vermont as during the past week.
>
> We are fairly satisfied that the corner has been turned and that truck sales will show a substantial and marked increase from now on. We can safely round it up in one small package by saying that public interest and attendance at the Boston show exceeded our fondest expectation by 100 per cent.[77]

In the fall of 1921, Clydesdale participated in one more still show, this time overseas. The Fifth International Motor Exhibition at Olympia, London, was one of the largest in Europe. Great Britain, historically, was the largest importer of American trucks compared to other European countries, so American manufacturers often attended the national shows. The trip, however, required time, money, and a market infrastructure that could support an international exhibit and sales. Clydesdale, of course, managed all of these resources, and exhibited, along with just 12 other American manufacturers.[78]

Ship-by-Truck

In addition to national truck tours and automobile shows, the Clydesdale Motor Truck Company also participated in industry efforts to improve roads and change national shipping practices. Clydesdale participated in the national Ship-by-Truck campaign for at least two

Don't Damn the Railroads— Use the Highways

WITH the whole world crying for greater production, and every artery of transportation fairly bursting from the load it must carry, the motor truck has surely come into its own.

No more is it a question of how long these conditions will last, but rather what can be done to relieve the pressure on our great common carriers. And the solution must be immediate, if our country is to avoid a traffic jam which will seriously affect our present prosperity.

The motor truck is rapidly becoming the master of today's situation. It is a strong thread in our commercial fabric, because it keeps the necessities of life from piling up in a useless heap at some congested freight terminal. It brings the farmer's product to market and keeps the city dweller from starving. It quickens the pulse of industry and opens the way to greater production. It stimulates investment in necessary enterprises by showing the possibilities of motor transportation to logical markets.

And finally, the motor truck has done more to convince our legislators of the necessity for good roads than has any other single factor.

So it behooves the owners of trucks to use them to the utmost, twenty-four hours if necessary, and thereby set an example which may be followed to the profit of business and the broad benefit of the people at large.

Clydesdale Motor Truck Company
Clyde, Ohio

"Don't Damn the Railroads — Use the Highways": This Clydesdale Motor Truck Company advertisement appeared in the June 26, 1920, issue of *Literary Digest*. It is one of a few special advertisements where the Clydesdale company issued an official statement on a policy issue, or in this case, an industry issue: shipping via truck compared to shipping via railroad. The "Ship-by-Truck" emblem appears on the left of the page. The Firestone Tire & Rubber Company had launched the "Ship-by-Truck" campaign annually since 1918 to encourage shipping by truck for long hauls. Truck shipments were cheaper and more efficient than rail shipments for distances under 300 miles.

The Literary Digest for July 24, 1920   109

Without Transportation Business Stands Still

EVERY community depends upon transportation for its development, indeed for its very existence. Every business man, large or small, depends upon transportation for every dollar he has invested.

Transportation by rail is at its peak. Freight cars are crowded to capacity, and the motor truck is serving the public as a very necessary adjunct to the railroads, both in collection and distribution of life's necessities.

Manufacturer, merchant, producer and consumer all must look to the motor truck as it directly influences their own lives. Without this servant everyone would be forced to sacrifice some modern day comforts and conveniences.

Therefore, no business can afford to stint its truck requirements. The same methods used to finance any essential to good business should be employed to secure adequate hauling equipment.

The bank which cares for your other business needs will clearly see the necessity of aiding you to solve the financial problem that may be holding back your transportation facilities.

THE CLYDESDALE MOTOR TRUCK COMPANY
CLYDE, OHIO

"Without Transportation Business Stands Still": This Clydesdale Motor Truck Company advertisement appeared in the July 24, 1920, issue of *Literary Digest*. It is another of the advertisements in which the "Ship-by-Truck" emblem appears on the left of the page. The Firestone Tire & Rubber Company had launched the "Ship-by-Truck" campaign.

A secondary purpose of the Ship-by-Truck campaign included raising awareness of road conditions across the country. After all, shipments by truck were challenging without proper roads. Road conditions varied with each location, with some locations offering less than desirable pavement, as shown here. With the Good Roads Movement already popular, the Ship-by-Truck campaign reinforced their agenda, advocating for safe and travel-friendly roads. The Clydesdale truck shown here has an open body. Notice the artillery wheels and the headlights — both important for traveling along a road like this one.

years, 1919 and 1920. Started as a marketing campaign by Firestone Tire and Rubber in 1918 to sell tires, Ship-by-Truck became an industry-wide movement, with supporters lobbying for better — in many cases this meant paved — roads, and the increased use of trucks for shipping and hauling materials short distances. As late as 1920, many manufacturers were limited to railroads for shipping. Railroads had long been established as practical and economical for long hauls. Railroad shipping for short hauls, or anything less than 300 miles, however, was impractical and expensive, which often resulted in higher costs for consumers. Railroad shipping for local deliveries was virtually impossible, given the distance between and frequency of railroad freight stops. Even long haul deliveries had a short haul at the end to deliver the product locally. American manufacturers quickly identified trucks as another option, more practical and less expensive than railroads for short hauls and local deliveries. One Clydesdale dealer described the "problem of the short haul":

> It is not the cost of raising crops that makes prices so high, but the cost of getting stuff to the consumer....
>
> This "short haul" is the problem to which the motor truck is the only known key. Statistics compiled by the government, and checked by various other sources, show that it costs more to deliver the average shipment *in* New York City than it does to get *to* the city.

Men from the Masson & Sons Fruit Company of Montreal, Quebec, Canada, load crates of fruit from a Clydesdale truck into a Canadian-Pacific Railroad car. The truck has a "Ship-by-Truck" logo in the windshield, so it is likely 1920. Also note the truck's unusual whitewall tires (*courtesy of the McCord Museum, Montreal, Quebec, Canada*).

> The National Motor Truck Development Tour proved that seven properly equipped trucks could feed a thresher better than ten teams with wagons and five more men. Taking grain to the elevators by truck is accomplished in ⅓ less time than by teams. These are merely other examples of "short hauls."
> At first the truck was considered a competitor of the horse. Now it competes with the railroads, and better yet, the railroads are welcoming the truck as an adjunct to the their business for they too have discovered that the "short haul" is unprofitable.[79]

At its time, the Ship-by-Truck campaign was the most concerted effort within the auto industry to raise awareness of the need for quality roads and truck shipping. A decentralized campaign for better roads all over the United States had already started in the late nineteenth century with the Good Roads Movement, as bicycles became popular and cyclists demanded higher quality roads. With the birth of the automobile, however, the movement gained traction. It was thrust into the national spotlight in 1916, when Woodrow Wilson included the need for quality roads in his presidential platform: "The happiness, comfort, and prosperity of rural life, and the development of the city, are alike conserved by the construction of public highways. We, therefore, favor national aid in the construction of post roads and roads for military purposes."[80]

The U.S. Army had launched several Transcontinental Motor Convoys, starting in 1917, which also helped to raise public awareness of the condition of the nation's roads. Prior to federal highway legislation, there were no guarantees of uniform, or even paved, roads in the country. It was up to each state, county, or community to maintain its own roads, so conditions varied between location. Truck makers quickly realized that in order for automobiles, especially trucks, to become widespread in every part of the country, roads had to be built and maintained at drastically increased levels of quality.

In expanding the Ship-by-Truck campaign from a corporate initiative to a national movement, Firestone established the Ship-by-Truck Association in March 1919, as well as the Ship-by-Truck Bureau. The bureau, with branch offices in 65 cities across the country, was charged with studying the "problems relating to the entrance on a sound business basis of the motor truck into our national, commercial, and economic life."[81] The bureau set out to promote the use of the truck "where it is economically feasible"; analyze efficient cost, operating, and business methods "with a view to advocating their general adoption"; plan cooperation with other forms or agencies of transportation "so that our country may have a complete, efficient, and economical scheme of transportation"; promote the construction and maintenance of roads "adequate for the proper use of the motor truck and the legitimate expansion of its service to encourage uniform and suitable legislation relating to the use of motor trucks, trailers, and the highways"; and cooperate with other agencies having "all of these policies or any one of them as their subject."[82]

The national movement's annual capstone was Ship-by-Truck Week, which occurred each year, starting in 1919. The week included parades in cities across the country, caravans to showcase trucks, and "Good Roads Sunday" sermons. There was a national essay contest for American high school students.

In 1919, Ship-by-Truck Week was actually three weeks long, and took place during the last week in September and the first two weeks in October. Thirty-two governors issued official proclamations in honor of the week in their states. There were parades in over 100 cities, with the largest stepping off in Brooklyn, with 3,051 trucks. The trucks then participated in longer tours.

The Clydesdale Motor Truck Company participated in at least two exclusive Ship-by-Truck tours. The first was in Buffalo, New York, and took place September 22–27, 1919. Sponsored by the Buffalo Truck Dealers Association, eighteen trucks traveled through nine counties and 48 cities. The purpose was to "educate the farmers and business men to the possibilities of highway motor transport, to demonstrate that trucks could be utilized to haul all commodities, and that a fleet could maintain a well-defined schedule."[83] The tour was a huge success. It passed through cities, reaching a combined one million New Yorkers. A band accompanied the tour and played concerts at night, which helped to attract interested crowds. "The fleet reached Hamburg to attend the Erie County fair, the officials of which presented an invitation to be present, and the trucks were paraded around the race track twice, which was some innovation for a fair."[84]

A couple of weeks later, Clydesdale trucks were participating in another Ship-by-Truck tour, in southern California. The Southern California Motor Truck Tour left Los Angeles on October 6, 1919. Thirty-seven trucks traveled a 65-mile route, carrying educational banners and capacity loads for delivery through thirty communities, including Long Beach, Pomona, San Bernadino, and Claremont. When the convoy arrived in Riverside, the mayor declared the day Motor Truck Day. "Everywhere the train was favored with the interest of the town and countryside. Farm work stopped while the caravan wound its long length of trucks carrying capacity loads that varied from drug store supplies to a colossus formed of baled hay."[85] The tour ended in Los Angeles on October 11, 1919. It was declared

STRENGTH

WITH PLENTY OF MARGIN FOR THE EMERGENCY

FROM the standpoint of materials, it is reasonable to assume that every motor truck is strong. The intelligent truck purchaser can judge material strength by appearance. But continuous performance demands strength of design to supplement strength of materials. It is an honest combination of the two which enables the Clydesdale truck to serve its owner faithfully without costly interruptions.

For instance, the Clydesdale frame is of pressed steel, *shaped so that the greatest strength comes at the point of greatest strain.* It is two inches deeper than the average, and is gusseted at every corner and cross member, so that no twist of road or load can possibly bend it. Compare this construction with rolled steel frames which cannot be so shaped, and one reason for Clydesdale sturdiness is apparent. Fewer repairs and slower depreciation are worth considering.

THE CLYDESDALE MOTOR TRUCK CO.
Clyde, Ohio

CLYDESDALE
MOTOR · TRUCKS

How This Controller Conserves Strength

The strength of most trucks is taxed to the utmost by the sudden strain put upon them when the motor is raced to get the load quickly under way. The speed of the motor is too great for the starting speed of the rear wheels, and every part is called upon to stand the shock until the speed is equalized. With the Clydesdale Controller to act on the gas supply, this cannot happen, since the motor starts the load *slowly* and picks up gradually to the speed set on the throttle No part is jerked into doing more than its share.

"Strength: with plenty of margin for the emergency": This advertisement from the September 25, 1920, issue of *Literary Digest*, and the three that follow, were a series that highlighted certain characteristics of the Clydesdale truck. The Clydesdale Automatic Controller is featured across the bottom of the page in each of these ads, which is unusual. Also unusual, these advertisements were signed by the artist, Ben Rino. He was a commercial artist hired by Clydesdale to draw the images in the foreground of the advertisement.

The Literary Digest for October 23, 1920 123

DEPENDABILITY

ONE TRUCK ON THE ROAD IS WORTH TWO IN THE SHOP

THE motor truck is only profitable if it is kept moving. To keep on the road and out of the shop, a truck must meet two important conditions: it must first be dependable in itself, and then it must be properly serviced. Dependability is paramount, though, for sometimes a truck must operate where service is not always instantly available.

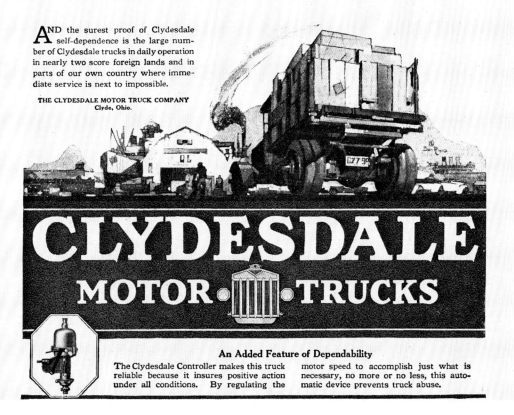

AND the surest proof of Clydesdale self-dependence is the large number of Clydesdale trucks in daily operation in nearly two score foreign lands and in parts of our own country where immediate service is next to impossible.

THE CLYDESDALE MOTOR TRUCK COMPANY
Clyde, Ohio.

CLYDESDALE
MOTOR ●|||||● TRUCKS

An Added Feature of Dependability

The Clydesdale Controller makes this truck reliable because it insures positive action under all conditions. By regulating the motor speed to accomplish just what is necessary, no more or no less, this automatic device prevents truck abuse.

"Dependability: One truck on the road is worth two in the shop": This advertisement is from the October 23, 1920, issue of *Literary Digest*.

PERFORMANCE
WHY DRIVERS SWEAR BY THIS TRUCK, NOT AT IT

WHILE the purchase of the first truck may not be influenced by the driver's opinion, the performance of that truck in the hands of the driver often determines the selection of a second one. Clydesdale preference among drivers is founded upon two facts—mechanical excellence which includes power, adequate speed and ease of adjustment, together with the Clydesdale Controller which enables the driver to forget everything but the road.

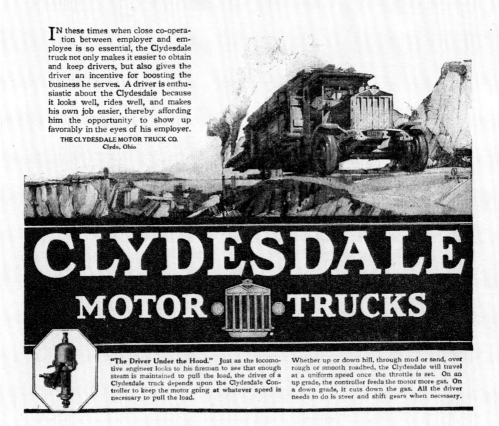

IN these times when close co-operation between employer and employee is so essential, the Clydesdale truck not only makes it easier to obtain and keep drivers, but also gives the driver an incentive for boosting the business he serves. A driver is enthusiastic about the Clydesdale because it looks well, rides well, and makes his own job easier, thereby affording him the opportunity to show up favorably in the eyes of his employer.

THE CLYDESDALE MOTOR TRUCK CO.
Clyde, Ohio

CLYDESDALE
MOTOR · TRUCKS

"The Driver Under the Hood." Just as the locomotive engineer looks to his fireman to see that enough steam is maintained to pull the load, the driver of a Clydesdale truck depends upon the Clydesdale Controller to keep the motor going at whatever speed is necessary to pull the load.

Whether up or down hill, through mud or sand, over rough or smooth roadbed, the Clydesdale will travel at a uniform speed once the throttle is set. On an up grade, the controller feeds the motor more gas. On a down grade, it cuts down the gas. All the driver needs to do is steer and shift gears when necessary.

"Performance: Why drivers swear by this truck, not at it": This advertisement is from the November 20, 1920, issue of *Literary Digest*.

The Literary Digest for December 18, 1920 83

ECONOMY

NOT MILES PER GALLON, BUT MILES PER TRUCK

WHILE the consumption of gas, oil and tires must figure in motor truck operation, the most important element is the length of a truck's life. Upon this element depends the answer to a vital question, "How much does my truck cost per ton-mile?" Clydesdale represents true economy in long life and low upkeep, with a record to prove it.

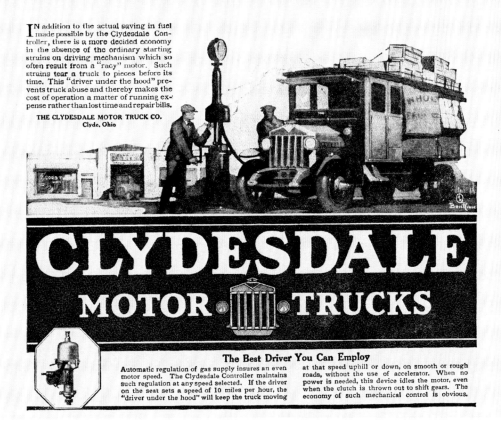

IN addition to the actual saving in fuel made possible by the Clydesdale Controller, there is a more decided economy in the absence of the ordinary starting strains on driving mechanism which so often result from a "racy" motor. Such strains tear a truck to pieces before its time. This "driver under the hood" prevents truck abuse and thereby makes the cost of operation a matter of running expense rather than lost time and repair bills.

THE CLYDESDALE MOTOR TRUCK CO.
Clyde, Ohio

CLYDESDALE
MOTOR TRUCKS

The Best Driver You Can Employ

Automatic regulation of gas supply insures an even motor speed. The Clydesdale Controller maintains such regulation at any speed selected. If the driver on the seat sets a speed of 10 miles per hour, the "driver under the hood" will keep the truck moving at that speed uphill or down, on smooth or rough roads, without the use of accelerator. When no power is needed, this device idles the motor, even when the clutch is thrown out to shift gears. The economy of such mechanical control is obvious.

"Economy: Not miles per gallon, but miles per truck": This advertisement is from the December 18, 1920, issue of *Literary Digest*.

a success and "may be taken to represent a great event in the growth and expansion of motor truck freighting on the Pacific Coast."[86]

At home in Clyde, Clydesdale officials took the Ship-by-Truck message to heart. Representatives implemented the use of trucks for short hauls in delivering supplies to the factory. They discovered a time and cost savings, compared to shipping parts by train, even though the railroad line was adjacent to the factory. An October 1919 issue of *Motor West* magazine noted how the company "spurns railroad":

> Some time ago, when the railroads were so short of cars that traffic was congested, the [Clydesdale Motor Truck Company], Clyde, Ohio, was so badly in need of axles for its trucks, that one of its 5-ton Clydesdale trucks was sent to the Timken-Detroit Axle Company, Detroit, for the parts. The trip was so successful that all axles have been so hauled ever since, and the company finds that it is cheaper and more convenient than shipping by railroad.[87]

Clydesdale company executives believed that an increased use of trucks for short hauls would actually be welcomed by railroads, which typically made more money on longer freight deliveries. If more railroad cars were emptied of less-profitable short hauls, they reasoned, there would be more room for long hauls, creating opportunities for larger profits. Ultimately, railroad traffic would move faster and more economically.

Ship-by-Truck Week took place in the following year during May 17–22, 1920, and was even grander, with more parades and events. The national essay contest attracted 250,000 entries. According to the *Pittsburgh Gazette*, over sixty truck trains traversed the United States, with each traveling an average of 300 miles.[88] The *New York Times* reported a glamorous parade that went down Broadway. In all, there were a combined 171 tours and parades during Ship-by-Truck Week in 1920.

The Clydesdale Motor Truck Company also participated in one Michigan truck train, which left Detroit on May 17, 1920. Fifty trucks participated in the tour, which made a loop around the state, first traveling north to cities such as Pontiac and Flint, then heading south toward Ann Arbor, traveling through cities such as Fenton, Milford, Novi, and Ypsilanti. When the train reached Ann Arbor, the city's Chamber of Commerce planned a dinner for everyone on the tour. After Ann Arbor, the caravan headed back toward Detroit, going through cities such as Adrian, Chelsea, Deerfield, Inkster, and Dearborn along the way. When the truck train returned to Detroit, five days later, the Detroit Automobile Dealers Association hosted a banquet for the travelers. Harvey Firestone was the keynote speaker.

The Ship-by-Truck campaign's inclusion of the Clydesdale Motor Truck Company's participation in related events and advertising ultimately did effect the passage of early American highway legislation. Senator Charles Townsend, from Michigan, recognized the need for a "broadened policy which will concentrate government funds on national highways, releasing state and county funds for the use on state and county roads. Nothing could be more valuable than a national discussion of this question such as that proposed during the National Ship By Truck-Good Roads Week."[89] The Federal Highway Act of 1921 increased federal funding for roads, and laid the groundwork for subsequent funding and the development of a national highway system.

In the span of just three years following World War I, Clydesdale proved just as active and successful in domestic markets as overseas and on the battlefield. By the end of

1921, the Clydesdale Motor Truck Company was truly at the height of prosperity — expanding production, taking the national stage in shows and tours, and building relationships with the millions of Americans transitioning from horse to truck. This foundation of international and domestic success would leave the company poised to face challenges in the years ahead.

4

New Directions (1922–1932)

On May 1, 1922, Clydesdale Motor Truck Company introduced a new truck: an all-steel model that they nicknamed the Model-10. After several years as part of the national tour and automobile show circuit, Clydesdale engineers had developed a fresh, innovative truck model especially for the everyday consumer and small business owner. It was billed, with considerable fanfare, as a lighter truck, with a carrying capacity of 3,850 pounds, but developed with larger carrying capacities in mind.

> From the Radiator, to the Rear Axle, the Design and Construction of the Model-10 combines the most advanced European and American Engineering Practice with the highest quality of materials to be had. All units and parts are "over size." The frame, for instance, is of the same size section as is usually used in the construction of trucks having a rated capacity of over two tons. Not only the top spring leaf, but ALL the spring leaves are of chrome vanadium steel. Only on large trucks of the highest quality (such as the other Clydesdale models) is there to be found a radiator made of expensive copper tubes. The castings used throughout are of steel instead of iron, thereby earning the name "THE ALL STEEL TRUCK."[1]

The new motor truck chassis was priced at $1,485, significantly lower than comparable trucks on the market at that time. It was priced to sell, and, according to Clydesdale officials, at a discount because of lower materials and production costs. Marketed as "speedy," the truck achieved a maximum speed of 35 miles per hour. "Light and graceful in design, the truck combines the reliability of the Clydesdale product with the flexibility and easy running qualities of a well built passenger car.[2]

Vice-president and general manager A.J. Banta explained how the new Clydesdale model contributed additions to the truck market, while maintaining the standards of quality that customers had come to expect:

> This chassis marks a distinct advance in the construction of light trucks, and a glance at its specifications will convince the most skeptical that it is built not for looks and speed alone, but on time-tried principles for hard practical service.
> Our announcement, I believe, will prove of interest to the hundreds of Clydesdale truck owners who have found the vehicles reliable, serviceable and efficient; as well as economical in upkeep. And I am sure we have in this All-Steel truck a vehicle that will uphold the reputation of the company and justify our pride in it.[3]

According to Clydesdale executives, the new truck received approval from "the most eminent automotive engineers in America." Engineers and designers alike "have pronounced the chassis one of the best offered the truck-buying public at a popular price."[4]

The new chassis still retained many of the same trademark features of earlier Clydesdale

Top: Clydesdale released this "Model-10" all-steel chassis in 1922. It was marketed as a lighter truck, an addition to the company's line of medium and heavy duty trucks. It had an overall capacity of 6,850 pounds, and was priced at $1,485. Company officials billed it "light and graceful in design, the new truck combines the reliability of a Clydesdale products with the flexibility and easy running of a passenger car." *Bottom:* Clydesdale Model-10 truck with a "type D" cab. Note the additional aluminum nameplate on the side of the cab.

Top: Clydesdale Model-10 truck with a cab and pickup body. Note the disc wheels and spare tire mounted on the driver's side of the cab, as well as the octagonal headlights. *Bottom:* A rare postcard view of a Clydesdale Model-10 truck with a pickup body and disc wheels.

Top: Clydesdale Model-10 truck owned by the Sandusky Gas & Electric Company, Sandusky, Ohio (*courtesy of the Sandusky Library Follett House Museum Archives, Sandusky, Ohio*). *Bottom:* Fleet of Clydesdale trucks, including two new Model 10As, owned by the Union Transfer Company, Philadelphia, Pennsylvania.

trucks, including the automatic controller and the copper tubing radiator. In addition, the model also offered new features, not always standard on previous Clydesdale models, including an electric horn, Bosch starting, lighting, and ignition, and pneumatic cord tires. Design wise, the Model-10 unveiled a longer wheelbase (138 inches) and an increased loading length (196 inches).[5] It also unveiled a more modern wheel style — steel discs with demountable rims, which would become widespread across Clydesdale models in subsequent years. Overall, it was a more modern-looking chassis, meant to accommodate many of the more streamlined bodies available to customers.

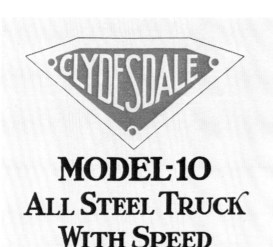

The release of the Model-10 marked a distinct shift in how the Clydesdale Motor Truck Company offered truck chassis to customers. Clydesdale began offering customers complete trucks — chassis, body, and cab. Standard bodies were offered alongside the chassis at an additional cost. This was a dramatic departure from the business model discussed in Chapter 2, in which Clydesdale customers were compelled to purchase separate customized truck cabs and bodies from third party manufacturers. With the Model-10, however, Clydesdale offered ten "express body" options that could be added to chassis orders and delivered to customers.

Body options included the "Full Canopy," which offered two different cab door options, or an open driver's seat option. There was also the "Full Canopy" with a rear seat, including rear steps; or the "Full Canopy" with a produce rack. The Clydesdale company also offered the "High Grain Box;" the "Open Cab with Curtains;" "Stake Sides" with an open driver's seat; the "Fully Enclosed Panel Body," with enclosed cab; or the "Flare Board Body." If these body options were not enough for customers, the Model-10 could be ordered with a cab only, open or enclosed, allowing for traditional body customization by third-party builders. All bodies and cabs were made of wood and steel, and cabs comfortably sat three people.

Clydesdale Motor Truck Company promotional brochure for the Model-10 truck, released in 1922.

Clydesdale motor coach at Plum Brook Country Club, Sandusky, Ohio (*courtesy of the Charles Frohman Collection, Rutherford B. Hayes Presidential Center, Fremont, Ohio*).

The Clydesdale Motor Truck Company's decision to offer standard cabs and bodies was not specifically outlined in company documents or press releases, and may never even have been recorded. Such actions, however, were in line with industry trends by 1922. Companies acknowledged a need to produce more "complete" motor trucks, including cabs and bodies, in order to satisfy customers, especially following the successful motor truck tours and shows highlighted in the previous chapter. "Much of the success of the finished product is going to depend upon the suitability of the outfit to the work. And in this respect, 'outfit' means more body than chassis."[6]

Poor Man's Limousine: The Motor Coach

Not long after the release of the Model-10, the Clydesdale company introduced a highway coach. The 1923 bus chassis was priced at $4,500. The coach body was constructed separately by nearby Fremont Metal Bodies, of Fremont, Ohio, for an additional $3,500. With a total cost of $8,000, the Clydesdale highway coach was quite expensive for the time, but was "top of the line." The completed coach could carry anywhere from 15 to 25 adult passengers, and featured 4-wheel brakes and a 6-cylinder Continental engine that could achieve speeds of up to 50 miles per hour. It included a ventilation system which circulated fresh air to passengers, even when the bus was crowded. The *Fremont Daily News* described

Top: Early Clydesdale bus owned by S. Conlan in Pleasant, New York. *Bottom:* Clydesdale motor coach with metal body made by Fremont Metal Body in nearby Fremont, Ohio. The chassis was priced at $4,500, and the metal body priced at $3,500, so the entire bus cost $8,000.

Top: Rear view of the Clydesdale motor coach highlights the trunk and overhead luggage rack (*courtesy of the Charles Frohman Collection, Rutherford B. Hayes Presidential Center, Fremont, Ohio*). *Bottom:* A look inside a Clydesdale motor coach. Notice that the coach has four doors on the passenger's side, and two doors on the driver's side.

Top: The Clydesdale motor coach chassis was not substantially different from the truck chassis in terms of construction. The overall length of the bus chassis was 271 inches, while the width was 56 inches, and the height from the ground was 28½ inches. The wheelbase was 198 inches. *Bottom:* Fleet of early Clydesdale buses at a Chicago dealership awaiting pick-up by representatives from the Carson Pirie Scott department store.

Top: Clydesdale vice president A.C. Burch (center) stands with colleagues in front of a motor coach. *Bottom:* Clydesdale motor coach in front of the Law Courts Motel in Dunedin, New Zealand, in 1924. The coach features a curved windshield and dual rear wheels.

the coach as "much like a streetcar," with electric lights and buzzer.[7] "Particular attention has been given to provide an easy riding vehicle which shall be as free as possible from vibration."[8]

While the motor coach chassis did not represent a significant change from the truck chassis in terms of construction, the bus was Clydesdale's only foray into strictly passenger, as opposed to commercial cargo-hauling, vehicles. The Clydesdale bus presented new opportunities for the company to market the attention to passenger comfort, which was a departure from marketing traditional motor truck, mostly technical, features:

> The highway coach lately introduced by the Clydesdale Motor Truck Company, Clyde, Ohio, aside from its features of mechanical construction and assembly, presents an appearance of sumptuous comfort, which compels immediate attention. The long and smooth body lines, together with the effect of the limousine-enclosure well paneled with plate glass, promises the prospective rider a passage of solid comfort.[9]

The bus was also viewed as a social equalizer, or for some, uplifting. Everyone could ride the bus, no matter his economic or social circumstances. "The motor bus is the poor man's limousine. It gives him all of the comforts and delights of closed-car motoring, with none of the expense. It is swift, sure, silent, comfortable, and even luxurious."[10]

The overall length of the Clydesdale bus chassis was 271 inches, while the height from the ground to the top of the frame was 28½ inches, width 56 inches, and wheelbase 198 inches. Entrance to the interior was gained through four doors on the right side of the bus, in addition to two doors on the left side. A running board lined the entire length of the bus to assist with passenger ingress and egress, and was low enough to negate the need for typical entrance steps. A baggage rack skirted the rear end of the roof, while a trunk was mounted over the 18-gallon gasoline tank, also in the rear. As well, "the distinctive Clydesdale radiator, hood and bumper design add considerably to the attention arresting characteristics of this job."[11]

Many of the Clydesdale Company's motor coach designs were used in communities. Some were used by schools to transport students, including those in Townsend Township and Jackson Township, Ohio.

Cover of a promotional brochure for the Clydesdale motor coach. In a rare display, the logo of the Clydesdale Motor Truck Company has been adjusted to read "Clydesdale Motor Coach."

Top: Many Clydesdale buses were customized for school transportation, as this one was from Jackson Township school in northwest Ohio. Note the heavy wooden artillery-type wheels with pneumatic tires. *Bottom:* Clyde Boy Scout troop with a Clydesdale motor coach outside of the Clyde Armory (*courtesy Clyde Heritage League, Clyde, Ohio*).

The Cleveland-Lorain Highway Coach ran daily between Cleveland and suburban Lorain, Ohio. This Clydesdale motor coach was the first bus in their fleet. The photograph includes a notation that the bus had traveled 35,000 without needing any repairs.

The new Clydesdale motor bus became the inaugural coach employed by the Cleveland-Lorain Highway Coach Company in 1923. H.A. Sanborn and H.G. Coleman started the company that year with one Clydesdale coach, which made daily trips between suburban Lorain, Ohio, and Cleveland. "This bus has been driven 35,000 miles without any upkeep," noted one company photograph.

In Calumet City, Illinois, real estate developer G. Frank Croissant used a Clydesdale motor coach to offer shuttle service to "Ford's new plant," located in nearby southeast Chicago's Hegewisch neighborhood. The Ford plant opened in 1924, and manufactured Model Ts in what was the largest factory outside of the River Rouge complex in Detroit. Nicknamed "America's Greatest Salesman," Croissant later developed parts of Fort Lauderdale and North Palm Beach Heights, Florida.[12] The Ford plant, meanwhile, remains the company's oldest continually-operating automobile manufacturing factory.

The new motor coaches were often viewed as competitors of street cars. This positioned the Clydesdale Motor Truck Company amid significant debates about which mode of trans-

Real estate developer G. Frank Croissant used a Clydesdale motor coach to launch daily service between Calumet City, Illinois, and "Ford's New Plant," which had just opened on nearby Chicago's south side in 1924.

portation was the most versatile and economical. The market relationship between buses and streetcars was complex, as each had distinct advantages and disadvantages, and were heavily controlled by industry leaders who enthusiastically believed their way was the way of the future. At least one Clydesdale executive envisioned a "trackless street:"

> Traffic congestion in large cities, it is pointed out, make the street car just as awkward and unnecessary as its predecessors, the horse car and the stage coach, and it will not be long before the large cities are trackless and free from the unsightly and abominable overhead wires with their appurtenances.
>
> A single street car out of order can hold up traffic for hours. When a motor bus is out of order, the passengers are simply transferred to another bus, and the derelict is repaired at their leisure by a wrecking crew or hauled to the garage. There is no break in the service, whose strength lies in its constancy. A fire can hold up an entire street car system, but motor buses are not subject to the limitation of tracks, and they can readily change their route to another street when one is closed to them.
>
> Motor buses mean faster service. While one bus is taking on passengers at a corner, the bus following can keep on going and pick up the passengers at the next corner. There is no waiting for one car to complete its loading and discharging of passengers before those behind can go ahead. In this way every motor bus bears its full share of the day's work, and the spectacle isn't seen of some crowded to the roof, while others go by empty.[13]

There are ten sound reasons
for the high earning power of a

CLYDESDALE COACH

1—DESIGN—built solely for motor-coach service; especially fitted to its work.

2—LOW OPERATING COST—insuring a higher NET.

3—ABSOLUTE RELIABILITY—protecting patronage.

4—LONG LIFE—safeguarding the investment.

5—APPEARANCE—Deluxe design; attractive to riders.

6—COMFORT—passengers delighted with its riding qualities

7—SAFETY in SPEED—low center of gravity; large brake surface; two sets on rear wheels; one set on front.

8—POWER—6-cylinder motor; ample power, not wasteful; smooth, rapid acceleration.

9—STRAIGHT FRAME—long, low frame, without a kick-up; perfectly straight-lined drive.

10—NOT EXPERIMENTAL—built by an old-established and experienced company.

Full Information on Request—Prompt Deliveries

THE CLYDESDALE MOTOR TRUCK COMPANY, Clyde, Ohio, U.S.A.

"There are ten sound reasons for the high earning power of a Clydesdale Coach": This advertisement for the Clydesdale motor coach appeared in the December 1923 issue of *Motor Coach* magazine. It appeared on page nine of the issue, with an advertisement for competitor White Motor Company on the next page. While White touted 5,000 buses in use, "more than any other make," Clydesdale showcased the characteristics of its new motor coach.

The Clydesdale vision of the "trackless street" did become a reality by the mid-twentieth century. In addition to being more flexible and able to access areas without tracks, motor buses were cheaper to build, maintain, and operate than streetcars, and promoted increased passenger safety with curbside loading and unloading.

Riding the Clydesdale School Bus

Several Clydesdale motor coaches were used as school buses, especially in communities close to the Clyde factory. Nearby Townsend Township School acquired one Clydesdale school bus, new, in 1923. Sandusky, Ohio, resident Milton "Milt" Opper recalled riding the bus as a child, and shared memories that provide a glimpse at not only bus riding in the 1920s, but also how Clydesdale motor coaches were part of significant everyday use. The Clydesdale bus was one of three motor coaches owned by the school, which also owned a Dodge bus, explained Milt. It was "really quite a step up" to get on the bus, he explained. He estimated that the height between the ground, running board, and coach door was two feet. The Clydesdale motor coach's Continental engine, he remembered, "made a little noise," but was not considered loud.

Inside the Clydesdale bus, Milt described, were hard bench seats with modest padding, a "nice cover." The ride, he recalled, was a bit bumpy, "like riding in a truck." The bus was not open air, but had windows, which opened and closed with a strap attached to the bottom of the window. In the spring and summer, passengers could pull up on the strap to raise and lower the window along a short set of tracks. In winter, heat came from the blower in the front of the bus, located close to the driver. A long mirror mounted above the driver allowed him to see the entire bus simply by looking upward, very similar to mirrors mounted in modern school buses. The motor coach doors opened with a handle operated by the driver, also similar to those used in modern buses.

The driver, reminisced Milt, was a regular employee of the school, who would store

Close-up of the Clydesdale school bus that Milt Opper remembers riding. It was used by Townsend Township School in northwest Ohio, a short distance from the truck factory.

Students at Townsend Township School in Ohio stand with buses in front of their school. The Clydesdale bus is first in the line.

and care for the bus at his home. In the morning, the driver would leave his home on the bus, pick up all of the students along the route, and then take them to school. After school, the same driver would take all of the students home, then return the bus to his home. The driver was also responsible for maintaining, washing, and cleaning the bus. The Clydesdale bus was generally very clean, noted Milt, who could not recall a time when the motor coach broke down. "Anything was better than walking," he chuckled, as he lived three miles from school.

He estimated that 35 to 40 students rode the bus each school day. Sometimes students would be called upon to assist the driver, explained Milt. At railroad or interurban tracks, it was difficult for the driver to see out of the Clydesdale's windows whether any rail traffic was approaching. High school students would be asked to step off the bus, look in either direction down the railroad tracks for rail traffic, and then signal the driver an "all clear" (or not). Students might also be asked to assist with operation of the manual windshield wiper, which attached to a lever inside the bus, which had to be moved across the window during rain or snow.

All of the students, suggested Milt, understood the significance of the Clydesdale bus. It, along with the Dodge bus, was one of the first for the school district, and replaced horse-drawn buggies. It was, he emphasized, "something special."[14]

New Laws Inspire Updates

During the same year, 1923, Clydesdale announced a complete update to all existing truck models in order to "conform to present day laws in the various States relative to tire size in relation to load capacity."[15] The new line included not only the recent motor coach and Model-10, but also four more trucks — the Model-8, Model-6, Model-4, and Model-2. The final truck included in the new line was nicknamed the "Oil-field Special." Company officials explained, "The new models retain the well-known Clydesdale characteristics and provide a range of sizes and wheel-bases to meet almost any haulage requirement from 500 pounds up to six tons."[16]

The Model-2, which could haul up to eight tons, including the body, was the most powerful of the new line. It had a wheelbase of 176 inches. The Model-6 was in the middle of the line with a carrying capacity of approximately five tons. Its wheelbase ranged from 163 to 180 inches, depending on customer needs. Compare these to the Model-10, which had been released first during the previous year, with a carrying capacity of approximately two tons, and standard wheelbase of 138 inches. The "Oil-field Special," named for its capacity to perform in the widely recognized strenuous environment of oil fields, was engineered very similarly to the Model-6, but offered a heavier frame and more gear options — seven forward, plus two reverse gears. Clydesdale models included pneumatic tires on all of the new trucks, which ranged from 36 to 40 inches, by four to seven inches wide, depending on the load capacity of the body. In addition to tire changes, the engines in several of the updated models were changed to accommodate heavier tires and load capacities. All Clydesdale models still included Continental engines, but one of four made by the company, including the K4, L4, S4, and B7.

In realigning their truck chassis to accommodate a variety of hauling needs, the Clydesdale Motor Truck Company was responding to industry and political concerns about truck sizes and weights. During this time, it was not uncommon for owners to overload their trucks. Depending on the truck, the load, and the condition of the road on which it traveled, overloaded trucks could threaten safety, or the road surface itself, if the truck was too heavy. As a result, by the early 1920s, individual states were enacting laws to regulate tire and truck sizes and load capacities. As early as 1918, states including Maine, Massachusetts, Pennsylvania, and Washington began regulating truck weights. In addition, Maine, Massachusetts, and Pennsylvania also enacted tire size limits. Such laws helped to ensure the safe hauling of freight, and, as large trucks were often heavy on asphalt, preserved conditions of new roads. "New road laws, aimed especially at truck men driving excess loads, have been passed by several of the eastern states. The increased traffic, the heavily-overloaded trucks pounding continuously day and night over the new state highways, have destroyed, in a comparatively short time, surfacing that under normal conditions would have lasted for years."[17]

Overall, Clydesdale, like most motor truck manufacturers, supported the new state laws, which would help to ensure that all trucks on the road were being operated and loaded in appropriate proportions to their construction. As a manufacturer, the Clydesdale company had no interest in customers overloading their trucks, lest improper use prevent the truck from operating properly. Such laws also helped to purge "misfit" trucks from the road, by compelling customers to buy a professionally designed truck chassis and body. This encouraged truck sales. Following the changes to accommodate the new state laws, and perhaps in an attempt to generate additional truck sales, the Clydesdale company announced that prices of all models would be fixed rates for at least one year. Prices ranged from $1,535 for the Model-10 to $4,880 for the Model-2.[18]

Clydesdale Situation Develops

By 1922, and certainly by 1923, business at the Clydesdale Motor Truck Company was changing. Amid the market and industry changes affecting the company from the outside, major personnel changes affected the company from the inside. Company vice-president and founder Louis Krebs resigned in 1922, departing Clydesdale to run the nearby Collier Motor Truck Company, in Bellevue, Ohio. In addition, company vice-president A.C. Burch resigned and took a position with the nearby Courier Cars Company, in Sandusky, Ohio. The few surviving Clydesdale advertisements from this period mark a distinct shift in the company's branding compared to earlier years, particularly with the release of the Model-10.

Many of the company's advertisements after 1922 place less emphasis on the famous "automatic controller," or "the driver under the hood," in favor of other characteristics of the truck. Generally, there appeared to be more emphasis on the qualities of the truck, and what those could mean to customers, rather than any particular part underneath the hood. Like small windows into history, many of the advertisements during this time feature testimonies and photographs from longtime Clydesdale owners.

A summer 1923 marketing campaign, during which a Clydesdale advertisement appeared each month in the trade magazine, *Management*, for example, included personal statements from Clydesdale owners about their satisfaction with their trucks. One advertisement featured Mr. K.A. Thomas, secretary and treasurer of the Interstate Forwarding Company of New York. His firm used five 5-ton Clydesdale trucks to haul freight around the state:

> Operating Clydesdales has two outstanding advantages that every truck owner will appreciate. First, the Clydesdale automatic controller prevents wasting gas and oil, and makes even a good driver more efficient by assuming part of his responsibility. Second, the service given Clydesdale users is prompt and dependable. On account of this excellent service, and the fine performance of our trucks, we expect to buy more Clydesdales as soon as our business needs them.[19]

Two months later, August 1923, the magazine featured another Clydesdale owner, C.B. Ward of the Ward Cartage Company of Detroit. He summarized his Clydesdale experience:

> Operating a general hauling business as we are doing, we must have trucks capable of handling any kind of a job. Our Clydesdale truck has shown wonderful endurance and speed. It has such an exceptional amount of power that we have geared the truck up quite a bit. This gives us a good deal more speed, and reduces the vibration of the engine. Actual repairs have been less than $100 in three years. I certainly wish my other trucks would operate as cheaply as the Clydesdale — and when I replace them, it will be by Clydesdales.[20]

Professionals from across the country told similar stories through advertisements that appeared in subsequent issues of *Management*. In September 1923, Mr. I.C. Baumann, in charge of maintenance for the Gridley Dairy Company in Milwaukee, testified that his company's 2-ton Clydesdale truck had "been on the job delivering milk to wholesale buyers for over 5 years," averaging approximately 20 miles per day. "We have found the Clydesdale a most dependable truck — and obtained very satisfactory service from it. Its job has been a hard one, covering a route on which horses lasted no time at all."[21] In perhaps the most glowing review, W.S. Ostrander, the secretary of the New York Piano Delivery Company, ranked his organization's Clydesdale truck above others on the market: "We are thoroughly familiar with the construction features of various makes of trucks and believe that the Clydesdale's better springs afford more protection to the engine than other trucks give.... Clydesdale construction originally sold us this truck — and it is keeping us sold."[22] His feature advertisement appeared in October 1923.

This seemingly modern method of crowd-sourced advertising continued into 1924, featuring similar stories and echoing sentiments, from customers. That year, however, the Clydesdale company boasted a new and distinctive tagline in much of their advertising: The Country's Most Dependable Truck. One advertisement highlighted Louis Aulicino, a butcher in New York, who calculated that his 3½-ton Clydesdale truck saved him $1,400 annually in hauling costs, and offered better service to customers that would have been

"No. 9" Clydesdale truck in the fleet owned by Atlas Plaster & Fuel Company, Louisville, Kentucky, with bridges over the Ohio River in the background.

impossible with horses. He praised his truck: "The Clydesdale has certainly proved a splendid truck for our work. It has a good motor which develops sufficient power to meet all demands upon it."[23] Stories like this, proclaimed Clydesdale officials, helped to establish a reputation as "The Country's Most Dependable Truck."[24]

While it seemed as though business was booming in Clydesdale advertising, other aspects of the company's outreach were not thriving in the same ways that they had in previous years. The company was no longer touring the country in motor truck development tours or exhibiting products at national truck shows. In fact, if the national truck shows were any indication of the market at large, the industry was changing. The National Automobile Chamber of Commerce did not schedule the traditional motor truck shows in conjunction with the national automobile shows in cities such as New York, Chicago, or Los Angeles. In 1922 and 1923, the national trade magazine, the *Commercial Car Journal,* advertised that the January issues of each year would serve as replacement motor truck shows. In other words, instead of buying booth space, companies bought advertising space. The Clydesdale Motor Truck Company purchased advertising space in both issues, and highlighted models from their new line.[25]

In addition to the decline in national motor truck shows, overall national automobile sales declined in the last half of 1921, making it difficult for manufacturers to sell their inventories. A national recession that began in 1920, caused primarily by the transition from supplying the war effort to providing for peace, began affecting truck manufacturers. One trade journal speculated, "Probably no line of business has been hit any harder than that of motor truck manufacturer."[26] Many manufacturers lowered prices, which, according to *Motor Age*, created a "decidedly jumpy" market.[27] The market was "jumpy" indeed. The *Automobile Trade Journal* reported in 1922 that the prior year's production total — for 1921 — was just 65 percent of the 1920 totals. Likewise, sales in 1921 were approximately 80 percent of 1920 totals.[28] Until that point, 1920 had been the most prosperous year on record for truck production and sales, and many industry experts were disappointed when 1921 numbers seemed to stabilize, rather than climb. Export records, however, told a brighter story. By the end of 1922, motor truck exports increased by 50 percent compared to 1921, and the automobile industry as a whole saw an overall doubling in the numbers of cars and trucks shipped overseas.[29] Nations such as Canada, Australia, Japan, and Mexico were the chief foreign markets for American motor trucks, as they had been in prior years. Amid this unpredictable market, the Clydesdale Motor Truck Company was still selling trucks, and reported annual profits of approximately $4 million each year.[30]

This was likely due, in part, to the efforts of the newly organized Clydesdale Operating Company, which Clydesdale Motor Truck Company officials had organized early in 1925 to expand sales to dealerships. The operating company would assist with the acquisition of new dealer customers, as well as manage dealer deliveries with consignments during the spring and summer months, "which always tax the capacity of the Truck Company."[31] In fact, during one week, the Clydesdale Motor Truck Company shipped several trucks to, and developed floor plans for, dealers around the world. One update from the local newspaper provided a snapshot of a week's activity at the factory:

> Five orders were received on Monday from our New York distributors for immediate delivery.
> M.E. Brackett was in Detroit in business on Friday.
> Howard Hawk of the service department was in Chicago on business the first of the week.
> Three trucks were shipped to dealers in San Juan, [Puerto Rico] Friday.
> Louis Snyder made delivery of a Model 2 chassis on Tuesday to [a] dealer in Detroit, Michigan.[32]

In addition to assisting with sales and delivery of trucks, the Clydesdale Operating Company was authorized to sell 15,000 shares of stock, which was valued at $10 per share, in an effort to increase capital for the Clydesdale Motor Truck Company.

> It is hoped that a considerable amount will be subscribed to the stock of the Operating Company by the business men of Clyde and by the stockholders of the Clydesdale Motor Truck Company.
> The prospects for the future success of the Clydesdale Motor Truck Company are better at this moment than they have been for several years, but they very much need the assistance that will be furnished them by the Clydesdale Operating Company.[33]

It seemed that long-term success of the Clydesdale company depended on the success of the Clydesdale Operating Company.

In the summer of 1925, the Clydesdale Motor Truck Company was sued by Continental Motors for "unpaid sundry notes" totaling $9,038.63.[34] Production at the factory stopped, and Judge John Killitts, of the U.S. District Court for the Northern District of Ohio in Toledo, appointed a receiver, Commerce Guardian and Trust Savings Bank of Toledo, to handle all of the company affairs.[35] According to the local newspaper, the company affairs seemed to be in order, and business profitable, in the years prior to the lawsuit: "Up to September 16th of this year, when the Receiver was appointed, the Clydesdale Company was turning out and selling trucks at the highest rate in eight years, and was in a fair way to establish a production and sales record, the advent of the Receiver, however, serving to temporarily suspend production."[36]

Court records indicate that the Clydesdale accounts were more complex. After completing the sale and reviewing more records, the court-appointed receiver later reported "creditors in addition to those contained" in the lawsuit.[37] Even with reported annual sales of $4 million, the Clydesdale Motor Truck Company had creditors claiming upwards of $503,000 in unpaid bills. Creditors included not only Continental Motors, but also the Timken-Detroit Axle Company, Glidden paints, and others. There were also employees claiming unpaid wages. Two employees with the largest claims — M.R. Pence, with a claim for $1,134.10; and Joseph Waldi, with a claim for $455.96 — testified in court as part of the receivership proceedings. In spite of these discoveries, and the lawsuit brought forth by creditor Continental Motors, the overall fiscal outlook for the Clydesdale company was relatively healthy. "The indebtedness of the company, according to its books, is considerably less than the value of its assets."[38] Executives at Clydesdale further admitted:

> The period after the war, beginning the latter part of 1920, affected the business of this Company materially, as it did in many industries especially in the motor truck business generally. Because of the heavy obligations incurred as a result of the slump of 1920, the Company has found, since 1920, it to be a difficult matter to readily meet the obligations incurred during the war period alluded to, and have been handicapped in providing sufficient working capital for their requirements.[39]

According to court records, the company had entered into negotiations in April 1925 with parties in Sacramento, California, to sell their holdings in the state, including the expansive dealership in San Francisco. The sale was finalized shortly after the receivership, resulting in a recorded $3,000. The California holdings had been appraised at approximately $14,000, but in the interest of prompt sale, or losing the sale altogether, the $3,000 sale price was accepted by the receiver and approved by the court.

Judge Killitts subsequently ordered the factory, and all of its contents and facilities, sold in order to pay creditors. According to court records, all of the creditors were willing to participate in the reorganization of the company, to the end that business and the Clydesdale brand could be preserved. Industrial Plants Corporation, professional liquidators from New York, began preparations for the sale, which was scheduled for January 19, 1926. They marketed the company as a prime investment: "It has always maintained a reputation for building a high grade product. Its present line of trucks is second to none in the industry and is so recognized by the trade, not only in the United States, but throughout the world. The Clydesdale truck is a truck of international reputation and distribution."[40] In fact, Clydesdale officials received welcome proof of the truck's international reputation and distribution in the summer of 1925.

Clydesdale Motor Truck Company officials received a copy of a full-page advertisement, which appeared in the *Eastern Province Herald*, a newspaper published in Port Elizabeth, Good Hope, South Africa. The advertisement featured a Clydesdale truck, and highlighted the brand's predominance in the country's market. "More heavy duty Clydesdales are in

Pursuant to an order of the UNITED STATES DISTRICT COURT for the Northern District of Ohio, Western Division in the matter of Continental Motors Corp. vs. Clydesdale Motor Truck Co., Equity Case No. 589.

Tues., Jan. 19, 1926
Starting at
11 A. M.
Eastern Standard Time

PUBLIC AUCTION

Land, Buildings, Service Parts, Business, Machinery, Equipment and Small Tools

of

The Clydesdale Motor Truck Co.

MANUFACTURERS OF

Clydesdale

MOTOR TRUCKS

FILED

JAN 26 1926

P. C. MILLER, Clerk
U. S. District Court, N. D. O.

AT
CLYDE, OHIO.

Exhibit "a"

Receivers: The Commerce Guardian Trust & Savings Bank, Toledo, Ohio

*Attorneys for Receivers: Marshall, Melhorn, Marlar & Martin
Toledo, Ohio*

Attorneys for Liquidators: Boggs & Doty, Toledo, Ohio

Under the Management of

Industrial Plants Corporation
AUCTIONEERS
NATIONAL LIQUIDATORS

**25 CHURCH STREET
NEW YORK, N. Y.**

**928 NICHOLAS BLDG.
TOLEDO, OHIO**

Following a lawsuit from engine supplier Continental Motors over approximately $10,000 in unpaid invoices in 1925, and in spite of reported annual sales of $4 million, the Clydesdale Motor Truck Company went into receivership. A federal judge ordered the factory, equipment, company, and Clydesdale name sold at public auction to help pay additional creditors. This public sale brochure was produced by sellers Industrial Plants Corporation (*courtesy of the National Archives at Chicago*).

daily use in South Africa successfully performing their functions than any other similar vehicle made. Large fleets of Clydesdales for railways, harbours, milling corporations, sugar and farm estates, merchants' forwarding of coal, timber, and mining products are in use."[41] Additional text noted that the Clydesdale truck had recently won first prize in a show in East London, home of the largest Clydesdale truck distributors to South Africa.

Company officials also received correspondence from Cox & Sons, a wholesale milk and cream contractor in Cardiff, Wales. Officials at Cox & Sons wrote to tell Clydesdale representatives that their fleet of Clydesdale trucks needed few repairs, and as "mutual monuments for efficient transportation," they would "continue to be our standard bearer."[42]

Accordingly, the company was marketed as a complete facility. "The method will be to sell the plant as a whole if possible," with hopes of the new owner "continuing to manufacture trucks under the Clydesdale name."[43]

Industrial Plants Corporation appraised the Clydesdale facility and inventory at $750,000 by the end of 1925. This figure included $350,000 worth of inventory, plus real estate, equipment, and copyrights. Beginning on January 15, 1926, the plant in Clyde, Ohio was opened to the public for two weeks for inspection. Prospective buyers from across the country appeared in Clyde to examine the facility. As the sale opened on January 19, approximately 150 interested parties arrived in Clyde by train and automobile, and crowded the factory engineering room where the auction was held. Reporters from the local newspaper

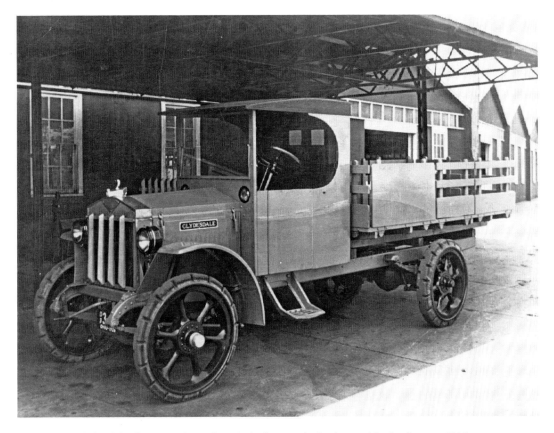

Clydesdale chassis with a cab and platform stake body outside the factory, 1926.

were on hand to record the day's events, and provide the most complete historical account of the company sale:

> Prospects that the big plant of the Clydesdale Motor Truck [Company] will operate again are said to be brighter at the present time than they have been for some months past.
>
> The auction sale of the Clydesdale factory, advertised profusely throughout the country, has been in progress at the plant since Tuesday morning when the Industrial Plants Corporation, professional liquidators of New York City, began a sale in charge of auctioneer Charles Kriser of New York.
>
> Hundreds of people, among them many from New York, Detroit, Toledo, and Sandusky, as well as local interests, have been bidding on material and equipment. The sale commenced at noon Tuesday when auctioneer Kriser offered the business in three lots, the first as an entire plant, together with real estate and machinery, second, the lands and buildings, and third the Clydesdale name and service department.
>
> Bidding on the whole plant was not very spirited but when the auctioneer's gavel fell a bid of $82,000 was recorded.[44]

Mr. H. Paltrowitz, president and treasurer of the Marine Metal and Supply Company of New York, bought the Clydesdale Motor Truck Company for $82,000, significantly below the appraised worth. He also paid an additional $14,000 for the real estate of the company as a separate bid. The court approved the sale, and Paltrowitz was eager to resume production at the facility. "Our purpose in buying the plant here is to continue the business," he explained to reporters. "We have investigated the value of the Clydesdale as a truck and have found it to be among the leaders in its field.... It would be a shame for the Clydesdale to die, and I am sure that we can put it in its rightful place on the truck market."[45]

In addition to the winning bid for the Clydesdale factory and real estate cast by Mr. Paltrowitz, equipment sales raised an additional $120,000 for the company. All of the sales were significantly lower than their appraised values, but approved and accepted by the court in favor of finalizing the receivership proceedings. In addition to bidding, another moment during the public sale caught the eye of reporters: "Quite a little stir was created among bidders when one enthusiastic fellow stated that Henry Ford was in the room. A man resembling Ford sat near the auctioneer but it wasn't Henry."[46]

Back to Business

Within approximately two weeks of the January 1926 public sale, employees at the Clydesdale Motor Truck Company were back to work. The company had been reorganized, and was taking orders for trucks, still with the help of the Clydesdale Operating Company. Clydesdale employee M.R. Pence reported several foreign and domestic orders in February 1926: "Agencies abroad have been cabled news of the purchase of the Clydesdale factory and expressions of satisfaction have been received by cable telegram from all parts of the world."[47] In one week during that month alone, Clydesdale sales representatives took orders for trucks totaling $60,000.[48] Some of the machinery at the factory had been sold in small lots during the public auction, so orders were filled accordingly, while replacement equipment was shipped immediately. By the end of February 1926, order deliveries were being promised to customers by March 1 of that year. By March 12, 1926, the first shipment of trucks left the Clydesdale Motor Truck Company factory for overseas shipment.[49]

Following the receivership, the Clydesdale company seemed to disappear from the historical record. The Clydesdale Operating Company was dissolved in 1927. Then, in 1930, several national trade journals announced that the company would "produce a new Clydesdale truck, which will be [marketed] both in foreign countries and the United States."[50] The announcements indicated that the Clydesdale factory had "been idle for a number of months," but would resume a full schedule of production by January 1931.[51] The factory would produce 125 trucks in just the first three months of 1931.[52]

It appears at this time that the Clydesdale factory was undergoing a common industry practice known as "mothballing," where facilities would stop production for a time, then resume production, without changing ownership, and once economic conditions improved.[53] By this time, the Clydesdale Motor Truck Company, along with automobile manufacturers and Americans generally, would have been facing the effects of another, more profound recession, the Great Depression. Following the initial market crash in 1929, the national economic outlook was bleak. The auto industry, in particular, faced devastation. During the first three years of the Depression, by 1932, automobile sales fell 75 percent. The net income of General Motors, to use the company as a weather vane, plummeted from $248.3 million in 1929, to less than $82.7 million in 1932, or less than one third of the 1929 totals.[54] Their stock fell from $73 a share on the New York Stock Exchange to just under $16.[55] Industry-wide, approximately one half of all automakers closed or were bought by larger companies within the same span of three years.[56]

Perhaps it is all the more remarkable, then, that the Clydesdale Motor Truck Company not only survived the early years of the Depression, but also released brochures, which promoted a new line of trucks to be released in 1931. The brochures detailed a full line of trucks, but there is no evidence that the trucks were ever physically produced. Nonetheless, the elaborately planned trucks shed light on what Clydesdale Motor Truck Company executives were considering during this time. The new Clydesdale truck models included six-cylinder engines, rather than four, and featured Lockhead internal expanding brakes on all four wheels, as well as an updated steel frame design. According to brochures, the new truck models would be available in six different carrying capacities: 1–2 ton range, 2-ton range, 2½–3 ton range, 3½–4 ton range, and 5–6 ton range. The smallest truck, the 1–2 ton range, or Model-20, would be designed to achieve the highest speeds — 45 miles per hour. The largest truck, the 5–6 ton range, or Model-120, would be designed to achieve a maximum speed of approximately 25 miles per hour.

Many of the new technologies which Clydesdale advertised as planned integrations into their new models — 6-cylinder engines, 4-wheel air brakes, pneumatic tires, and advanced chassis and body designs — followed industry upgrades that catered to the burgeoning commercial trucking industry. Despite what was happening to the auto industry during the Depression, the trucking industry was relatively profitable and able to provide a modest market to manufacturers. Prior to the 1930s, what we know as commercial trucking tended to be handled by private carriers. Under these arrangements, manufacturers and company owners bought and maintained their own trucks, and employed their own truck drivers, to ship materials, make deliveries, and haul supplies. Independent for-hire trucks and truck drivers, commonplace today, comprised just 15 percent of the market. In the midst of an economic depression, however, the independent truck drivers suddenly found more customers.[57] Reminiscent of the 1920 Ship-by-Truck campaign, trucks offered manufacturers and shippers a cheaper rate for all but long-distance hauling. Inde-

CLYDESDALE 5-6 TON RANGE

Six Cylinder　　　**Gross Vehicle Weight, 26,000 Pounds**　　　**Model 120**

SPECIFICATIONS

Axle, Front — I-beam section. Extra heavy drop forged alloy steel. Especially designed to meet stresses produced by four wheel brakes. Timken roller bearings at spindles.

Axle, Rear — Double reduction drive, heavy duty, full floating type, axle shafts removable without taking off wheels. Axle shafts 2½" in diameter, chrome nickel steel. Timken roller bearings at differential and double Timken bearings at wheel hubs. Gear ratio; standard, 9.92 to 1; optional, 8.9 to 1 and 11.4 to 1.

Axle, Rear — Model 120-W heavy duty worm drive, full floating type; axle shafts removable without taking off wheels. Chrome nickel steel worm, mounted in three roller bearings; worm wheel of chilled bronze. Timken roller bearings in differential and double Timken bearings at wheel hubs. Gear ratios; standard, 11⅔ to 1.

NOTE — Model 120-W is furnished with identically the same specifications as Model 120 with the exception of the rear axle.

Braking System — Westinghouse air brakes on all four wheels, operated by foot control valves. Brake chambers are mounted directly on the axles in accordance with the latest approved practice. Drums are 17¼" in diameter and 5" in width. The finest and most expensive brakes built today. Hand brake unusually powerful. A 16" ventilated disc on the transmission shaft is acted upon by four opposed brake shoes, one set shoes can be connected with service brake.

Carburetor — Zenith balanced latest type. Choke mounted on instrument panel.

Clutch — Standard Dry discs. Extra large friction surfaces insure long life without adjustment. Clutch brake facilitates shifting of gears. Designed for severe truck service.

Drive — Through radius rods. Ball and Socket type.

Equipment —

Bumper	One spare wheel
Starter	Jack
Generator	Front fenders
Battery	Metal running
Electric head and	boards
tail lights	Side and front splash
Horn	aprons
Air cleaner	Tools
Oil filter	Clydesdale Con-
Wheel and tire carrier	troller or Governor
Ignition switch	Ammeter
Speedometer	Temperature
Oil gauge	indicator

The instruments listed above are mounted in a single indirectly lighted panel.

Frame — Special alloy steel. Gives maximum strength with minimum weight. Vertical section 9", width of flange 3½", thickness of material throughout ¼". Six cross members, including two of special construction at the most advantageous points, give great strength, yet permit the frame to absorb any "weaving" motion.

Promotional piece for one of the six-cylinder gasoline trucks that Clydesdale announced in 1930. There is no evidence that these trucks were ever produced.

pendently hired trucks were especially valuable for hauling the less-than-railcar sized orders that many manufacturers were receiving and shipping.[58] Independent carriers also tended to make longer trips, as most private hauls, such as delivery services, were less than 100 miles. The ability of independent carriers to accommodate both of these conditions — varied loads and longer trips — allowed the industry to grow rapidly. In addition, cutting-edge technological advances in trucks like those produced by the Clydesdale Motor Truck Company made hauls more efficient, thereby increasing payloads for each truck. By the end of 1931, this prompted *Business Week*, which had conducted a survey of the trade, to recognize "an unusual maturity in so young an industry."[59] The trucking industry was increasingly ready to compete with railroads for business in the declining transportation market. Truck registrations in the United States subsequently continued to increase significantly, even during the Depression. Registrations grew from 3 million in 1934 to approximately 4.5 million by 1940.[60] The number of long-haul truck trips also exploded by 1940, increasing to five times their recorded frequency in 1925.[61]

In addition to the technological and structural changes planned by the new Clydesdale truck models, the brochures showcased noticeable design changes. The announced Clydesdale trucks were strikingly modern in appearance, compared to the chassis produced in prior years. They featured longer, streamlined bodies, with fewer corners and more curves. They also featured modern wheels with metal spokes that seemed to pay homage to the spoke wheels that appeared in earlier models. For an additional cost, however, steel disc wheels, like those on other, more contemporary Clydesdale models, were also available.

In revealing design plans for such modern-looking trucks, the Clydesdale Motor Truck Company was part of an industry-wide shift from "horseless carriages" to stylized automobile designs during this time. More than one scholar has recognized this distinct historical trend in automobile production: "In the century of the automobile, then, the depression years represent a period of the most pronounced transition in automobile styling.... From a boxy object dominated by its technology at the beginning of the depression, the automobile evolved into a rounded, enclosed shape...."[62] In fact, 80 percent of automobiles manufactured at the beginning of 1920s were "open," or having no enclosed cab. By the end of the same decade that figure reversed — 80 percent of manufactured automobiles were enclosed, while just 20 percent remained open. By the 1930s, however, open air automobiles comprised just 1 percent of the market.[63] The science of "streamlining," or producing shapes that would allow air to flow easily around them for optimal aerodynamic efficiency, was increasingly popular by 1930, and contributed to the enclosed and rounded styling of not only Clydesdale trucks and vehicles generally, but also trains, and everyday housewares such as toasters and refrigerators. According to one scholar, "This first attempt at 'streamlining' was tentative at best. Still, the rounded style represents a less direct response to technological knowledge gained in wind tunnel research than the beginning of a tendency progressively taking shape through much of the depression era."[64]

Outside of the science of streamlining, but within the auto industry, there was also encouragement to differentiate models and brands through design. During a 1930 speech to the Society of Automotive Engineers, society manager L. Clayton Hill observed, "General proportion, panel contours, roof sweeps, window shapes, belt molding treatments — these and other points which give to a body its distinguishing characteristics have reached such a state of similarity, in most cases, as to confuse the buying public."[65] He dared auto manufacturers to strive for individuality, particularly through radiator and hood designs. By 1933, most radiators were no longer suggestive of simple mechanical functions, but incorporated into the automobile body proper, almost extensions of the increasingly stylized hood.

Perhaps these examples help to provide a larger context for the striking design changes that took place with Clydesdale's advertised release of the 1930 6-cylinder models. Regardless of whether the announced truck designs were executed, their concepts would continue to influence the company's trucks for the rest of its existence. It seemed as though the Clydesdale Motor Truck Company was making a dramatic statement about its place in the industry, and in the modern truck market. Following the announced release of the modern 6-cylinder models, by 1932, however, the company seemed to disappear from the historical record. Despite the lack of press, no one could deny that in little more than one decade, the company had transformed from a postwar motor truck chassis manufacturer to a modern motor coach and truck maker.

5

The Diesel Experiment (1932–1939)

By the mid–1930s, diesel technology was the latest and greatest innovation in the American truck manufacturing industry, and it seemed that anyone who was anyone was jumping on the bandwagon, including Clydesdale. The company started their "several years of research into the possibilities of greater economics in truck operation" as early as 1932. Former Clydesdale Motor Truck Company vice president A.C. Burch had returned to his position by this time, and told local newspapers that he "was convinced of Diesel Engine operating economy and he started engineering work to develop a line of modern motor trucks, suitable for present day hauling conditions."[1] So the Clydesdale Motor Truck Company shifted gears, and engineers developed a diesel truck. The Clydesdale Motor Truck Company would ride the wave of the future.

The first diesel engine had been invented in Germany by Rudolf Diesel in 1892. He developed and patented the first internal combustion compression-ignition engine, which still bears his name today. His engine worked by heating and compressing fuel, not gasoline, and causing it to ignite. Unlike in gasoline engines, sparks were not necessary to ignite fuel to power the diesel engine. Because the diesel engine was, and still is, driven solely by high compression in its cylinders, it was generally more energy-efficient, quieter, and required less maintenance and fewer repairs than other internal combustion engines.

In 1897, brewmaster Adolphus Busch bought the American rights to Rudolf Diesel's technology, and arranged for companies to pay him not only for licenses to use the technology, but also royalties for any profitable developments or inventions that resulted from further engineering. Not surprisingly, U.S. companies were reluctant to develop new technology under these conditions, so by the time his monopoly expired in 1912, Busch had failed to establish the Diesel empire he had envisioned, despite Rudolf Diesel's prediction that his invention would find its "greatest usefulness in America."[2] Busch sold licenses to just 260 diesel engines over the previous decade. Industry-wide, this arrangement simply stifled diesel technology development in the United States.

After Busch's licensing agreement expired, diesel engines grew in popularity, but slowly. For every believer in the new technology's potential to change the automobile industry, particularly truck manufacturing, there was a skeptic. Editors at *Popular Mechanics* in 1925, for example, forecast the "diesel motor as auto power" would save fuel.[3] Two years later, in 1927, the Society of Automotive Engineers was devoting sessions to diesel technology at their annual meeting.[4] General Motors began extensive testing of diesel engines the following year. *Fortune* magazine, years later, however, declared the still relatively new technology "distinctly unpromising" for automobiles — any cost savings in fuel would be canceled by high initial costs.[5] In addition, diesel engines, which were most popular with heavy industrial marine projects, were labeled a "bourgeois brutus," limited to "middle class" applications.[6]

"The tone in the business press had begun to shift by 1934," explained Cummins Engine Company historians Jeffrey Cruikshank and David B. Sicilia:

> *Scientific American*, for one, gave the automotive diesel more serious attention. While it was doubtful that diesels would be common "for some time to come," the magazine's writers noted significant progress with trains and trucks. And even if the automotive diesel had "yet to win its spurs," it nevertheless had "accomplished feats which have stirred the imagination." When *Fortune* revisited the industry in the same year, it found "a piece of machinery ... as exciting as a weekend visit with your maiden aunt." Nevertheless, *Fortune* grudgingly conceded, this was one of the few expanding segments in the national economy, a "vastly encouraging industry" that was "seething and boiling with ideas." "The Diesel industry today is about where the automotive industry was in 1914," *Fortune* concluded — in other words, on the brink of a revolutionary expansion.[7]

The diesel industry continued to grow, in spite of the economic climate of the Great Depression. In 1935, *Business Week*, like *Fortune* during the prior year, noted, "At least one branch of the durable goods industries has ceased to talk about the depression — the diesel power industry."[8] The same year, *Popular Mechanics* reported 800 diesel trucks in the United States, bolstered by the success of diesel engines in farm tractors: "What's around the corner in diesels for light trucks and small tractors is in the laboratories and test fields of some of the big manufacturers at this very minute, perhaps. They are all working on it. So are the auto engineers of firms with names that are household names."[9] In 1936, Clessie Cummins, the famed Indiana engine maker, told national Rotary Club members, "We are on the brink of one of the major shifts in the world's sources of power."[10] It was, he prophesied, "the upturning wave."[11]

Given this backdrop, it was not surprising, when the Clydesdale Motor Truck Company announced, in the fall of 1934, a focus on diesel engine trucks. Diesel fuel offered tremendous advantages to gasoline with respect to powering truck

In 1934, the Clydesdale Motor Truck Company announced a focus on diesel engine trucks. The company claimed to have developed the first completely diesel truck, rather than adapting a gasoline engine truck to accommodate a diesel engine.

engines. The most significant advantage was fuel consumption. Diesel engines used approximately half as much fuel as gasoline engines, which significantly lowered fuel costs. Diesel fuel also boasted a lower heat quotient than gasoline, which meant cooler running temperatures for large, often easily overheated engines. It was also less flammable than gasoline, and did not require a spark to start the engine, which made starting the engine safer. In addition, diesel-powered trucks did not require a carburetor, so maintenance time and costs were reduced. They also produced less carbon monoxide exhaust, which offered increased public health benefits.

Critics, however, pointed out that diesel engines were larger and heavier than gasoline engines, which necessitated their use in larger devices, including larger vehicles. They were also more expensive to purchase than gasoline engines, so concerns of increased diesel fuel

When the Clydesdale Motor Truck Company announced a new focus on diesel engine trucks in 1934, they updated not only the engine technology, but the design of the truck. This round cloisonné emblem appeared on later Clydesdale truck models. It was a change from the pentagonal nameplate that appeared on earlier trucks.

costs offsetting the initial extra cost were not uncommon. Diesel engines were also slower in many ways than their gasoline counterparts. George Green, vice president for engineering at General Motors in 1931, panned the "lack of acceleration or pick-up," along with the engine's "giving off a dense cloud of black smoke when running at full load."[12] In fact, Green was right. Diesel engines were very slow with starting and stopping over short distances. They performed best at constant running speeds on long trips, rather than variable speed short trips.

The Clydesdale Motor Truck Company claimed to be "the first Motor Truck Company in the country to specialize exclusively on Oil Engine powered trucks."[13] While the authors were unable to verify Clydesdale's claim through historical research, they also found nothing pointing to the contrary. It is entirely possible that the Clydesdale Motor Truck Company was the first manufacturer to focus exclusively on diesel engine trucks, particularly given that the trucks were engineered from the outset to operate with diesel power. "For with Clydesdale, Diesel Trucks are neither a sideline nor an adaptation."[14] Many truck manufacturers at this time simply retooled gasoline engine chassis to accommodate the new diesel technology. Clydesdale, however, developed a diesel truck, rather than repurposing their gasoline chassis. "Clydesdales are not conventional trucks with Diesel motors added — they are Designed and Built as Diesel Trucks Throughout," extolled advertisements.[15]

To assist with the development of modern diesel engine motor trucks, Clydesdale executives invited two industry experts to join the engineers in Clyde: E.B. Arnsbarger, of the Willys Overland manufacturing company, and C.A. Fulmer, of the Simplex Motor Car Company. Both men had extensive experience engineering and selling automobiles, including industrial products powered by diesel engines. Fulmer, specifically, had been drafted during World War I to serve as of the "Dollar a Year men" to work out the carburetion and

Aquí está

El **CLYDESDALE**

El Camión con Motor Diésel . . .

Ofrece nuevas oportunidades para lucrativas ventas en el campo de transporte por camión . . . .

LOS compradores de camiones, en todas partes del mundo, serán los primeros en reconocer y admitir la extraordinaria importancia de los camiones Clydesdale con motor de tipo diésel en todo género de transporte. El AHORRO DE COMBUSTIBLE llega hasta 70%. La POTENCIA ES MUCHO MAYOR, pues los motores diésel desarrollan su esfuerzo de rotación máximo a velocidades comparativamente moderadas, que es cuando más se necesita su FUERZA. Su EFICACIA general y ECONOMIA DE TRANSPORTE han sido comprobadas por millares y millares de kilómetros de servicio y por los registros de sus dueños en numerosos campos industriales, dueños cuyos negocios dependen en gran medida de la utili-

zación de los mejores camiones del mercado. Los nuevos Clydesdale están proyectados como camiones con motor diésel, de parachoque a lamparita trasera. No son camiones de tipos corrientes provistos sencillamente de motores de tipo diésel. Están cuidadosamente ideados, perfectamente equilibrados y completamente ensayados. Se ha provisto mayor "capacidad en reserva" en los embragues, cambios de marcha, árboles propulsores, ejes traseros y otras partes del chasis, para responder a los requisitos de la fuerza del motor diésel. Y los ingenieros del Clydesdale se han guiado por la tendencia hacia camiones de lindo aspecto. Por esta razón, los Clydesdale son de estilo perfilado.

La presente serie de camiones Clydesdale con motor diésel comprende modelos de 1½ a 12 toneladas de capacidad. Invitamos a los comerciantes del extranjero a estudiar detenidamente las posibilidades de ganancias de nuestros productos, los cuales están actualmente estableciendo nuevos precedentes en funcionamiento y en ventas en el campo de transporte por camión. Estamos ahora nombrando concesionarios en el extranjero. Las firmas de acreditada solvencia en el extranjero quedan cordialmente invitadas a pedirnos por carta o por telegrama información detallada, precios y pormenores de nuestra representación.

CLYDESDALE
MOTOR TRUCK COMPANY
Fábrica: Clyde, Ohio, E.U.A.
Dirección telegráfica: Clydesdale

The Clydesdale Motor Truck Company first marketed their new diesel trucks overseas, most prominently in South America. This advertisement for Clydesdale Diesel Motor Trucks is written in Spanish, and appeared in an Argentine magazine in August 1935. Graphically, it exhibits a dramatic departure from the line drawings that were used in earlier advertisements.

*Ofrecen extraordinario valor de transporte
y nuevas oportunidades para grandes ganancias . . .*

CLYDESDALE

CAMIONES Y OMNIBUS

CON MOTOR  DIESEL

LOS CLYDESDALE SON CAMIONES DIESEL — DE PARACHOQUE A LAMPARITA TRASERA

NO cabe la menor duda de que ha llegado la era de los camiones y ómnibus con motores de tipo diésel. Los camiones y los ómnibus Clydesdale con motores de tipo diésel han despertado extraordinario interes entre el comercio de automóviles y dueños de camiones y ómnibus en todas partes del mundo . . . Y con mucha razón, pues estos nuevos modelos Clydesdale tienen todo lo que se necesita . . . todo lo que tiende a facilitar las ventas en beneficio de sus activos distribuidores y representantes . . . todo lo que los compradores de camiones y ómnibus exigen en el sentido de mejor transporte moderno . . . Cuando se considera que los nuevos modelos Clydesdales producen economías en consumo de combustible hasta de 70%—que ofrecen mayor potencia, desarrollando su máximo esfuerzo de rotación a bajas velocidades de motor, que es cuando más se aprovecha la fuerza— que su eficacia y economía se han demostrado por millares de millas de funcionamiento irreprochable al servicio de sus dueños—que nuestros ingenieros, al proyectar los nuevos modelos Clydesdale, los han embellecido con un estilo perfilado, en armonía con la actual preferencia por vehículos más hermosos . . . Cuando se reflexiona sobre todo ésto, se comprende entonces la extraordinaria oportunidad para un negocio permanente y lucrativo que se presenta en la representación de los nuevos camiones y ómnibus Clydesdale provistos de motores de tipo diésel . . . A responsables organizaciones distribuidoras en el extranjero ofrecemos excelentes mercados. Si Uds. se interesan, sírvanse pedirnos, por carta o por telegrama, información detallada. Comuníquense directamente con la CLYDESDALE MOTOR TRUCK COMPANY, Clyde, Ohio, E. U. A.—Dirección telegráfica: "CLYDESDALE".

CAPACIDADES—1½, 2, 2½, 3, 4, 5 TONELADAS Y OTRAS HASTA DE 12 TONELADAS

CLYDESDALE MOTOR TRUCK CO., Clyde, Ohio, E.U.A. Dirección telegráfica: "CLYDESDALE"

Advertisement for Clydesdale Diesel Motor Trucks in Spanish that appeared in an Argentine magazine in November 1935. The company's extensive overseas sales network that had been established during World War I was the first market for the new Clydesdale diesel truck in 1934.

Top: Clydesdale diesel truck that was purchased by the president of the Dominican Republic for use on his farm. This truck was later featured in a 1936 advertisement for Clydesdale Diesel Engine Motor Trucks. *Bottom:* Clydesdale diesel truck working as a transport truck in Bilbao, Spain. The side of the body folded down to allow for more versatile hauling, very similar to the dumping bodies on earlier Clydesdale trucks. This truck was later featured in a 1936 advertisement for Clydesdale Diesel Engine Motor Trucks.

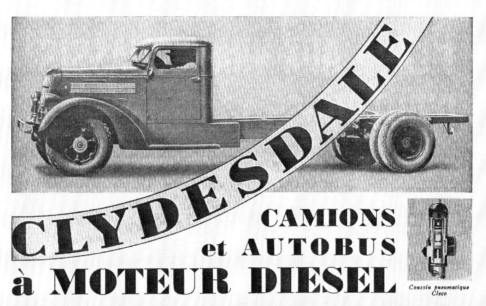

CAMIONS et AUTOBUS à MOTEUR DIESEL

Coussin pneumatique Cleco

Etudiés spécialement pour moteur Diesel

ECONOMIE DE CARBURANT—allant jusqu'à 70% par rapport aux moteurs à essence de même régime . . . PLUS GRANDE PUISSANCE—moteur développant un moment de rotation maximum lorsque la force est la plus nécessaire—comme, par exemple, lorsqu'il s'agit de tirer une charge en prise directe (mais au ralenti), ce qui calerait un moteur à essence courant de même régime . . . MOTEUR TOURNE PLUS LENTEMENT—assurant une durée plus grande au moteur—une consommation réduite en huile—moins d'usure au châssis . . . ECHAUFFEMENT MOINDRE—échappement sans fumée—minimum d'entretien et de réparation. . . . Tous ces points de supériorité ayant été prouvés par des milliers de kilomètres de parcours dans les domaines les plus variés. C'est là le record des CAMIONS ET AUTOBUS CLYDESDALE A MOTEUR DIESEL.

Superbe profilage . . . pare-brise en V . . . plus grande visibilité . . . protection efficace contre les intempéries . . . ventilation idéale . . . coussins très confortables . . . pneus de fort calibre . . . grande stabilité . . . Coussins pneumatiques CLECO ajoutant au confort et permettant de transporter sans danger les articles fragiles et les denrées périssables. Tous ces avantages sont offerts comme équipement standard sur tous les véhicules CLYDESDALE.

Le Clydesdale *n'est pas* un nouveau-venu, car il a fait ses preuves sur plus d'un marché. C'est un vétéran à même de fournir un *meilleur* travail tout en assurant une économie d'argent. Conçus de fond en comble pour moteur Diesel, les véhicules CLYDESDALE possèdent des embrayages, des transmissions, des arbres à cardan, des ponts-arrière et autres pièces de châssis, qui offrent une réserve de capacité répondant aux exigences d'emploi du moteur Diesel. Capacités offertes: 1½ à 20 tonnes. Tout genre de carrosserie, avec fini de diverses couleurs.

Conditions d'agence fournies aux distributeurs actifs, de réputation établie. Ecrire ou câbler sans tarder.

Boite de cinq vitesses pour poids lourd Clydesdale

Pont à double réducteur pour poids lourd Clydesdale

Joint universel à roulement à aiguilles

Direction à came et levier

CLYDESDALE MOTOR TRUCK CO.

CLYDE, OHIO, U. S. A.   Adresse télégraphique: "CLYDESDALE"

LE CLYDESDALE EST CONCU DIESEL DE FOND EN COMBLE

This 1936 advertisement for Clydesdale Diesel Motor Trucks was one of the last produced exclusively in Spanish, as the company's diesel line was released in the United States the following year.

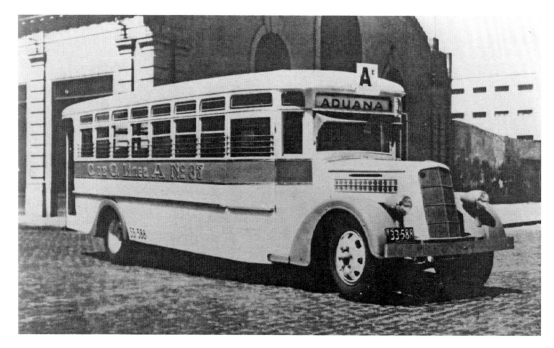

In addition to a full line of diesel trucks, Clydesdale offered a diesel bus. This Clydesdale Model 44-D diesel bus transported passengers in Aduana, Ecuador.

charging of Liberty airplane engines at the U.S. Bureau of Standards.[16] According to Clydesdale vice-president A.C. Burch, "For over 15 years he has been a technical consultant on fuels, and engine operation for various oil companies as well as the larger manufacturers of Diesel Engines. His experience over this period of time on Diesel Engine design and operation classes him as an outstanding expert on Diesel Engine practice."[17]

Between the Clydesdale Motor Truck Company's announcement of the diesel specialization and the actual appearance of diesel engine trucks in the United States, approximately three years passed. There were few public announcements from the company between 1934 and 1937, though those that have been identified suggested diesel truck development was taking place during these years. Advertisements from Argentina dated August and November 1935 suggest that the Clydesdale Motor Truck Company led the development and release of their diesel engine trucks overseas, more specifically, in South America. In an advertisement addressed to potential dealers, Clydesdale marketers insist "truck buyers all over the world will be the first to recognize and acknowledge the extraordinary importance of Clydesdale trucks in every kind and type of transport."[18] Clydesdale diesel trucks were also available in the Dominican Republic, Spain and Sweden. The company maintained the extensive overseas market that had sustained them during World War I, and was now allowing them to break into the diesel scene.

Also during this time, Clydesdale officials no doubt mourned the passing of company founder and motor truck engineer J.C.L. "Louis" Krebs. Louis Krebs died on April 16, 1936, at his home in Tampa, Florida. He and his family had moved there in 1925, several years after he had vacated his position at the Clydesdale company. According to his family, he had been ill for just 17 days prior to his death. He was survived by his wife, Louise,

Clydesdale Motor Truck Company diesel truck exhibit at an automobile show in the Netherlands. The exhibit highlights the Hercules engine. Signage indicates that the truck on display was imported into the country by a dealer named van Leewaarden, has a 6-cylinder engine, was made in America, and, according to the sign in the window, is "verkocht," or "sold." There is no indication of a date in the photo, but it most likely would have been 1935 or later. Clydesdale did introduce diesel trucks in the United States in 1937, but had been selling them overseas in the years prior.

and their four children, Marie, Loretta, Bertha, and Edmund. Louis Krebs was buried at the Loma Vista Mausoleum in Tampa.

Diesel Engine Motor Trucks

In a scene reminiscent of twenty years earlier, then successful in an overseas market during World War I, in 1937 the Clydesdale Motor Truck Company burst onto the American automobile manufacturing scene with their long-awaited diesel engine motor trucks. Company officials quickly recognized, and acknowledged, the somewhat rocky acceptance of diesel technology in the truck market, and described the Clydesdale trucks as "distinctive in appearance," then suggested, "They naturally attract special attention because people are not yet accustomed to seeing Diesel Engine trucks on the road."[19] Yet all signs pointed to full faith in the new technology. Perhaps in a most official manner, for the first time in the company's history, company officials formally trademarked the Clydesdale brand and logo. The "Clydesdale" trademark was issued October 12, 1937, and included everything in the company's production history up until that time: "Diesel and Gasoline Motor Trucks, Diesel and Gasoline Buses, Trailers, and Commercial Truck Bodies, Clydesdale Motor Truck Company, Clyde, Ohio."[20]

Announced just a year ago —
CLYDESDALE
DIESEL ENGINE MOTOR TRUCKS
Have won immediate widespread acclaim —

ACCEPTANCE! Clydesdale Diesel Engine Motor Trucks are answering the needs and demands of buyers of modern truck transportation the world over. Illustrated are a few of the many Clydesdales shipped abroad since their introduction just a year ago. . . . Their widespread acclaim was absolutely justified when you consider that Clydesdale Diesel Engine Trucks are not conventional trucks with Diesel motor added—but are designed and engineered specially throughout for Diesel Power . . . that they effect tremendous FUEL SAVINGS—they give more than double the miles per gallon. . . . That they offer GREATER POWER, for Clydesdales develop maximum torque at low engine speeds—where POWER is most needed. . . . That their all 'round EFFICIENCY and HAULING ECONOMY have been proven by the records of truck operators in many industries. . . . Overseas territories are now being offered to aggressive, responsible sales organizations—write or cable immediately for full details.

A Clydesdale Diesel Truck purchased by His Excellency the President of the Dominican Republic, for use on his own farm.

In Northern Spain—Here's another Clydesdale Diesel drop side lorry truck used for general hauling service.

A Clydesdale Diesel purchased by the Government of Santo Domingo.

CLYDESDALE
MOTOR TRUCK COMPANY
Factory: Clyde, Ohio, U.S.A.

Cable address: Clydesdale

All Sizes and Capacities . . .
. . . Special Trucks for Every Purpose

A Clydesdale Diesel in service as a garbage truck for the Department of Health and Sanitation in the Dominican Republic.

This Clydesdale Diesel Engine Motor Trucks advertisement appeared in the August 1936 issue of *The American Automobile* magazine. It was one of the first domestic ads for the diesel trucks and features Clydesdale diesel trucks from around the world, which reminded customers of the company's extensive overseas market. The trucks in the advertisement, from the top, include: a Clydesdale diesel truck bought by the president of the Dominican Republic for use on his farm; a drop side lorry Clydesdale diesel truck for hauling in Northern Spain; a Clydesdale diesel truck purchased by the government of Santo Domingo; and a Clydesdale diesel garbage truck used by the Department of Health and Sanitation of the Dominican Republic.

In what was the largest offering of trucks ever included in one line for the company, Clydesdale Motor Trucks offered nine different diesel truck models. The range of hauling capabilities and functions paralleled earlier offerings of gasoline models. Three smaller Clydesdale diesel trucks included the 30-D, with a carrying capacity of 1 to 2 tons; the 34-D, with a carrying capacity of 1½–2½ tons; and the 44-D, with a carrying capacity of 2½–4 tons. Mid-size models included the 75-D, which could accommodate loads of 3½–5 tons; the 80-D, which could accommodate loads of 5–7 tons; and the 90-D, which could accommodate loads of 5–7 tons. The three largest Clydesdale diesel trucks included the 105-D, which offered a capacity of 7–9 tons; the 125-D, which offered a capacity of 9–12 tons; and the 150-D, which offered the largest capacity of 12–20 tons.[21] The trucks were powered

Hercules Engine Company employee badge. Hercules supplied the diesel engines that went into Clydesdale diesel trucks.

by 4- or 6-cylinder Buda or Hercules diesel engines. Compared to Clydesdale's earlier gasoline models, all of the diesel models were quite speedy, with the 30-D achieving a maximum speed of 41 miles per hour, the 75-D achieving the highest maximum speed of 63 miles per hour, and the 150-D achieving 48 miles per hour.[22]

Even though the new diesel technology negated the need for the automatic controller that proved so distinctive among earlier models, all of the Clydesdale diesel trucks shared exclusive components. All of the models included 4-wheel hydraulic brakes, except for the two largest trucks, the 125-D and the 150-D, which included Westinghouse air brakes. Standard chassis equipment included the front bumper; head, parking, and tail lights; front fenders; short running boards; a "kit of tools"; and a tire jack. The lighted instrument panels included an ammeter, oil gauge, fuel gauge, temperature indicator, speedometer, and tachometer. Also within the driver's reach were light controls, the instrument panel switch, and a cigar lighter. A round, rather than the earlier pentagonal-shaped, cloisonné enamel nameplate identified all chassis as "Clydesdale Diesel" trucks. According to company literature, all of the Clydesdale chassis were painted a standard Clydesdale Golden Tan. Wheels were painted yellow. Finally, dual tires added balance in the rear of the chassis.

Clydesdale diesel trucks could be customized in much the same way as their earlier gasoline trucks. Though no actual Clydesdale diesel trucks appear to have survived, there are photographs and records of Clydesdale diesel dump trucks, moving trucks, and flatbed trucks. Similar to the customizable body options available in the past, Clydesdale offered several body types to customers at an additional cost, or customers were free to hire third party builders, or develop their own.

The truck bodies offered by the Clydesdale Motor Truck Company bore a strong resemblance to those manufactured by nearby Indiana Trucks. The company produced trucks

Top: One of the first Clydesdale diesel trucks to leave the factory for domestic orders. This truck was owned by S.A. Hemker and was featured in a 1937 advertisement for Clydesdale Diesel Engine Motor Trucks. It was described as "a short coupled half cab-over-engine tractor in the 18,000 lb. gross range. Offering a short wheelbase without the added expense of full cab-over-engine, yet offering full engine accessibility for service." *Bottom:* Clydesdale diesel dump truck owned by the Medusa Portland Cement Company, Cleveland, Ohio.

Model 90-D diesel dump truck outside the factory in Clyde, Ohio.

and truck bodies in Marion, Indiana, from 1911 until 1939. During that time, the Cummins Engine Company used several Indiana trucks for long-distance diesel tests, which made headlines. While there is no record of a partnership between the two companies, Clydesdale Motor Truck Company may have been heavily influenced by the diesel testing and the Indiana Truck company.

One of the custom bodies that Clydesdale offered to diesel customers was the bus, or motor coach, body. Clydesdale buses were particularly marketable as efficient and safe in light of new diesel technologies:

> Clydesdale Diesel Buses are designed for the Operators who demand — SAFETY FOR PASSENGERS, LOWER OPERATING COSTS, HIGHER PROFITS, TIME SCHEDULE PERFORMANCE, and EASY CONTROL for the Driver at all speeds.
> They reduce fire hazard by using non-explosive fuel, which lowers insurance rates, adds to the passengers' comfort, and provides safety for baggage, express and mails.
> Clydesdale Buses are engineered in many styles and offered with Diesel Power. They have quick acceleration, quick deceleration, and provide the most practical engineering science embodied in their design.[23]

While the bus advertising made note of diesel's advantages relevant to passenger transport, advertising for the other Clydesdale models recognized the company's historic record of performance and reliability. This, combined with the cutting-edge technology of diesel, made the Clydesdale diesel advertisements relatively earnest, in contrast to the seemingly pithy cleverness in earlier marketing campaigns. One advertisement, for example, read:

Top: A rear view of the Model 90-D Clydesdale diesel truck. *Bottom:* Clydesdale diesel truck, Model 44-D. This truck features a streamlined deluxe stake body and cab with skirted rear wheels. The body maker was likely Gar Wood Industries of Michigan.

Top: Front view of the Clydesdale diesel truck. Note the modern, streamlined design. *Bottom:* The Clydesdale diesel bus was marketed in much the same way as the earlier gasoline motor coach. This promotional illustration for the Clydesdale diesel bus highlights some of its features.

First American Trucks, Buses, and Moving Vans completely engineered for Oil Engine power and offered to World Markets. They have proven their dependability — Power — Longer Life — Lower Maintenance Costs and Economy over equivalent Gasoline Engine Units in every conceivable type of Field Service. They are engineered by designers using the most modern and scientific knowledge from Foreign and American experience, They eliminate fire hazards by using non-explosive fuels.

They are good looking, stylish and streamlined trucks, offering advanced designing that embodies every element of practical and scientific research engineering....

Clydesdales long have been favorites with the world's outstanding Transportation Engineers, who want dependability in motor trucks, buses, or vans, for delivering their products in World Markets, and who demand safety and economical performance. Clydesdale Diesels are rugged and sturdy-built trucks, offering operators the smoothest, non-smoking, easiest starting Diesel power ever presented....

If you want completely engineered transportation and quality with Dependability — Economy — Long Life....

Select a World-Proven Motor Truck.[24]

The "world-proven motor truck" quickly gained a foothold within the international diesel truck market. They were, after all, reminded Clydesdale Motor Truck Company executives, "seasoned veterans and engineered by designers using the most modern and scientific knowledge from Foreign and American experience."[25] Like a list of customers reminiscent of Clydesdale's post-war boom, diesel truck shipments were made to Mexico, Argentina, France, Finland, Uruguay, Santo Domingo, Cuba, Manila, Java, South America, and Spain. Subsequent company advertising urged customers to "Consider Clydesdale Trucks," which received "amazing performance records ... from the ends of the earth."[26]

The first domestic Clydesdale diesel orders went to a local straw and hay provider, S.A. Hemker, and to the Cleveland Pneumatic Tool Company, in Cleveland, Ohio.[27] A subsequent order called for shipment of a Clydesdale diesel truck to Honolulu. "Present orders, together with the increasing popularity of the Clydesdale Diesel Trucks, assures this company of a very successful year," quoted the local newspaper.[28] Additional diesel orders included trucks for Denny Motor Transfer Company, which operated a trucking company between Louisville, Kentucky, Indianapolis, and South Bend, Indiana; and Medusa Portland Cement Company of Cleveland, Ohio.

Diesel Motors, Inc, in Detroit, Michigan, was named one of the first distributors of Clydesdale diesel trucks. In selling the "only complete line of Diesel trucks in America," the distributor focused exclusively on diesel products and serviced every vehicle they sold, and even offered classes on operation and routine maintenance.[29] "It's purely a matter of low cost transportation and power," representative Mr. Moyer declared: "The Diesel makes half-price fuel go twice as far. Its simplicity still further cuts costs. On any power assignment in steady use Diesel economy simply can't be ignored. On long-haul intercity truck runs Diesel will soon become practically mandatory. As a source of power, Diesel performance is simply outstanding"[30]

The Clydesdale truck, in particular, served as a "splendid example of modern haulage equipment and Diesels, through and through." Company officials encouraged diesel truck buyers to use their Clydesdales in the "widest possible variety of service," in an effort to test the products.[31] They also encouraged customers to document truck performance in order to report back with information or feedback: "We must also know that the amazing record each in sure to establish shall be carefully kept."[32]

Top: The Clydesdale diesel bus chassis used the same steel frame that carried the larger trucks. *Bottom:* Clydesdale Motor Truck Company diesel truck display inside a dealer showroom. The engine and air brakes are prominently featured.

145

CLYDESDALE

DIESEL ENGINE
MOTOR TRUCKS

Below—Glow plug side of Clydesdale Diesel Engine showing an 84 horsepower full Diesel engine with vacuum pump installed, also special five speed transmission assembly with large diameter band brake with 5/16" lining operating on a cast iron drum.

Above—A short coupled half cab-over-engine tractor in the 18,000 lb. gross range. Offering a short wheelbase without the added expense of full cab-over-engine, yet offering full engine accessibility for service.

"CLYDESDALES
are Not conventional trucks with Diesel motors added --- they are Designed and Built as Diesel Trucks Throughout - - -"

Four years of specialization on Diesels exclusively—three years of field service all over the world—in competition with the best Europe offers—are further proof that DIESEL ENGINES in motor trucks can be successful only when the chassis as a whole is designed and built exclusively for Diesel Power.

The new series of Clydesdale Diesel Engine Trucks includes models from 1½ to 15 tons capacity. Offered in the conventional type — two wheel rear drive, cab-over-engine, half cab-over-engine, six wheel four wheel rear drive, four wheel four wheel drive and six wheel six wheel drive.

We invite fleet operators to investigate the profit making possibilities of our line, which today is setting new standards of performance and sales in the truck transportation field. Territories are now being allocated to responsible and aggressive sales organizations. Write for detailed literature.

CLYDESDALE
MOTOR TRUCK COMPANY

Factory: Clyde, Ohio, U.S.A.   *Cable Address*: Clydesdale

"All Sizes and Capacities . . . Special Trucks for Every Purpose"

COMMERCIAL CAR JOURNAL
APRIL, 1937

This advertisement for Clydesdale Diesel Engine Motor Trucks appeared in the April 1937 issue of *Commercial Car Journal.*

CLYDESDALE
DIESELS

First Completely engineered American Trucks, Buses and Moving Vans offered to World Markets. They have proven their Dependability—Power—Long Life—and Economy—for Years—Over equivalent Gasoline Motor Units in every Conceivable Type of Field Service. They give 28 to 35% Lower Net Per Mile Operating Costs and offer complete elimination of Fire Hazards by using non-explosive fuels.

They are seasoned veterans and engineered by designers using the most modern and scientific knowledge from Foreign and American experience. They are manufactured by a Company that has enjoyed an enviable reputation for over 28 years.

They are good-looking, Stylish and Streamlined Trucks, offering advanced designing that embodies every element of practical and scientific research engineering. They are offered in Two-wheel, Four-wheel and Six-wheel drive models and in capacities of 1-ton to 20 and are engineered to fit your business.

When you want engineered transportation and quality with

DEPENDABILITY ● ECONOMY ● LONGER LiFE — SELECT
A WORLD PROVEN MOTOR TRUCK

Desirable territories open write or wire

CLYDESDALE MOTOR TRUCK COMPANY
CLYDE, OHIO, U. S. A.

This advertisement for Clydesdale Diesel Engine Motor Trucks appeared in the November 1937 issue of *Commercial Car Journal*. It is one of the last advertisements for the Clydesdale Motor Truck Company to appear in a national trade journal.

Clydesdale Motor Truck Company exhibit at the 4th Annual National Motor Truck Show, Newark, New Jersey, November 6–13, 1937. The truck features a streamlined stake body with skirted rear wheels. The body was likely made by Gar Wood Industries of Michigan.

In stark contrast from a focus on the individual truck owner, Clydesdale marketed their diesel trucks primarily to fleet operators. Many company advertisements from this time period were invitations directed toward fleet managers who might consider ordering not just one Clydesdale diesel truck, but several. In other words, replace the fleet, and switch to diesel. With so many distinct advantages over gasoline-powered engines, it was not difficult for the Clydesdale Motor Truck Company to persuade customers to make the switch. "Clydesdale Full-Diesel Engine Trucks Bring Amazing Savings," and "Clydesdales Cut Costs," were common advertising headlines.[33] At least one advertisement even asked customers if they had "a run that will permit a Clydesdale Diesel to conspicuously prove its amazing economy?" Customers were then invited to write or call the company, in order to allow the Clydesdale diesel truck to do just that — prove its economy.[34]

Clydesdales at the Big Truck Show

"The Clydesdale Motor Truck Company will feature one of the foremost designed Diesel trucks at the National Motor Truck Show, to be held November 6 to 12 at Newark, New Jersey, according to E.B. Arnsbarger, first vice president of the Clydesdale Company," reported the front page of the *Clyde Enterprise* on September 30, 1937.[35] A decade had passed since Clydesdale trucks last appeared at a national automobile or motor truck show. They appeared again on the national stage, this time with completely redesigned and fundamentally different trucks.

The National Motor Truck Show in 1937 was one of the major automobile shows happening that year. Organized by the New Jersey Motor Truck Association and National Motor Truck Show, Inc., the show followed New York's National Automobile Show, which had taken place earlier in October. Clydesdale Motor Truck Company did participate with other manufacturers in a special diesel exhibit as part of the October New York show, which highlighted the latest technology in truck manufacturing. Following the New York show, the three Clydesdale diesel trucks in the exhibit were sent to Newark for the motor truck show, which was more specialized than the New York show and sure to reach more truck-oriented attendees.

Clydesdale's display at the Newark show was strate-

Interior of the Clydesdale diesel truck cab at the Newark Motor Truck Show. Note the single driver's seat. The front heater can be seen in the foreground.

gically planned. After all, they were participating in a national exhibition with the industry's largest manufacturers of trucks, trailers, engines, and accessories. Truck executives and engineers from around the world were expected to attend, as the regional meeting of the Society of Automotive Engineers was also taking place at the same time. The company partnered with the Ex-Cell-O Corporation of Detroit to make the Clydesdale Motor Truck Company exhibit "one of the finest displays ever presented to the motor truck world."[36] Ex-Cell-O

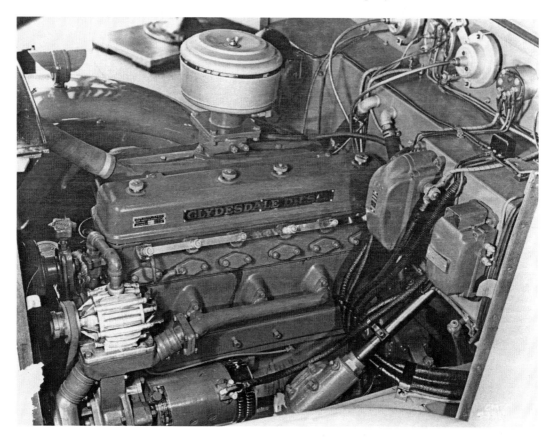

A close up of the 6-cylinder Buda or Hercules engine rebadged as a Clydesdale diesel engine for the Newark Motor Truck Show.

manufactured the fuel injection pump used in most Clydesdale diesel trucks.[37] Engineers were eager to showcase the Ex-Cell-O fuel injection pump as part of the popular Clydesdale.

The Newark National Motor Truck Show opened with 92 participating exhibitors. Of those, 25 were truck manufacturers, including Clydesdale. The show began with a "Parade of Transportation" down Newark's Broad Street. New Jersey governor Harold Hoffman declared it Transportation Week in the state.[38] Organizers strived to showcase trucks that performed a variety of everyday tasks, including trucks that delivered milk, fuel, coal, and beverages, as well as sales trucks. In addition to trucks on display, the Pennsylvania Railroad exhibited streamlined trains at its Newark station. There was also a display of the latest aviation equipment at the Newark airport. Like past automobile shows, there was an emphasis on new transportation technologies, including diesel engines, but also safety glass, non-skid tires, refrigeration, and improved signals, air brakes, and carburetor cleaners.

According to industry leaders, the Newark National Motor Truck Show was perhaps the grandest of all of the truck shows that occurred in 1937. It took place in Newark's Center Market Building, which offered 78,000 square feet of exhibit space. The show space was "elaborately decorated to illustrate the tremendous advances by the motor truck industry in the field of transportation."[39] Decorations were described as "unique and original in treatment."[40]

The building was transformed into a showcase of not only the advances in transportation technologies, but the evolution of humans from the Stone Age to the present day. This was achieved through a large mural and panoramic paintings on the wall, which were designed by Samuel Asch, a well-known national auto show decorator at that time. It was a noble, albeit less than accurate, even hyperbolic story, with early humans fashioning primitive wooden vehicles in order to improve their hunting and gathering lifestyles. Trade journals explained the elaborate progression, titled "The Romance of Transportation:"

Beginning at a height of ten feet from the floor, the murals pictorialize man's early battle for existence, the struggle against the elements, the limitations of life itself because of the lack of transportation. The early man was confined to his immediate surroundings to seek what food and sustenance and shelter could be found in his vicinity. He had to carry what he could find.

As man progressed he harnessed what animals were found in his region. Later on he built from the timber sources in his locale the type of vehicle his ingenuity could create. As the human race grew in numbers and in adopted area, each established their own civilization and national existence and each fashioned their means of locomotion in their own way. The murals show the means of transportation among the Phoenicians, the Assyrians and the Egyptians, each in their own adaptation of the chariot and other means of transportation; the Chinese who had their own civilization, used the sedan and manpower to carry. The East Indians pressed their elephants into service not only for the heavy type of work done today by giant trucks, but also for the transportation of their princes and potentates....

The construction of wagons and coaches did not begin until the 10th century and from that period on man's progress has been more rapid. The story of transportation as pictorialized in this frieze measures 800 feet in length, covering both sides of the Center Market Building....

The Indian drag, the oxteam carts, the stage coach, the pony express, the covered wagon, the early wood-burning trains, the horse car in the large cities, the various forms of bicycle and the first automobile and its subsequent development are all covered in detail including man's conquest of the air, sea and the subjugation of the elements of nature to the needs of civilization. This pictorialized story goes on with our giant zeppelins, trucks, conveyances of every sort including our monster seaplanes, our streamlined trains, streamlined automobiles and streamlined motor trucks.... This march of transportation in its tremendous expansion covers all lands, all climes and all regions.... Those who see this mural will have a new conception of the great strides and accomplishments the motor industry has made and the phenomenal blessings it has brought to the peoples of the earth.[41]

One of the diesel truck trailers manufactured by the Clydesdale Motor Truck Company by 1937. The company exhibited these trailers at the 1937 American Trucking Association annual meeting in Louisville, Kentucky.

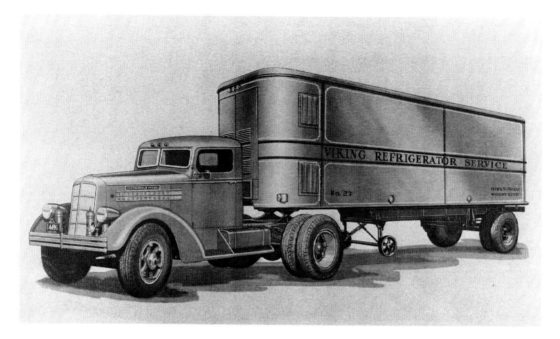

Top: The modern trucking industry that we know today was growing when Clydesdale released their semitrailer. Here is an illustration of a Clydesdale diesel truck pulling a trailer for the Viking Refrigerator Service. This may have been created for a brochure or customer presentation. *Bottom:* Photograph of the Denny Motor Transfer Company Clydesdale tractor trailer, from New Albany, Indiana.

Top: Clydesdale diesel truck pulling a tandem axle flatbed trailer of sugar cane in Hawaii. *Bottom:* Clydesdale diesel truck with a semi-trailer chassis.

Top: When the Clydesdale Motor Truck Company was granted the federal contract with the U.S. Navy, they had already sold at least one diesel truck to the government. This Clydesdale diesel truck is in service for the U.S. Navy in Bilbao, Spain. *Bottom:* One of the four wheel, 4-wheel drive Clydesdale diesel trucks customized for the U.S. Navy. This was the smaller of the two models designed for the military.

Detailed front view of the four-wheel, four-wheel-drive Clydesdale diesel military truck.

Top: Clydesdale employee Dominic Vartorella, left, stands with a colleague outside the factory in front of the 6-wheel diesel trucks manufactured for the U.S. Navy. *Bottom:* Front view of one of the Clydesdale diesel trucks engineered for the U.S. military.

It took nine months to research and to assemble the friezes. The mural, at 800 feet long and 10 feet tall, was thought to have been record-breaking. There were also murals paying homage to the "hundreds of thousands of men [who] are given employment and billions of dollars expended in materials and labor."[42] One additional mural, 40 feet long and 20 feet tall, depicted "The Motor Industry in its conquest of the world." The mural showcased how the automobile industry brought technology to many otherwise remote parts of the world. The "Goddess of Transportation" stood in the center of the scene, bestowing blessings on people from around the world. In addition to the artwork, modern lighting helped show-case the trucks. Over 500 lights were used throughout the show, which filled two floors.

Immediately following the show in Newark, the Clydesdale Motor Truck Company diesel trucks participated in the other major truck show of 1937 — the Truck and Accessories Show at the Annual Meeting of the American Trucking Association, in Louisville, Kentucky. The show took place November 15–18 at the Louisville Armory.[43] The truck and accessories show drew approximately 40 exhibitors from fifteen states, including truck, trailer, and accessories manufacturers. The meeting of the American Trucking Association, recently established in 1933, drew 4,000 trucking attendees.

By this time, the Clydesdale Motor Truck Company had introduced a steel frame trailer for use with their diesel trucks. It was very similar to today's semi truck trailers, but flat, ready for customization. Company representatives exhibited two of these trailers, with "each displaying the latest in design," according to *Motor Truck News.*[44]

Highlights from the Louisville show included a night parade of trucks, which took place on the show's opening night. It was five miles long.[45] The parade was themed to include five phases of transportation: first, historical means of transportation; second, the practical everyday utility of trucks; third, floats carrying messages about the economic importance of the trucking industry; fourth, "The Parade of the States;" and fifth, a display of outstanding equipment of local companies.[46] Grand Marshal of the parade was "safest truck driver" Andrio, who had been chosen from among the 1,500 truck operators entered in a safety contest.

Another show highlight was the "truck rodeo," which was directed by Colonel H. Norman Schwarzkopf. Entrants in the rodeo demonstrated expert driving by maneuvering trucks through narrow openings, figure eights, twists, turns, and challenging stops. There is no record of any Clydesdale trucks participating in the truck rodeo, but representatives certainly would have attended the event.

A Federal Test

In the spring of 1937, the Clydesdale Motor Truck Company, having "been engaged in building Diesel powered trucks sold in foreign markets," and "Having met with suc-cess all over the world," received two large orders for trucks from the United States gov-ernment. With the contract totaling approximately $215,000, the company raced to "build test trucks at once."[47] The first order was for 22 Clydesdale six-wheel, 6-wheel drive 7½-ton models, complete with cabs and cargo bodies, each equipped with winches and other special tools. The second order was for a number of four-wheel, 4-wheel drive trucks, also complete with cabs and cargo bodies, and also equipped with special tools. "Both orders consist of special design vehicles to meet the United States government specifications. One

Bottom view of the Clydesdale diesel military truck, as it is winched up inside the factory.

Top: Clydesdale diesel model 128D embarks on testing for the U.S. Navy by carrying several Clydesdale engineers to the test site. *Bottom:* Testing of Clydesdale diesel military trucks continues.

Top: A Clydesdale military-grade diesel truck speeds across a field during testing. *Bottom:* A company representative inspects a Clydesdale military tandem diesel truck during testing in 1937 (*courtesy Clyde Heritage League, Clyde, Ohio*).

Top: Clydesdale diesel truck following field testing for the U.S. military. *Bottom:* Clydesdale president A.C. Burch, right, with Mr. Robert Brown, who arrived in Clyde in the fall of 1937 to inspect the diesel trucks that had been contracted for order from the U.S. Navy (*courtesy Clyde Heritage League, Clyde, Ohio*).

each is to be built in the shortest time possible for test purposes by the War Department inspectors."[48] Due to the special materials required to fulfill the orders, Clydesdale estimated it would take 90 days to complete the first two trucks. To fulfill the rest of the order, production would occur at a rate of two 6-wheel trucks and four 4-wheel trucks each week. "Present orders, together with the increasing popularity of the Clydesdale Diesel Trucks, assures this company of a very successful year," reported the local *Clyde Enterprise.*[49]

Engineers at the Clydesdale factory immediately began developing, building, and testing the trucks. They designated a "test field" nearby, and drove the trucks in as many conditions as they could manage, including up hills, down hills, and through brush. Some of the "special equipment" on the trucks, aside from their hulking size, included spare tires, screen guards across the radiator — the trademark Clydesdale radiator had been modernized years before, but did not appear on these trucks — and wide mirrors. In the fall of 1937, the U.S. Navy granted the Clydesdale Motor Truck Company an official test, and the company was ready. Mr. Robert Brown of Baltimore would inspect the Clydesdale models as they pulled, climbed hills, drove through mud, and otherwise demonstrated "great strength in the truck."[50] Two more inspectors, Mr. John Albrecht of Cleveland and Mr. J. Sarbar of Detroit, assisted Mr. Brown.

Between the fall of 1937 and spring of 1938, or the time following the federal test, the Clydesdale Motor Truck Company disappeared from the historical record. One might assume that the company was waiting on results of the inspection and continued to fill

Employees load a Clydesdale diesel truck engineered for the U.S. military into a rail car for possible shipment.

orders. In May of 1938, however, the Clydesdale factory personnel received disappointing, and devastating, news. The federal government was canceling the contract, and would not be taking receipt of the trucks that had been so meticulously developed and tested. The newspaper reported, "Company Has New Program — Government Cancels Contract with Clydesdale; Company Needs New Operating Funds."[51] "The United States Government has cancelled its contract with the Clydesdale Motor Truck Company for building trucks for the War Department."[52] Congressional records indicate that the Clydesdale contract was not the only such diesel truck contract in existence, or canceled, so whether there was an ultimate need to thin the ranks of contractors, or to eliminate a particular focus on Clydesdale, is uncertain. Further examination of the historical record suggests that the cancellation may have been a somewhat mutual decision between Clydesdale and the U.S. government:

> Investigation of the contract by the company, indicated that completion would result in a substantial cash loss for the company, Burch said, and that the contract was cancelled as a result of a later investigation made by the government. It was said that the cancellation would facilitate the securing of new funds with which to carry on operation of the local concern.[53]

It became clear that the Clydesdale Motor Truck Company had poured all of its resources into developing the trucks under the government contract. Both of the two models intended for government purchase had been custom designed for military use, so they could not be easily produced and marketed to Clydesdale's usual clientele. The 6-wheeled, 7½-ton truck, in particular, was a monstrous model, too large and heavy for the daily needs of most individual or commercial customers.

To be sure, the cancellation of the federal contract was the death blow to the Clydesdale Motor Truck Company. In fact, the company had borrowed additional funds both in the fall of 1937 and in the spring of 1938 in order to help pay for some of the costs of developing an essentially new and specially-designed product. Still optimistic, Mr. Burch reported "'a substantial amount' of inquiries on hand for new business."[54] Following the cancellation, production at the Clydesdale factory stopped. "The factory is reported to be not operating at present."[55] Clydesdale officials were hopeful, however, that a new "program," or business plan, would allow the employees of the factory to resume production. The company's assets still exceeded any debts, and all told, the company was worth approximately $150,000. But this was not enough money to develop a new truck line and all of the accompaniments. Company officials submitted an official offer to shareholders in an attempt to "secure new and additional funds with which to carry on its business."[56] While there is no record of any shareholder coming forth to supply funds, one might assume that sufficient funds were arranged to keep the company in production for at least several months. As the new year dawned in 1939, Clydesdale president A.C. Burch, while acknowledging that the company had been "operating meagerly for several months," remained optimistic about the planned reorganization. "He stated that the cooperation of the company's sources of machinery, equipment, and supplies has been very encouraging, showing that the manufacturers supplying the Clydesdale have confidence that the company will eventually 'get on its feet.'"[57]

6

Winding Up Affairs (1939–1943)

On September 20, 1939, Clyde lawyer and Clydesdale creditor Fred Huffer filed suit in the county court to formally dissolve and "wind up the affairs" of the Clydesdale Motor Truck Company.[1] Following the federal government's cancellation of its contract, and the company's subsequent appeal to shareholders to acquire additional funds and credit, the Clydesdale Motor Truck Company simply never recovered. Whether the company solicited enough funds and credit from shareholders to continue doing business for a few more months is uncertain. The Clydesdale Motor Truck Company disappeared from the public record. By the fall of 1939, however, it was certain that Clydesdale Motor Truck Company was ending production for good. "It was reported financial conditions of the company made it impossible for a re-organization, and the officers desired clos[ing] of the company's affairs to the best interests of all concerned."[2]

Clydesdale Motor Truck Company officers by this time included an assembly of familiar names, men who had been with the company for years, if not decades. Longtime Clydesdale engineer and industry expert A.C. Burch was president; veteran Clydesdale engineer Amos White was vice-president; and J.H. Traxler, an engineer from Cleveland, was secretary. Finally, J.H. Morris of Amherst, Ohio, was director. Privately, they voted to end production at the Clydesdale factory, and as the newspaper reported, "wind up" affairs.

The county court judge assigned to the case, A.V. Baumann, ordered Clydesdale officers or other company officials to appear in court and explain, for any reason, why they thought the dissolution of the company should be stopped:

> Notice is hereby given that on the 20th day of September, 1939, Honorable A.V. Baumann, Judge of the Court of Common Pleas of Sandusky County, Ohio, issued an order, in case number 23373 on the appearance docket of said court, in which F.D. Huffer is plaintiff and the Clydesdale Motor Truck Company is defendant, requiring all officers, directors, and shareholders of the Clydesdale Motor Truck Company to appear in said court and show cause on the 27th day of September, 1939, why said corporation should not be dissolved.[3]

No one appeared. So court proceedings advanced. The Clydesdale Motor Truck Company was formally dissolved by the end of September 1939.

Court documents reveal details of a dire financial situation at the factory that started as early as 1937, during the heaviest diesel truck development, and only intensified in the months following the cancellation of the government contract. The Great Lakes Acceptance Corporation, a mortgage lender in Cleveland, held three liens, or chattel mortgages, against the Clydesdale Motor Truck Company, with property and equipment as collateral. The first

Lewis Snyder outside his garage with a finished Clydesdale chassis. Following the dissolution of the Clydesdale Motor Truck Company in 1939, Snyder helped to assemble several remaining chassis for a shipment overseas to Finland (courtesy of Robert Snyder, Port Clinton, Ohio).

lien was dated October 20, 1937, and was the most significant of the three, and amounted to $133,625. It had, by 1939, also accrued unpaid interest in the amount of $48,266. The other two liens were dated April 28, 1938, in the amount of $1,500; and April 29, 1938, in the amount of $2,500. In addition to the liens, at least one contracted Clydesdale supplier pursued outstanding balances. On December 6, 1938, the Glidden Company, which supplied paint to the Clydesdale factory, obtained a judgment against the Clydesdale company in the Municipal Court of Cleveland for $540 in unpaid costs plus interest.[4]

According to the local newspaper, one public sale of machinery, equipment, parts, and office furniture took place on October 18, 1939.[5] Additional equipment sales continued until April 16, 1942, when the dissolution case was finally closed. Much of the Clydesdale equipment was sold to employees, local businesses, or nearby firms. Sale prices varied, subject to best offers presented, which were sometimes significantly below market value. Court records indicate, for example, that Mr. Ben Parker purchased a combination rip saw for $125. Meanwhile, Lee's Auto Wrecking Company of Clyde purchased a number of items, including one pattern for a windshield, master clock, gas tank, log chain, and steel cable, along with cab parts, cab doors, two fenders, two gas tank brackets, a variety of castings, and two gallons of gear lube, all for $10. By this time, any money that could be generated to pay creditors, while removing equipment from the factory space, was welcomed.

As production at the Clydesdale factory was winding down, there remained one particularly complex outstanding order for trucks. The order was from a buyer in Finland, already paid, and needed to be completed and shipped overseas. Owners of a local garage agreed to assemble the trucks in an attempt to fulfill the order. On August 5, 1939, Highway Garage co-owners Lewis Snyder and Paul Beier delivered one 3-ton Clydesdale diesel truck and trailer to New York, where it would later be shipped to a buyer in Helsingfors, also known as Helsinki, Finland. "The Clydesdale Company last year received the truck order from the Finland firm, but was unable to complete the job, because financial difficulties slowed down activities at the factory.... The [Highway Garage] practically built all of the trailer," Mr. Snyder said. "The work was completed in two weeks and was taken to New York immediately."[6]

As Snyder and Beier at the Highway Garage completed one remaining order for trucks, the life of the Clydesdale Motor Truck Company also seemed complete. There were few, if any, public announcements of the company's dissolution. In fact, international Clydesdale dealers continued to write to the company, particularly for replacement parts, until at least 1943.

Little is known about what happened to Clydesdale employees. Mr. M.R. Pence, former Clydesdale sales representative, went on to become an automotive advisor to the U.S. military during World War II. After the war, he became the regional sales manager for Willys-Overland Motors. He also pursued a venture partnership with Mr. H.C. Bacon, and the two established the Bacon-Pence dealership in Louisville, Kentucky.

Clydesdale vice-president and director of sales A.C. Burch took a position as manager of market research for Thew Shovel Company, Lorain, Ohio. The Thew Steam Shovel, invented by Captain Richard Thew in 1895, is credited as being the first fully revolving excavator in the United States. Thew shovels were used around the world, especially along the Great Lakes shipping channel, for moving ore shipments, as well as during construction of the Panama Canal. Burch worked for Thew until his death on March 12, 1948. According to a few announcements in trade journals, he died following a heart attack in his Sandusky, Ohio, home.

The dissolution of the Clydesdale Motor Truck Company was not unexpected given the climate of the automobile manufacturing industry. Locally, the city of Clyde had been watching production at the company start and stop for some time. Certainly the closing of the factory was a blow to the local economy, as the closing of the Elmore Manufacturing Company had been decades earlier. Nationally, many independent car and truck manufacturers, still reeling from the Great Depression, had gone bankrupt, been formally dissolved, closed, or bought by larger companies by 1939. In fact, in his now classic 1941 history of the industry, Edward D. Kennedy identified just five "active producers" among independent truck makers that had survived.[7] The Clydesdale Motor Truck Company falls somewhere between the exception and the rule, developing trucks until 1939. By the end, however, it had become another casualty of, yet leaving its mark upon, a rapidly changing industry.

Epilogue

It is estimated that there are fewer than ten Clydesdale trucks left in existence today. True to the Clydesdale Motor Truck Company's global customer base, at least one existing truck was located in New Zealand. The rest are located in the United States, near Clyde, Ohio, where they were manufactured. All of the recorded existing Clydesdale trucks are gasoline models made before 1930. No late model gasoline 6-cylinder or diesel Clydesdale trucks have ever been located. Most of the Clydesdale trucks are privately owned and maintained. At least one, however, is preserved in a museum, open to the public.

Fully restored 1920 Clydesdale fire truck that was used by the Clyde Fire Department, Clyde, Ohio. It was in service until it was decommissioned in 1947, and was sold by the city. Upon the truck's sale, the fire chief removed all of the unique equipment and put it in storage. The truck was recovered from a collector, Theodore Gruener, in 1967, who donated it back to the city for complete restoration. City officials located all of the original equipment and remounted it on the truck. Since then, the truck has made frequent appearance in parades. It is housed at the Clyde Museum, operated by the Clyde Heritage League, with the truck itself maintained by the Clyde Fire Department.

(1) Rear view of the Clyde Fire Department's 1920 Clydesdale fire truck; (2) Close-up of the cast aluminum foot plate on the floor of the Clyde Fire Department's Clydesdale fire truck; (3) Close-up of the cast aluminum hood handles and octagonal headlights of the Clyde Fire Department's Clydesdale fire truck; (4) Close-up of the distinctive "Clydesdale" nameplate on the Clyde Fire Department's fire truck. The same nameplate appeared on most Clydesdale trucks made prior to 1924.

Top: Former Clyde Kraut Company Clydesdale chassis owned by Norm "Jake" Warner of Vickery, Ohio. *Bottom:* Former Clydesdale quarry truck restored by Mike Bushong of Fremont, Ohio.

Restored Clydesdale truck owned by a collector from New Zealand, Bryce Manderson.

The city of Clyde, Ohio, at the Clyde Museum, still maintains the Clydesdale fire truck that served the local fire department starting in 1920. Members of the Clyde Fire Department still perform regular maintenance on the truck to ensure that it is in working order. Its preservation in the museum is somewhat fortuitous, as the truck did not stay continuously in Clyde since 1947. It was returned to the city in 1967, following a rather dramatic search, by a private collector who had bought the truck years earlier.

After its purchase by the department in 1920, the Clydesdale fire truck served the fire department for 25 years, and was decommissioned in 1947. In 1949, city officials authorized the sale of the truck, which until that time had been stored in then Fire Chief Frank Fultz's garage. Three local men purchased the out-of-service Clydesdale fire truck for $75. Before delivering the truck, however, Chief Fultz removed all of the mounted unique fire equipment, including the hand siren, bell, lantern, and hose fittings, and stored the parts at Clyde's City Hall. A local business owner displayed the truck in front of his filling station along U.S. Route 20. Antique truck collector Theodore Gruener, of Chardon, Ohio, stopped by one day and bought the Clydesdale fire truck from the new owners for $350.

Clyde city officials began searching for the truck in 1966 at Chief Fultz's urging. He had been informally searching for the truck ever since he learned it had left the community following the city's sale. As word of the city's search made area news, one of Mr. Gruener's employees shared an article with him, and asked if he happened to own the truck. He did, and soon contacted Clyde city officials. "He asked if the village was looking for a Clydesdale fire truck, motor number 24380.... "'Well, I have it.'"[1]

Mr. Gruener agreed to donate the Clydesdale fire truck to the city for restoration. Since the time he had purchased the truck, it had never been fully restored. When Clyde city officials took possession of the truck in 1967, it had been sitting on blocks, not running, for ten years. City officials drove to Chardon to pick up the truck, with a local resident donating a flatbed truck for transportation. "We found the gentleman, walked into his barn, and there it sat up on blocks," recalled John Ashton, a former city finance director who assisted with bringing the truck back to Clyde. "It was a basketcase."[2]

Upon its return to Clyde, the truck was fully restored, including all of the mounted unique parts — hand siren, bell, lantern, and hose fittings — that had been saved decades earlier. The restored Clydesdale fire truck is one of few physical reminders of the Clydesdale Motor Truck Company surviving in Clyde, Ohio. The Amanda Street factory facility was gradually dismantled and torn down, with the last piece, the company water tower, torn down in 1975. The fire truck, along with the other restored Clydesdale trucks still in existence, and a few meticulously curated archival collections, are all that remain of the once thriving Clydesdale Motor Truck Company and their "Driver Under the Hood."

How I Learned
About Clydesdale Trucks
by James M. Semon

I am a transportation enthusiast — railroads were my main area of interest, until I ran into the Clydesdale truck. Pursuing its history for over forty years has brought me many adventures and many new and lasting friendships. It began with Bruce Dicken, who worked with me at American Greetings Corporation in Cleveland, Ohio. He was also a railroad enthusiast, and showed me pictures of his father on a rail car on the New York Central Railroad — a rail car that just happened to be holding crates of Clydesdale trucks. I learned that Hugh Dicken, Bruce's father, had worked in the shipping department of the Clydesdale Motor Truck Company in Clyde, Ohio. Bruce's uncle, Merlin Pence, had also worked for the Company as assistant sales manager. I wanted to learn more about this unique Clyde company.

Start of Many Friendships

I visited the Clyde Public Library and found additional information on Clydesdale trucks. I learned from my former boss, Roger Kuns, while visiting him and his wife Pat at their home near Clyde, that the Clyde Volunteer Fire Department had a restored Clydesdale fire truck that they used in parades. I was able to get a few indoor photographs of the fire truck in Clyde in the fall of 1988, while attending a Nickel Plate Railroad Historical and Technical Society Convention at the Mad River Museum in nearby Bellevue, Ohio.

That fueled my interest! I contacted Dave Moyer, then chief of the Clyde Volunteer Fire Department, and he arranged an outdoor photo session for me with the Clydesdale fire truck in the summer of 1991. Dave also suggested that I contact Norm "Jake" Warner in Vickery, Ohio, who had found and preserved a Clydesdale truck that had once been owned by the now-shuttered Clyde Kraut Company. Jake invited me to his farm to see his original Clydesdale flatbed truck, where I took indoor photographs and made many notes. He also showed me a Clydesdale Motor Truck Company promotional piece — a replica ashtray, which he found at a toy show many years ago. Jake still owns the truck, and we have remained good friends.

In 1992, I visited the Clyde Heritage League Museum and introduced myself to Curator

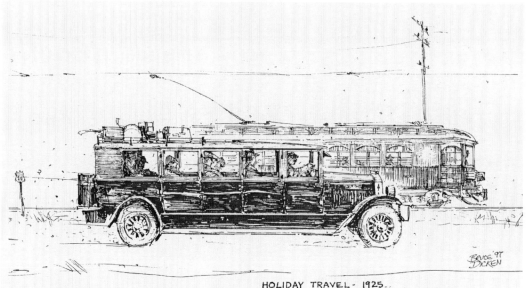

Top: Sketch of a Clydesdale bus riding alongside a Lake Shore Electric rail car, by Bruce Dicken, 1997. Bruce's father, Hugh Dicken, worked for the Clydesdale Motor Truck Company as a young man. The Clydesdale Motor Truck Company released the motor coach by 1925, and the Lake Shore interurban car had at least one Clydesdale line truck. *Bottom:* Promotional Clydesdale Motor Truck Company aluminum ashtray. The promo replica is likely one of the earliest made by a truck company. The cab holds a matchbox, while the back of the truck collects ashes. Author James Semon saw several of these ashtrays owned by collectors in the decades that he researched the Clydesdale Motor Truck Company.

Top: Author James Semon with his Clydesdale truck prior to restoration. With the radiator removed, there is a clear view of the cooling fan in the front of the truck. *Bottom:* Author James Semon's Clydesdale truck prior to complete restoration. The distinctive Clydesdale radiator is prominent at the front of the truck.

Close-up of the engine of author James Semon's Clydesdale truck prior to restoration.

Ralph Rogers, who encouraged my interest in the history of the Clydesdale truck and the Clydesdale Motor Truck Company. Ralph and his wife Betty became very dear friends. Ralph also told me about Dominic Vartorella, of nearby Berlin Heights, Ohio, who had worked at the Clydesdale factory during the diesel years in the late 1930s.

Dominic was preparing to donate a large collection of Clydesdale truck and company photos to the Clyde Heritage League Museum. I visited Dominic and his wife Mary at their home in Berlin Heights, Ohio. These two wonderful people also became good friends, and Dominic shared many stories and photos of his experiences with the Clydesdale company during the diesel years. I subsequently nominated Dominic for a Founders Award from the American Truck Historical Society (ATHS). The award recognizes living trucking pioneers, or people who began working in the industry prior to October 1, 1935, and con-

Restored Clydesdale truck owned by Tom and Georgie Ward. The Wards completed restoration of author James Semon's Clydesdale truck in 2012.

tinued to work in the industry during their entire career. Dominic received the Founder's Award at the ATHS's annual convention in Milwaukee in 1993.

I also visited Sandusky, Ohio, historian Virginia Fuller Steinemann, whose grandfather, Burton A. Becker, was a founder of the Elmore Manufacturing Company in Clyde. As a predecessor to the Clydesdale Motor Truck Company, the Elmore Manufacturing Company was a starting place for many later Clydesdale engineers. She shared the history of her family's involvement as designers and manufacturers of the Elmore Automobile, and later as stockholders of Clydesdale Motor Trucks. She, too, showed me a Clydesdale replica ashtray, which had been given to her by her grandfather, and encouraged me to photograph it.

Building a Collection

I continued to collect every photograph, article, trade ad or bit of memorabilia I could find on Elmore automobiles, Krebs Commercial Car Company trucks, and Clydesdale trucks. To date, my collection stands at 360 photos, 70 articles, 58 company brochures, 65 trade ads, 2 Clydesdale parts books and other memorabilia, including an ashtray (a gift for my 55th birthday), folding rulers, badges, builder's plates, a radiator guard bar and business cards. In April of 1994, I was invited by the Clyde Heritage League to develop a presentation about Clydesdale trucks. My friend Roger Chapman of Hamilton, Ontario, Canada, made slides of my collection of black and white photos of Clydesdale trucks and memorabilia. That was the first of many presentations about Clydesdale trucks and the Clydesdale Motor Truck Company.

I even bought a Clydesdale truck of my own. I missed an auction in Michigan on a 1924 Clydesdale Model 10-A, but Ralph Rogers contacted me about another for sale in Indiana. It turned out to be the same truck from the Michigan auction, but new owner Leo Flory had decided not to tackle the restoration. My wife Bonnie and I visited Leo and his wife, Florence, and their marvelous collections of antiques and automobile memorabilia. We decided that we could not pass up the chance to own a real Clydesdale.

Transporting the Clydesdale truck required the help of four people, including myself and our son, Jim, along with Aud Balogh and our son-in-law, Bob Stacy, who volunteered his pickup truck and trailer. The three of them helped me to get the truck to our Sandusky, Ohio, shop. I worked on restoring the engine, frame and wheel rims, but after 13 years of trying to locate parts and estimating the work involved, I decided it was more than I could handle. I offered the truck to Dominic Vartorella's daughter, Georgie Ward, and her husband Tom. He had already restored Dominic Vartorella's Garford truck and several other antique trucks. Georgie Ward bought the truck from us in 2008, and Tom had it completely restored by the fall of 2012.

In the meantime, I co-authored with my friend Bruce Dicken three full color railroad books, two on the Nickel Plate and one on the Baltimore & Ohio, which were published by Morning Sun Books between 1995 and 1998. This encouraged my longtime desire to write a book about Clydesdale trucks.

A Book About Clydesdale Trucks

When I first met Ralph Rogers we talked about writing a book on the history of Clydesdale Trucks. That has always been my goal, but I wanted help. After reading the excellent book that McFarland published on the Jordan Automobile in 2005, I contacted them. They expressed interest, following up on my proposal annually while I continued to search for help with the manuscript.

In 2010, I was fortunate to meet Jill McCullough, Adult Services Librarian for the Clyde Public Library, at a Firelands Postcard Club meeting in Sandusky, and I later made my slide presentation on Clydesdale trucks at the Library. We discussed my goal of writing a book. Jill knew that a Clyde native now living in Chicago, Tiffany Willey Middleton, was interested in writing about the history of her hometown, and suggested her when I asked about possible local authors. She thought Tiffany might be interested in writing a history of Clydesdale trucks and the Clydesdale Motor Truck Company. She was!

After several exchanges of information with Tiffany, I knew that I had found the person that would make the Clydesdale book a reality. Tiffany's research has filled in many holes in the Clydesdale story, and with support from Jill and me, she has been able to develop a comprehensive history of the company and its people. My ultimate goal has been to share the unique Clydesdale story, a company with "The Driver Under the Hood" that refused to go away, for future generations to know and appreciate.

Appendix A: U.S. Patent #1117759 for Engine Governor

UNITED STATES PATENT OFFICE
FRANK X. BACHLE AND WALTER W. WELLS OF CLYDE, OHIO ASSIGNORS TO THE
KREBS COMMERCIAL CAR COMPANY, OF CLYDE, OHIO, A CORPORATION TO
OHIO

Engine Governor
Patent 1,117,759
Patented November 17, 1914
Specification of Letters Patent. Application filed July 11, 1913. Serial No. 778,443.

To all whom it may concern:

Be it known that we, FRANK X. BACHLE and WALTER W. WELLS, citizens of the United States, and residents of Clyde, in the county of Sandusky and State of Ohio, have invented a certain new and useful Engine-Governor; and we do hereby declare the following to be a full, clear, and exact description of the invention, such as will enable others skilled in the art to which it appertains to make and use the same, reference being made to the accompanying drawings, and to the characters of reference marked thereon, which form a part of this specification.

This invention relates to engine governors, and particularly to means of this class adapted for use in connection with the internal combustion engines of automobiles, but is not restricted to such use as it may be used in any connection for which it may be adapted or appropriate.

The object of our invention is the provision of simple and improved means of this class, which is operable to accurately regulate the speed at which it may be desired to run an engine, and which is capable of easy and quick adjustment from the driver's seat in the associated vehicle, or from any other convenient point, to change the speed limit at will, thus making our improved governing means of particular value for use in motor-driven commercial and pleasure vehicles.

A further object of our invention is the provision, in combination with a governor of the class described, of simple and efficient means for automatically controlling the time of ignition in proper accordance with the varying conditions of speed and load, whereby the engine will work at its maximum efficiency at all times.

The invention is fully described in the following specification, and while, in its broader aspect, it is capable of embodiment in numerous forms, a preferred embodiment thereof is illustrated in the accompanying drawings, in which,—

Figure 1 is a side elevation of an apparatus embodying our invention, with parts broken away. Fig. 2 is a plan of an engine and associated parts embodying the invention. Fig. 3 is an enlarged central vertical section of a steering mechanism with associated control parts of the invention, and Fig. 4 is a face view of the timer mechanism.

Referring to the drawings, 1 designates a portion of the supporting frame of a vehicle with

F. X. BACHLE & W. W. WELLS.
ENGINE GOVERNOR.
APPLICATION FILED JULY 11, 1913.

1,117,759.

Patented Nov. 17, 1914.
2 SHEETS—SHEET 1.

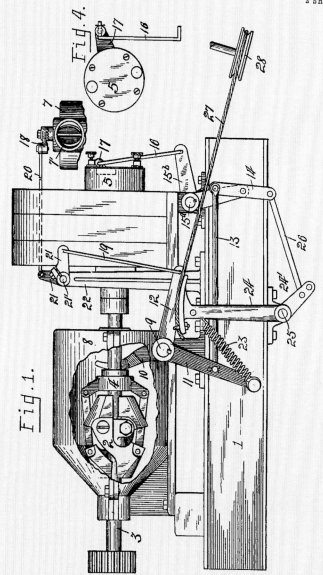

Fig. 4.

Fig. 1.

WITNESSES:
D. C. Watter
F. E. Aul.

INVENTORS
Frank X. Bachle,
Walter W. Wells.
By Owen & Owen.
Their attys.

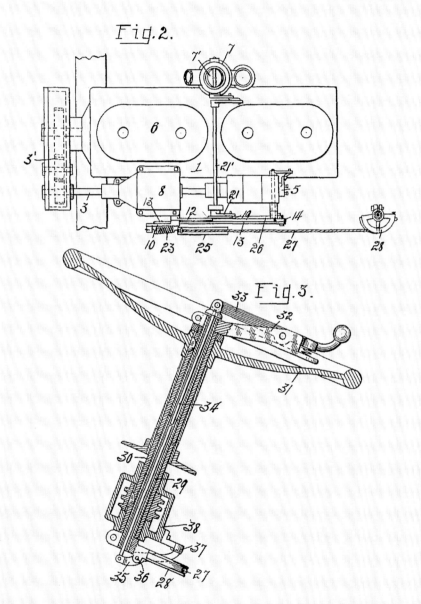

F. X. BACHLE & W. W. WELLS.
ENGINE GOVERNOR.
APPLICATION FILED JULY 11, 1913.

1,117,759.

Patented Nov. 17, 1914.
2 SHEETS—SHEET 2.

Fig.2.

Fig.3.

WITNESSES:
D. C. Walter
F. E. Aul.

INVENTORS
Frank X. Bachle,
Walter W. Wells.
By Owen & Owen,
Their attys.

which our improved mechanism is associated, or it may constitute any other suitable supporting part; 2 governor weights of any suitable form, which are rotatable with a shaft 3 and are connected to a sleeve 4 mounted for longitudinal sliding movements on said shaft, such movements being actuated by the governor weights upon a changing of the speed of running the shaft; 5 the timer mechanism for the ignition circuit of an associated engine 6 which mechanism may be of any 7 suitable type, and 7 the engine carburetor having the customary throttle valve. The governor shaft 3 is geared to the engine shaft, as at 3', or otherwise suitably connected thereto.

Projecting up within the governor case 8 from a rock-shaft 9 is an arm 10, the upper or free end of which is forked to adapt it to straddle the shaft 3 and bear against the outer side of the governor sleeve 4 whereby an outward movement of such sleeve from the governor weights effects a rocking of the arm 10 and shaft in one direction. The shaft 9 is mounted in the base of the governor case 8, or in any other suitable part, and has arms 11 and 12 projecting there from in bell-crank lever form and adapted to have rocking movements there with. The arm 11 is connected by a rod or link member 13 to the upper end of a lever 14, which is pivoted substantially centrally of its ends to a crank-arm 15 on one end of a rock-shaft 15a, which is mounted in a convenient frame part. An arm 15b on the other end of such shaft is connected by a rod or link member 16 to the movable part 17 of the timer mechanism, whereby the time of sparking of the ignition circuit of the engine is advanced or retarded, as the throttle is opened or closed, as is well understood in the art.

The lever-arm 12 is connected to the throttle-valve arm 18 of the carburetor in any suitable manner, as, for instance, through the rods 19 and 20 and the interposed bell-crank lever connection 21, the shaft 21' of which is mounted on a bearing-standard 22 and carries the lever arm at opposite ends thereof. It will, of course, be understood that the form of the connection arms 12 and 18 may be changed according to the relative positions of such arms. It is thus evident that a rocking of the forked arm 10 by an outward movement of the governor sleeve 4 effects an adjustment of both the timer mechanism and the carburetor throttle to suit the speed of desired running of the engine:

The centrifugal force of the revolving mass of the governor, which mass, in the present instance, comprises the weights 2, is opposed or counterbalanced by a coiled contractile spring 23, or other suitable means of an elastic nature, which connects the free end of the lever-arm 11 and an adjustable part, which part, in the present instance, is in the form of a rocker-arm 24 that is pivoted to the frame 1, as at 25, the tension of the spring on the arm 11 being changed by a movement of the part 24 in one or the other direction relative to said arm. The arm 24 has an extension or finger 24 projecting from its fulcrum end, and this finger is connected by a rod or link-member 26 to the opposite end of the lever 14 from that to which the rod 13 connects, for the purpose hereinafter described.

It is evident from the above that any increase of speed in the engine increases the centrifugal force of the weights so that they are no longer balanced by the pull of the spring, thus permitting the weights to move out farther from the axis of rotation, and this movement of the weights is communicated as hereinafter described, or in any other suitable manner, to the throttle or means controlling the supply of energy to the engine, an outward movement of the weights reducing the supply of energy by closing the throttle, and an inward movement increasing the supply by opening the throttle. Since the outward movement of the weights increases the radius of the circle in which they rotate, and since centrifugal force varies directly as the radius of rotation, the tension of the spring must be increased a like amount in order that it will be able to pull in the weights and effect an opening of the throttle as soon as the speed falls below normal. A spring could be used that is just stiff enough to balance the weights in either their inner or outer or any intermediate position, at exactly the same speed, thus providing what is known as an isochronous governor; but with such a spring a very slight change of speed causes the weights to move to their extreme position, and hence they would be constantly moving from one extreme position to another, a condition known as a "hunting" governor. It has been common practice to make the spring a little stiffer than is required to actually balance the weights so that the speed when the engine is fully loaded is about 2 percent less than when running idle, that is, for example, if the engine makes 98 R.P.M. under full load (weights in) and half of the load is thrown off, the speed will increase to 99 R.P.M., and then the spring will balance the weights in their middle position. Throwing off all the load allows the engine to speed up slightly and the weights reach their outer position and effect a closing of the throttle when the speed reaches 100 R.P.M. If a spring more flexible than required for isochronous governing were used, the centrifugal force and spring tension would balance at one speed with the weights in their outer position and at a higher speed with the weights in their inner position with the result that the engine would run with the throttle wide open until the speed reaches the maximum, and then the weights would move out closing the throttle tight until the speed dropped to the lower limit, then open wide again, etc., making a bad case of "hunting." Since centrifugal force varies as the radius of rotation and also as the square of the number of R.P.M. it will be seen that it is necessary to employ different springs or different weights or a different relation between the weights and spring if it is desired to use the governor at different speeds. For instance, at 1000 R.P.M., centrifugal force is twenty-five times as great as at 200 R.P.M. hence, the spring must be twenty-five times as stiff, or have twenty-five times as much leverage on the weights, if it is to govern to the same degree of accuracy.

With our improved governing mechanism different springs or weights are not required, but instead thereof the position of the spring is shifted, so as to change the leverage with which it acts, and this shifting is done while the engine is in motion and carrying its load, giving accurate automatic control of the speed regardless of changes of load and throughout a wide range of speeds.

In order to control the movements of the part 25 from the driver's seat in the associated vehicle, in the present instance, a cable or other suitable draft means 27 is attached at one end to the free end of the arm 24 and at its other end to the periphery of the wheel segment 28, which is carried at the lower end of the hollow shaft 29 that extends up through the steering column 30 of the vehicle, being suitably mounted therein. The upper end of the shaft 29 projects without the upper end of the steering column 30 above the steering wheel 31 and has an arm 32 projecting laterally there from, as shown in Fig. 2, whereby a swinging of such arm effects a rocking of the segment 28 to move the cable 27. A lever member 33 is fulcrum to the arm 32 within a longitudinally extending surface recess therein and has its inner end attached to the upper end of a rod 34, which extends down through the shaft 29 and attaches at its lower end to a latch-lever 35, which is fulcrum to the hub portion of the segment 28, as at 36, and is adapted to have rocking movements with said segment and also relative thereto. The free end of the latch-lever 35 is adapted to engage within any one of the notches of a segmental rack 37, which is fixed to a stationary part of the vehicle, as to a casting 38, thus causing the control parts to be held in adjusted position. It is evident that a shifting of the control arm 32 effects adjustment of the anchoring parts 24 to change the tension of the spring 23 and also its leverage on the arm 11 on the shaft 9, so that one spring accurately controls the engine for all proper positions and through a wide range of speeds.

The operation of our improved governing mechanism is as follows: when the governor is at rest the carburetor throttle 7 stands in what may be termed "full open" position, but which need not be full open position with relation to the carburetor, as it is only necessary that the throttle be open to such an extent as to enable it to have a closing or throttling down movement when the slide part 4 of the governor is moved outward, so that the engine, after a starting thereof, may be brought or throttled down to the speed at which it is desired to be run. The adjustment of the timer mechanism is also in accordance with the throttle movements. The full open position of the carburetor enables the engine to be easily started, and upon starting the outward movement of the governor part 4, which is caused by the rotation of the governor, imparts a movement to the arms 11 and 12, which in turn respectively move the timer lever 17 to advance the spark, and the throttle 7 to reduce the engine charges a sufficient extent to run the engine at the desired speed. If it is desired to increase or diminish the speed of running of the engine it is easily and quickly accomplished by simply moving the lever 33 to released position and then moving the control arm 32 to proper position to change the tension and leverage of the spring 23 on the lever arm 11 as desired, thus admirably adapting this control mechanism for use in motor driven vehicles, as it permits the changing of the speed of running of the same while the car is in motion and without the driver leaving his seat therein.

It is evident that the use of our improved governor makes possible an ideal automatic control of the time of ignition of the charges of an internal combustion engine. An automobile engine is required to operate under widely different conditions of speed and load, every change requiring a change in the time of ignition, if the spark is to work at its maximum efficiency. An expert driver can keep his "spark lever" in such a position as will enable the engine to deliver approximately its maximum power, but it is impossible for him to recognize and allow for every change of condition; and with the ordinary driver and ordinary conditions the timing is so far from ideal that some manufacturers prefer to use a fixed spark which may be right for the average speed with the average load, but which cannot be correct for other conditions. A little earlier spark than is necessary does not appreciably reduce the power nor interfere with the smooth working of the engine, but it does cause unnecessary wear on the engine, as shown by tests in which the indicated horsepower is increased as much as 3 percent by advancing the spark, while the brake horsepower remains practically the same. Some attempts have been made to secure an automatic timing of the ignition by means of a governor controlled circuit breaker on the magneto, but these have not come into general use, probably because they take account of only one of the variables hereinafter referred to-that is, the speed variable. The correct time for ignition depends upon three conditions as follows: 1. The size and shape of the combustion chamber and location of spark plug. Constant. 2. The density of the explosive mixture, and percentage of burned gas. Varies with the throttle position, especially on a four cycle engine. 3. Speed of motor. Varies at the will of the driver.

In our governing mechanism there is one lever, namely, 11, the position of which varies with the position of the throttle, due to the connection there between. This lever is also connected with the timer in such manner as to adjust the spark according to the density referred to in section 2 above. The position of another lever, namely, 24 determines the speed of the engine. This lever is also connected with the timer to take care of the changes in speed referred to in section 3 above. Inasmuch as both of the members 11 and 24 are connected to the timer, the time of ignition is changed with every change in density and speed, thus taking care of both variables 2 and 3 and giving the necessary advance under all conditions more accurately than the most expert driver.

We wish it understood that our invention is not limited to any specific construction or arrangement of the parts except in so far as such limitations are specified in the claims. Having thus described our invention, what we claim is new, and desire to secure by Letters Patent, is —

1. In combination, an internal combustion engine, a governor driven by the engine and controlling the supply of gas thereto, said governor having rotatable centrifugal parts, a spring, and leverage connection between said spring and parts, the spring resisting the centrifugal action of said parts and being adjustable to change the leverage on the parts at the same time its tension is changed.

2. In combination, an internal combustion engine, a governor driven by the engine and controlling the supply of gas thereto, said governor having rotatable centrifugal parts, a non-rotatable spring, and leverage connection between said spring and parts, the spring resisting the centrifugal action of said parts and being adjustable to change the leverage on said parts at the same time its tension is changed.

3. In combination, an internal combustion engine, a governor driven by the engine and controlling the supply of gas thereto, said governor having rotatable centrifugal parts, a non-rotatable spring, and leverage connection between said spring and parts, the spring resisting the centrifugal action of said parts and being adjustable to change the leverage on said parts.

4. In combination, an internal combustion engine, a governor driven by the engine and having rotatable centrifugal parts, a non-rotatable contractile spring, a lever connecting said parts and spring, said spring serving to resist the centrifugal action of said parts, anchorage means for said spring adjustable to change both its tension and leverage on said lever, and means actuated by the governor for controlling the supply of gas to the engine.

5. In combination, an internal combustion engine, a governor driven by the engine and having rotatable centrifugal parts, a non-rotatable spring, leverage connection between said spring and parts, the spring resisting the centrifugal action of said parts, an oscillatory anchorage member for said spring movable to change the tension of the spring and its leverage on said connection, and means actuated by the governor for controlling the supply of gas thereto.

6. In combination, an internal combustion engine, a governor driven by the engine and having rotatable centrifugal parts, a spring, leverage connection between said spring and parts, said spring cooperating with said connection to resist the centrifugal action of said parts, means operable to adjust the spring during a running of the engine to change its tension and also to change its leverage action on said connection, and means actuated by the governor for controlling the supply of gas to the engine.

7. In combination, an internal combustion engine, a fuel feed throttle therefore a governor driven by the engine, a lever movable in one direction by said governor when running, connection between said lever and throttle whereby throttling movements are communicated to the throttle upon a running of the governor, and means yieldingly resisting a governor actuated movement of said lever and adjustable to change both the tension and leverage of such resistance.

8. In combination, an engine, a fuel feed throttle therefore, a governor operated by the engine, means connecting said governor and throttle for communicating predetermined movements to the throttle when the governor is operated, said means having a rocker-arm, a spring attached to and co_operating with said arm to resist a governor actuated movement of said means, a movable anchor member for said spring, and means operable at a distance from said anchor member during a running of the engine to move said member to change the tension of the spring and its leverage on the rocker-arm.

9. In combination, an internal combustion engine, a fuel feed throttle therefore, a governor driven by the engine, connection between said governor and throttle for controlling the movements of the throttle by a running of the governor, means yieldingly resisting a throttle actuating movement of said connection, a movable anchor member for said means, and mechanism operable during a running of the engine and at a distance from said anchor member for moving the latter to change both the tension and leverage of said means on said connection.

10. The combination with the timer and throttle valve of an internal combustion engine, of a governor mechanism actuated by the engine and having a part the position of which varies with the position of the throttle valve and a part movable to change the speed of running of the engine, and means connecting both of said parts with the timer and operable upon a movement of either to change the time of ignition.

11. The combination with the timer of an internal combustion engine, of a governor having rotatable centrifugal parts, a spring, and leverage connection between the spring and said parts and timer, the spring resisting the centrifugal action of said parts, and means manually adjustable to change the tension of said spring, and connection between said means and timer.

12. In combination, an internal combustion engine, a fuel feed throttle therefore, an ignition timer for the engine, a governor operated by the engine, means connecting the governor to said throttle and timer for imparting movements to each upon a running of the governor, and manually controlled means yieldingly resisting governor actuated movement of said first means and being adjustable to change such resistance.

13. The combination with the timer of an internal combustion engine, of governor actuated by the engine, a lever member movable by the governor, an adjustable control lever, a spring connecting said control lever and member to resist a governor actuated movement of said member, and means connecting both said lever member and control lever to the timer to cause a movement of the timer when either said member of control lever are moved.

14. The combination with the timer of an internal combustion engine, of a governor actuated by the engine, a lever member movable in one direction by the governor, and adjustable control lever, yielding connection between said member and control lever, and mechanism connecting said timer to said member and control lever, said mechanism comprising a lever having one arm in connection with the timer and its other arm in connection with both said member and control lever whereby movements of either will impart movements to the timer.

15. The combination with the timer of an -internal combustion engine, of a governor actuated by the engine, a lever member movable in one direction by the governor, an adjustable control part, a spring connecting said part and member, the tension of the spring and its leverage action on said member being changed by an adjustment of said part, a lever, connection between one arm of said lever and the movable part of the timer, a cross-arm pivoted intermediate its ends to the other arm of said lever, and links projecting from the opposite ends of said cross-arm, one having connection with said lever member and the other having connection with said part whereby movements of either said member or part communicate movements to the timer to advance or retard the spark.

16. The combination with the throttle valve of an internal combustion engine, of a governor actuated by the engine, a three-arm lever having one arm in connection with the governor whereby the lever is moved upon a movement of said governor in one direction, connection between another of said arms and the throttle valve for communicating movements from one to the other, and an adjustable control member having yielding connection with the remaining arm of said lever for resisting a governor actuated movement thereof.

17. The combination with the throttle-valve of an internal combustion engine, of a governor, a lever having connection with and movable in one direction by said governor, connection between said lever and throttle valve, and manually controlled means having spring connection with said lever to resist a governor actuated movement of the lever and being adjustable to vary both the spring tension and the leverage action of the spring connection on said lever.

In testimony whereof, we have hereunto signed our names to this specification in the presence of two subscribing witnesses.

FRANK X. BACHLE
WALTER W. WELLS

Witnesses:
HOMER METZGAR
J.C.L. KREBS

Appendix B: Clydesdale Motor Truck Specifications

The following factory specifications were taken from original Clydesdale literature as noted. We assumed the information and descriptions to be correct at the time the literature was printed. We also realize that changes could have occurred after production began and have not tried to document those changes from other automotive sources.

1918

UTILITY MODEL 30 — ONE & ONE QUARTER TON NET LOAD

ENGINE: Four Cylinders, 3½" × 5", S.A.E. rating 19.6 HP, Develops 25HP at 1200 R.P.M.

IGNITION: Lauraine waterproof high tension magneto.

CARBURETOR: Zenith.

RADIATOR: Cast aluminum tanks and sides. Straight tube core.

FAN: 16" Pressed steel mounted on ball bearings.

CLUTCH: Enclosed multiple disc clutch operating dry.

TRANSMISSION: In unit with engine, three speeds forward and one reverse.

STEERING: Screw and nut type, 20" hand wheel.

FRAME: 5½" deep pressed steel.

REAR AXLE: Worm gear drive.

FRONT AXLE: Drop forged I beam section.

BRAKES: Internal & external.

TANK: 15 gallons capacity.

SPRINGS: Silico manganese, 36" × 2¼" front, 34" × 5' rear.

WHEELS: Heavy wooden artillery type.

TIRES: Solid pressed on, 34" × 3½" front, 34" × 5' rear.

WHEEL BASE: Standard 134".

CHASSIS WEIGHT: 2950 pounds.

BODY WEIGHT: Allowance 1,000 pounds.

MODEL 45 — ONE & ONE HALF TO TWO TONS

ENGINE: Four Cylinders, 4⅛" × 5¼", S.A.E. rating 27.2 HP, Develops over 40 HP on test.

IGNITION: Lauraine waterproof high tension magneto.

CARBURETOR: Zenith.

RADIATOR: Cast aluminum tanks and sides. Straight tube core.

FAN: 18" aluminum mounted on ball bearings.

CLUTCH: Enclosed multiple disc operating dry.

TRANSMISSION: Four speeds forward and one reverse.

STEERING: Right hand, screw and nut type, 20" hand wheel.

FRAME: Pressed steel 6" deep.

REAR AXLE: Overhead worm gear drive.

FRONT AXLE: Single piece steel drop forging I beam section.

BRAKES: 18" × 3½" internal expanding duplex type.

TANK: 30 gallons capacity, 3 gallons in reserve.

SPRINGS: Silico manganese, 40" × 2¼" front, 50" × 3" rear.

WHEELS: Heavy wooden artillery type.

TIRES: Solid pressed on, 36" × 3½" front single, 36" × 6" rear single.

WHEEL BASE: Standard 144".

CHASSIS WEIGHT: 4290 pounds.

BODY WEIGHT: Allowance 1,500 pounds.

MODEL 65 — TWO TON HEAVY DUTY

ENGINE: Four Cylinder, 4⅛" × 5¼", cast en bloc, S.A.E. rating 27.2 HP, Develops over 40 HP on test.

IGNITION: Lauraine waterproof high tension magneto.

CARBURETOR: Zenith.

RADIATOR: Cast aluminum tanks and sides. Straight tube core.

FAN: 18" aluminum cast, mounted on ball bearings.

CLUTCH: Enclosed multiple disc operating dry.

TRANSMISSION: Four speeds forward and one reverse.

STEERING: Right hand, screw and nut type, 20" hand wheel.

FRAME: Pressed steel 8" deep.

REAR AXLE: Worm gear drive.

FRONT AXLE: Single piece steel drop forging, I beam section.

BRAKES: 18" × 3½" internal expanding duplex type.

TANK: 30 gallons capacity, 3 gallons reserve.

SPRINGS: Silico manganese, front 44" × 3", rear 52" × 3".

WHEELS: Heavy wooden artillery type.

TIRES: Solid pressed on, 36" × 4" front single, 36" × 7" rear single or 36" × 4" rear dual.

WHEEL BASE: 163", extra long 180".

CHASSIS WEIGHT: 5180 pounds.

BODY WEIGHT: Allowance, 1,500 pounds.

MODEL 90 — THREE & ONE HALF TON NET LOAD

ENGINE: Four Cylinder, 4½" × 5½", cast in pairs, S.A.E. rating 32.4 HP, Develops over 45 HP on test.

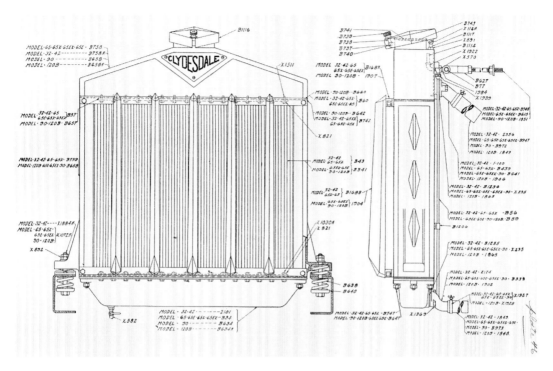

Diagram of the Clydesdale radiator.

IGNITION: Lauraine waterproof high tension magneto.

CARBURETOR: Zenith.

RADIATOR: Cast aluminum tank and sides. Straight tube core.

FAN: 20" aluminum, mounted on ball bearings.

CLUTCH: Enclosed multiple disc clutch operating dry.

TRANSMISSION: Separate unit, four speeds forward and reverse.

STEERING: Right hand, screw and nut type, 22" hand wheel.

REAR AXLE: Worm gear drive.

FRAME: Pressed steel 8" deep.

FRONT AXLE: Steel drop forged I beam section.

BRAKES: 21" × 3¾" internal expanding duplex type.

TANK: 30 gallons capacity, 3 gallons reserve.

SPRINGS: Silico manganese, front 44" × 3", rear 54" × 3½".

WHEELS: Heavy wood artillery type.

TIRES: Solid pressed on type, 36" × 5" front single, 40" × 5" rear dual.

WHEEL BASE: Standard 180", Optional 170".

CHASSIS WEIGHT: 6650 pounds.

BODY WEIGHT: Allowance 2,000 pounds.

MODEL 120 — FIVE TON NET LOAD

ENGINE: Four Cylinders, 4½" × 5½", cast in pairs, S.A.E. rating 32.4 HP, developing 45 HP on test. Cylinders are L head type with large valves.

IGNITION: Lauraine waterproof high tension magneto.

CARBURETOR: Zenith.

RADIATOR: Cast aluminum tank and sides — straight tube core.

FAN: 20" aluminum, mounted on ball bearings.

CLUTCH: Enclosed multiple disc clutch operating dry.

TRANSMISSION: Separate unit, four speeds forward and reverse.

STEERING: Right hand, screw and nut type, 22" hand wheel.

FRAME: Pressed steel 8" deep.

REAR AXLE: Overhead worm gear drive.

FRONT AXLE: Drop forged I beam section.

BRAKES: 24" × 4" internal expanding duplex type.

TANK: 30 gallons capacity, 3 gallons in reserve.

SPRINGS: Silico manganese, 44" × 3" front, 56" × 4" rear.

WHEELS: Heavy wood artillery type.

TIRES: Solid pressed on type, 36" × 6" front, 40" × 6" dual rear.

WHEEL BASE: Standard 180", Optional 170".

CHASSIS WEIGHT: 8100 pounds.

BODY WEIGHT: Allowance 2,000 pounds.

OPTIONAL AND EXTRA EQUIPMENT:

CLOSED CAB:

Four passenger cab with half doors supplied as original equipment at an extra cost of $100.

STEEL WHEELS:

Hollow spoke cast steel wheels can be supplied on Models 45, 65, 90 and 120 at extra cost.

PNEUMATIC TIRES:

Pneumatic tires can be supplied at extra cost on the sizes of Clydesdale trucks as follows: Model 30, 45 and 65.

GAS HEAD LIGHTS:

Gas head lights and acetylene tank installed on any chassis.

HYDRAULIC HOIST:

Hydraulic Hoist and steel dump bodies can be installed on all models of the Clydesdale chassis. Prices upon application. In writing for prices, state material to be hauled so that proper size can be determined.

HUB ODOMETER:

This instrument accurately measures the total amount of mileage covered by the truck in operation. It replaces the hub cap and is guaranteed by maker indestructible.

1922–1923

The following factory specifications were taken from original Clydesdale literature. While it is undated, we believe this literature was published in 1922–1923 for new model numbers from 2 to 10/10A. It is interesting that the higher number carried the lightest load and the lower number carried the heaviest load. This is a complete change from the 1918 numbering system, where the lowest number carried the lightest load and the highest number carried the heaviest load. We also noted the number and type of specifications varied from model to model. Some of this literature also carried the notation "ALL OF THE ABOVE DATA SUBJECT TO CHANGE WITHOUT NOTICE."

MODEL 10 & 10A

BRAKES: Internal Expanding, 2 sets on each rear wheel. 15" diam., 2½" wide.

CAPACITY: Chassis weight 3100 lbs. Gross weight including chassis, body and load, 6850 lbs. Body and payload capacity, 3750 lbs.

CARBURETOR: Zenith. Float feed truck type.

CLUTCH: 10" dry plate

DASH: Designed integral with windshield, carries instrument board.

EQUIPMENT: Standard chassis includes front fenders, engine steps (no running boards), speedometer, electric horn, tools, jack (no seat).

FENDERS: Heavy gauge pressed steel. Extra heavy brackets.

FINAL DRIVE: Spiral bevel gear and pinion truck type.

FRAME: Pressed steel; 5½" deep, 2¾" × ³⁄₁₆" section. Heavy gusset plates and cross members.

FRONT AXLE: I–Beam, drop forged, heat treated. Timken taper roller bearings.

FUEL FEED: Vacuum tank.

GOVERNOR: Clydesdale Automatic Controller. "No other Truck has it."

GASOLINE TANK CAPACITY: 12 gallons.

IGNITION: American Bosch. Distributor.

LAMPS: Substantial Truck Type, Head lamps mounted on radiator. Tail lamp and instrument lamp.

LOADING SPACE: Back of driver's seat 109", platform height 31"

MOTOR: Continental Red Seal. 22.5 HP S.A.E. rating. Develops 34 HP at 2000 R.P.M. 3¾" bore by 5" stroke. Three point suspension.

COOLING: Thermo-syphon, large fan mounted on engine.

CRANKSHAFT: Drop forged, heat treated.

LUBRICATION: Circulation splash system, gear driven pump.

PISTONS: Gray iron, 3 ring, ³⁄₁₆" wide.

SPARK PLUGS: ⅞" S.A.E. Standard.

VALVES: 1¹¹⁄₁₆" diameter. Poppet type; alloy steel.

PAINTING: Standard gray.

PROPELLER SHAFTS: Tubular. 3 universal joints.

RADIATOR: Clydesdale design. Copper tubes without fins. Water capacity 22 quarts.

REAR AXLE: Spiral, bevel gear driven, semi–floating. Timken roller bearings.

SPEED CONTROL: Hand lever.

SPEED: 35 miles per hour.

SPRINGS: Semi Elliptic, chrome vanadium steel; bushed throughout. Front 36" long by 2¼" wide. Rear 52" long by 2½" wide.

STEERING GEAR: Worm and nut type. Wheel 18" in diameter.

TIRES: Pneumatic cord 34 × 5 all around.

TRANSMISSION: Selective type. Three speeds forward and one reverse in unit with engine.

TREAD: 56".

TURNING RADIUS: 26 feet.

WHEELBASE: Standard 138".

WHEELS: Steel disc, demountable rims.

MODEL 9, CAPACITY 1½— 2 TONS

BRAKES: Internal Duplex expanding, two sets on each rear wheel; 16" diameter by 3¼" wide.

CAPACITY: Chassis weight 4600 lbs. Gross weight including chassis, body and load 9800 lbs. Body and payload capacity 5200 lbs.

CARBURETOR: Float feed, truck type 1¼" Zenith.

CLUTCH: Brown-Lipe, multiple disc; 10 dry plates, 10" diameter.

CONTROL: Center, left hand drive standard. Right hand drive optional.

DASH: Three-ply veneer, both sides covered with sheet metal. Instrument panel mounted on same.

EQUIPMENT: Standard chassis includes front fenders, steps, speedometer, horn, tools, jack,
bunk seat and Motormeter.

FENDERS: Heavy gauge pressed steel, 11" wide. Extra heavy brackets.

FINAL DRIVE: Timken top worm.

FRAME: Pressed steel; 32 ½" wide in front and 34 ½" wide in rear. Side rails are 6" deep, 3" wide, ¼" thick, and has five cross members making frame very strong.

FRONT AXLE: Timken I-Beam, drop forged, heat treated, roller bearings.

FUEL FEED: Vacuum, 12 gallon gasoline tank under drivers seat.

GOVERNOR: Clydesdale Automatic Controller. "The DRIVER under the HOOD."

IGNITION: New type Bosch, high tension magneto with impulse coupling.

LIGHTING: Electric Head, Dash, and Tail lights, with Generator, Ammeter and 90 Ampere, 6 Volt Battery.

LOADING SPACE: Back of cab 143" on 160" wheelbase, 120" on 148" wheelbase.

LUBRICATION CHASSIS: Dot high pressure lubricating fittings throughout.

MOTOR: Continental type S-4, 4 cylinders, 4¼" bore × 4½" stroke. removable head, three point suspension. Cylinder cast en-bloc. Horsepower S.A.E. rating 28.90, 50 at 2200 R.P.M.

COOLING: Centrifugal pump circulation, large fan mounted on engine.

CRANKSHAFT: Heat treated, drop forged.

PISTONS: Gray iron, 3" rings, ¼" wide.

SPARK PLUGS: ⅞" S.A.E. standard.

VALVES: 1⅞" diameter.

PAINTING: Standard gray.

PROPELLER SHAFT, SPICER: Tubular heat treated. Three universal joints.

RADIATOR: Aluminum cast tanks, straight copper tubes without fins, guard bars, spring suspension.

REAR AXLE: Timken worm drive. Timken roller bearings. Drive through radius rods.

SPARK CONTOL: Hand Lever.

SPEED: Governor set to 24 MPH.

SPRINGS: Semi-elliptic, all leaves chrome vanadium steel, bushed throughout. Front 40" long by 2½" wide. Rear 52" long × 3' wide.

STEERING GEAR: Ross, new cam and lever type. 18" diameter wheel.

TIRES: Pressed on S.A.E. standard, front 34" × 4" solid. Rear 34" × 6" single solid.

TRANSMISSION: Brown-Lipe, selective type U.P.P. four speeds forward and one reverse.

TREAD: Front 56", Rear 60".

TURNING RADIUS: 30 feet.

WHEELS: Metal hollow spoke type.

WHEELBASE: Standard 160", Optional 148". When pneumatic tires are specified, we recommend sizes 32" by 6" at net extra cost.

MODEL 8, CAPACITY 2 — 2 ½ TONS

BRAKES: Internal Duplex expanding, two sets on each rear wheel; 18" diameter by 3 ½" wide.

CAPACITY: Chassis weight 5300 lbs. Gross weight including chassis, body and load 11,800 lbs. Body and payload capacity, 6500 lbs.

CARBURETOR: Zenith float feed truck type 1¼".

CLUTCH: Brown-Lipe multiple disc, 12 dry plates, 10 diameter.

CONTROL: Center. Drive–Left hand standard; right hand optional.

DASH: Three-ply veneer, both sides covered with sheet metal. Instrument panel mounted on same.

EQUIPMENT: Standard chassis includes front fenders, steps, speedometer, horn, tools, jack and bunk seat.

FINAL DRIVE: Top worm.

FRAME: Pressed steel, 32½" wide in front and 34½" in rear. Side rails are 6 deep, 3 wide, ¼" thick and has 5 cross members making frame very strong.

FRONT AXLE: Timken I-beam, drop forged, heat treated, Timken roller bearings.

FUEL FEED: Vacuum, 30 gallon tank under driver's seat.

GOVERNOR: Clydesdale Automatic Controller. "No other Truck has it."

IGNITION: Bosch high tension magneto with impulse starter.

LIGHTING: Two oil dash lights and tail lamp.

LOADING SPACE: 118½" on 156 wheelbase; 142¼" on 170 wheelbase.

MOTOR: Continental type K-4, 4⅛" bore by 5¼" stroke. Three point suspension.

COOLING: Centrifugal pump circulation. Large fan mounted on engine.

CRANKSHAFT: Heat treated; drop forged three bearing type.

LUBRICATION: Force feed.

HORSEPOWER: 27.2 S.A.E. rating. B.M.H. 35 at 1300 R.P.M.

PISTONS: Gray iron, 4 rings ¼" wide.

SPARK PLUGS: ⅞" S.A.E. Standard.

VALVES: 1⅞" diameter.

PAINTING: Standard gray.

PROPELLER SHAFT: Spicer tubular. Four universal joints.

RADIATOR: Aluminum cast tanks, straight copper tubes without fins; guard bars; spring suspension.

REAR AXLE: Timken worm drive; full floating, roller bearings. Drive through radius rods.

SPARK CONTROL: Hand lever.

SPEED: 20 M.P.H.

SPRINGS: Semi-elliptic, chrome vanadium steel; bushed throughout; oil cups. Front 40" long by 2½" wide, Rear 52" long by 3" wide.

STEERING GEAR: Ross new cam and lever type; 20" wheel.

TIRES: Pressed on; S.A.E. Standard. Front, 36" × 4". Rear, 36" × 8" solid.

TRANSMISSION: Brown-Lipe selective type; four speeds forward and one reverse, placed amidships.

TREAD: Front 58 12". Rear 58½"
TURNING RADIUS: 30 feet.
WHEELBASE: Standard 156". Long wheelbase 170".
WHEELS: Metal hollow spoke type.

MODEL 6-X , CAPACITY 2½— 3 TONS

BRAKES: Internal expanding, two sets on each rear wheel; 18" diameter by 3½" wide.

CAPACITY: Chassis weight, 5700 lbs. Maximum gross weight, including chassis, body and payload, 14,350 lbs. Body and payload maximum capacity 8500 lbs. Body weight allowance 1500 lbs.

CARBURETOR: Float feed vertical type, 1¼" Zenith.

CLUTCH: Brown-Lipe multiple disc, 16 dry plates, 10" diameter.

CONTROL: Center. Left hand drive standard; right hand optional.

DASH: Three ply veneer ¾" thick. Both sides covered with sheet metal. Instrument panel mounted on same.

EQUIPMENT: Standard chassis includes front fenders, steps (no running board), speedometer, hand horn, tools, jack, bunk seat, and Motor-meter.

FENDERS: Fenders of heavy gauge pressed steel, 12" wide with extra heavy brackets.

FINAL DRIVE: Timken top worm.

FRAME: Pressed steel, 33⅜" wide; side rails are 8" deep by 3" wide by ¼" thickness. Frame has 6 cross members making frame very strong.

FRONT AXLE: Timken I-beam, drop forged, heat treated, Timken roller bearings.

FUEL FEED: Vacuum; 30 gallon tank under driver's seat.

GOVERNOR: Clydesdale Automatic Controller. "The Driver Under the Hood."

IGNITION: New type Bosch high tension magneto with impulse coupling.

LIGHTING: Electric Head, Dash and Tail lights, with Generator, Ammeter and 90 Ampere, 6 volt battery.

LOADING SPACE: Back of cab, 132" on 163" wheelbase; 166½" on 180" wheelbase.

LUBRICATION CHASSIS: Dot high pressure lubricating fittings throughout.

MOTOR: Continental type K-4; four cylinders 4⅛" bore by 5¼" stroke, removable head, three point suspension, cylinders cast en bloc.

COOLING: Centrifugal pump circulation. Large fan mounted on engine.

CRANKSHAFT: Heat treated: drop forged, three bearing type.

LUBRICATION: Force feed.

HORSEPOWER: 27.2 S.A.E. rating; B.H.M. 35 at 1300 R.P.M.

PISTONS: Gray iron, 4 rings, ¼" wide.

SPARK PLUGS: ⅞" S.A.E. Standard.

VALVES: 1⅞" diameter opening.

PAINTING: Standard gray.

PROPELLER SHAFT: Spicer, four universal joints.

RADIATOR: Aluminum cast tanks, straight copper tubes, guard bars; spring suspension.

REAR AXLE: Timken worm drive, Timken roller bearings, drive through radius rods.

SPARK CONTROL: Hand lever.

SPEED: Governor set to 17 M.P.H.

SPRINGS: Semi-elliptic, all leaves chrome vanadium steel; bushed throughout. Front 44" long by 3" wide; rear 52" long by 3" wide.

STEERING GEAR: Ross new cam and lever type, 20" diameter wheel.

TIRES: Pressed on S.A.E. Standard. Front 36" × 4" single solid; rear 36" × 8" single solid.

TRANSMISSION: Brown-Lipe selective type; four speeds forward and one reverse. Amidships mounting, Timken bearings.

TREAD: Front 58½"; rear 58½".

TURNING RADIUS: Short wheel base 24 feet, long wheel base 26 feet.

WHEELBASE: Standard 163", long 180".

WHEELS: Metal hollow spoke type.

MODEL 6 CAPACITY 2½—3½ TONS

BRAKES: Internal expanding — 2 sets on each rear wheel. 18" diameter by 3½" wide. Duplex type.

CAPACITY: Chassis weight 5850 lbs. Gross weight including chassis, body and load, 14,350 lbs. Body and pay-load capacity, 8500 lbs.

CARBURETOR: Zenith float feed truck type 1¼"

CLUTCH: Brown-Lipe multiple disc, 16 dry plate, 10" diameter.

CONTROL: Center. Drive-Left hand standard. Right hand optional.

DASH: Three-ply veneer, ¾" thick, both sides covered with sheet metal. Instrument panel mounted on same.

EQUIPMENT: Horn, tools, jack, oil dash and tail lamps, speedometer. Seat and riser.

FENDERS: Front fenders of heavy gauge pressed steel with extra heavy brackets.

FINAL DRIVE: Timken top worm.

FRAME: Pressed steel 8" deep; heavy gusset plates and cross members.

FRONT AXLE: Timken I-beam, drop forged, heat treated, roller bearings.

FUEL FEED: Vacuum, 30 gallon tank under driver's seat.

GOVERNOR: Clydesdale Automatic Controller. "No other Truck has it."

IGNITION: Bosch high tension magneto with impulse starter.

LIGHTING: Two Oil Dash Lights and Tail Lamp.

LOADING SPACE: 131" with 163" wheelbase, 165½" with 180" wheelbase.

MOTOR: Continental Type L-4, 4½" bore by 5½" stroke. Three point suspension.

COOLING: Centrifugal pump circulation. Large ball bearing fan mounted on engine.

CRANKSHAFT: Drop forged, heat treated, three bearing type.

HORSEPOWER: 32.4 S.A.E. rating. B.H.P. 43 at 1300 R.P.M.

LUBRICATION: Force feed.

PISTONS: Gray iron, 4 ring, ¼" wide.

SPARK PLUGS: ⅞" S.A.E. Standard. Valves — 2" diameter.

VALVES: 2" diameter.

PAINTING: Standard gray.

PROPELLER SHAFT: Spicer tubular. Four universal joints.

RADIATOR: Aluminum cast tanks, straight copper tubes, without fins; guard bars, spring suspension.

REAR AXLE: Timken worm drive; full floating type, roller bearings, drive through radius rods.

SPARK CONTROL: Hand lever.

SPEED: 17 M.P.H.

SPRINGS: Chrome vanadium steel; bushed throughout, oil cups. Front 44" long by 3" wide. Rear 52" long by 3" wide.

STEERING GEAR: Ross new cam and lever type; 20" wheel.

TIRES: Pressed on S.A.E. Standard. Front 36" × 5" single. Rear 36" × 5" dual.

TRANSMISSION: Selective type, four speeds forward and one reverse. Amidships mounting. Timken bearings.

TREAD: Front 58½". Rear 58½".

TURNING RADIUS: Standard 24 feet, Long 26 feet.

WHEELBASE: Standard 163". Long wheelbase 180".

WHEELS: Metal hollow spoke type.

MODEL 4-X , CAPACITY 3½ — 4 TONS

BRAKES: Internal Duplex Expanding. Two sets on each rear wheel. 21" diameter by 3¾" wide,

CAPACITY: Chassis weight 7300 lbs. Maximum gross weight including chassis, body and payload 20,500 lbs. Body and payload maximum capacity 13,200 lbs. Body weight allowance 2500 lbs.

CARBURETOR: Float feed, vertical type, 1¼" Zenith.

CLUTCH: Brown-Lipe Multiple Disc, 16 dry plate, 10" diameter.

CONTROL: Center, Left -hand drive standard, Right-hand drive optional.

DASH: Three-ply veneer ¾" thick. Both sides covered with sheet metal. Instrument panel mounted on same.

EQUIPMENT: Standard chassis includes front fenders, steps (no running boards), speedometer, hand horn, tools, jack, bunk seat and Motor-meter.

FENDERS: Fenders of heavy gauge pressed steel, 12" wide with extra heavy brackets.

FINAL DRIVE: Timken top worm.

FRAME: Pressed steel, side rails are 8" deep. 3¼" wide and ¼" thickness. Frame has 6 cross members making frame very strong.

FRONT AXLE: I-beam, drop forged, heat treated, Timken roller bearings.

FUEL FEED: Vacuum, 30 gallon gasoline tank under driver's seat.

GOVERNOR: Clydesdale Automatic Controller — "The Driver Under the Hood."

IGNITION: New type Bosch high tension magneto with impulse coupling.

LIGHTING: Electric Head, Dash and Tail lights with Generator, Ammeter and 90 Ampere, 6 Volt Battery.

LOADING SPACE: Back of cab 142" on 177" wheelbase and 165½" on 197" wheelbase.

LUBRICATION CHASSIS: Dot High Pressure, lubricating fittings throughout.

MOTOR: Continental type L-4, 4½" bore by 5½" stroke. 4 cylinders. Three-point suspension. Removable head.

COOLING: Centrifugal pump circulation. Large ball bearing fan mounted on engine.

CRANKSHAFT: Drop forged, heat treated, three bearing type.

HORSEPOWER: 32.4 S.A.E. rating. B.H.P. 42 at 1200 R.P.M.

LUBRICATION: Force feed.

PISTONS: Gray iron, 4 ring, ¼" wide.

SPARK PLUGS: ⅞" S.A.E. Standard.

VALVES: 2" diameter.

PAINTING: Standard gray, optional.

PROPELLER SHAFT: Spicer, four Universal Joints.

RADIATOR: Aluminum cast tanks, straight copper tubes without fins, guard bars, spring suspension.

REAR AXLE: Timken worm drive, Timken roller bearings, drive through radius rods.

SPARK CONTROL: Hand lever.

SPEED: Governor set to 15 M.P.H.

SPRINGS: Semi-elliptic. All leaves Chrome Vanadium steel, bushed throughout. Front 44" long by 3" wide. Rear 54" long by 3 ½" wide.

STEERING GEAR: Ross, new type cam and lever. Wheel 22" diameter.

TIRES: Pressed on S.A.E. Standard. Front 36" × 5" single solid. Rear 40" × 5" dual solid.

TRANSMISSION: Brown-Lipe new maximum type transmission, selective. Seven speeds forward, two reverse. Mounted amidship.

TREAD: Front 66½". Rear 65¼".

TURNING RADIUS: Short 31 feet, long 34 feet.

WHEELS: Metal, hollow spoke type.

WHEELBASE: Standard 177"; long 197".

MODEL 2 , CAPACITY 5 — 6 TONS

BRAKES: Internal Duplex expanding, two sets on each rear wheel. 24" diameter by 4" wide.

CAPACITY: Chassis weight, 9750 lbs. Maximum gross weight including chassis, body and payload, 27,750 lbs. Body and payload maximum capacity 18,000 lbs. Body weight allowance 2500 lbs.

CARBURETOR: Float feed, vertical type, 1½" Zenith.

CLUTCH: Brown-Lipe, multiple disc, 16 dry plates, 10' diameter.

CONTROL: Center, left hand drive standard.

DASH: Three-ply veneer, ¾" thick, both sides covered with sheet metal. Instrument panel mounted on same.

EQUIPMENT: Standard chassis includes front fenders, steps (no running boards), speedometer, hand horn, tools, jack, bunk seat and Motor-meter.

FENDERS: Fenders of heavy gauge pressed steel, 12" wide with extra heavy brackets.

FINAL DRIVE: Timken top worm.

FRAME: Pressed steel, side rails are 10" deep, 3¼" wide, 5⁄16" thick with (6) cross members which makes frame very rigid.

FRONT AXLE: Timken, I-beam, drop forged, heat treated, Timken roller bearings.

FUEL FEED: Vacuum tank, 30 gallon tank under driver's seat.

GOVERNOR: Clydesdale Automatic Controller. "No other truck has it."

IGNITION: New type Bosch, high tension magneto with impulse coupling.

LIGHTING: Electric Head, Dash and Tail lights, with Generator, Ammeter and 90 Ampere, 6 Volt Battery.

LOADING SPACE: Back of driver's seat 131" on standard, 207" on long. Distance from back of driver's seat to center line of rear axle 88" on standard, 116" on long.

LUBRICATION CHASSIS: Dot high pressure lubricating fittings throughout.

MOTOR: Continental B-7, 4 cylinder, 5" bore by 6" stroke. S.A.E. rating of 40 H.P. Develops 55 H.P. at 1400 R.P.M. Three point suspension. Removable head.

COOLING: Centrifugal pump circulation. Fan mounted on engine 20" diameter.

CRANKSHAFT: Drop forged, heat treated, 3 bearing type.

CYLINDERS: Gray iron, cast in two blocks.

LUBRICATION: Force feed.

PISTONS: Gray iron, 4 rings, ¼ wide.

SPARK PLUGS: ⅞" S.A.E. standard.

VALVES: 2⅛" diameter.

PAINTING: Standard gray.

PROPELLER SHAFTS: Spicer. Four universal joints.

RADIATOR: Aluminum cast tanks, straight copper tubes without fins, guard bars, spring suspension.

REAR AXLE: Timken worm drive, Timken roller bearings. Full floating drive through radius rods.

SPARK CONTROL: Hand lever.

SPEED: 15 miles per hour.

SPRINGS: Semi-elliptic, all leaves chrome vanadium steel, bronze bushed at ends. Front 3" wide by 44" long. Rear 4" wide by 56" long.

STEERING GEAR: Ross new type cam and lever. Wheel 22" diameter.

TIRES: Pressed on. S.A.E. Standard, front 36" × 6" single, Rear 40" × 7" dual.

TRANSMISSION: Brown-Lipe new maximum type transmission, selective. Seven (7) speeds forward and two (2) reverse. Mounted amidship with Timken bearings.

TREAD: Front 68⅜". Rear 69½"

TURNING RADIUS: Standard 30 feet. Long 33 feet.

WHEELBASE: Standard 176", Long 204".

WHEELS: Metal, hollow spoke type.

Note:

Oversize solid tires or pneumatic tires, "Presto-Lite," electric starting systems, bodies, hoists, and other special equipment supplied at extra cost upon request.

CLYDESDALES are built in various sizes and capacities to meet all requirements.

CLYDESDALE DIESEL ENGINE MOTOR TRUCK SPECIFICATIONS

The following factory specifications were taken from Clydesdale company Bulletin No.1037. While undated, we believe it was issued in October of 1937. We also utilized Ramco Truck and Bus Listings to determine diesel engine manufacturer for each diesel model. We have been unable to determine production figures for any of these Clydesdale diesels but assume the number was low due to the short time these trucks were available.

MODEL 30-D 1 to 2 TONS

GROSS LADEN WEIGHT: 11,000 Lbs.

CHASSIS WT. STANDARD WHEELBASE: 3,850 Lbs.

WHEELBASE — STANDARD: 138", OPTIONAL 160"

ENGINE TYPE: HERCULES 4-Cylinder Full Diesel, Displacement 196 Cu. In. (3.2Liters)

BORE & STROKE: 3⅝" × 4¾"

TAX HORSEPOWER: 21.03

MAXIMUM BRAKE HORSEPOWER: 60 at 2600 RPM

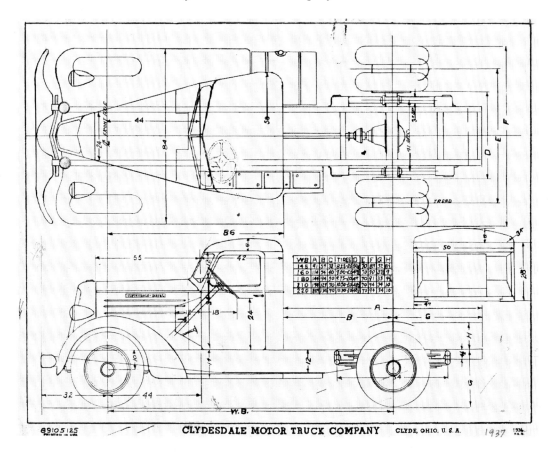

Drawing of a Clydesdale motor truck chassis.

MAXIMUM TORQUE-FOOT Lbs.: 130 at Peak

LUBRICATION: Full Pressure

ELECTRICAL EQUIPMENT: 12 Volt

FUEL INJECTION — MECH. PUMP: Bosch or Excello

CLUTCH-SIZE & TYPE: 11" Single Plate

TRANSMISSION — STANDARD TYPE: Underdrive, 4 Speeds Forward, 1 Reverse

TRANSMISSION — EXTRA: Overdrive

UNIVERSAL JOINTS — TYPE: Needle Bearing

FRONT AXLE-TYPE: Drop Forged I-Beam

REAR AXLE STAND. TYPE: Full Floating-Bevel

REAR AXLE — OPTIONAL-EXTRA: 2 Speed and Double Reduction

SERVICE BRAKES — STANDARD: 4 Wheel Hydraulic, Front 16" × 2¼", Rear 16" × 2¼"

POWER BRAKE — OPTIONAL, EXTRA: B.K. Vacuum Booster

EMERGENCY BRAKE-TYPE-SIZE: 8" × 2½"

SPRINGS: Front 40" × 2½", Rear 50" × 3"

HELPER SPRINGS: Standard

AIR SPRINGS — FRONT — OPTIONAL-EXTRA: Gruss Cleco

STEERING GEAR-CAM & LEVER: Roller Mounted Type

RADIATOR-TYPE: Flat Fin & Copper Tube

FRAME-DIMENSIONS: 8" × 2¾" × ³⁄₁₆"

FUEL TANK CAPACITY: 30 U.S. Gallons, 25 Imperial Gallons, 94 Liters

WHEELS — STANDARD-TYPE: Cast Steel Spoke, Optional: Budd-Michelin

TIRES: Front 6.00 × 20, Rear 6.00 × 20

MAXIMUM ROAD SPEED: 41 MPH (66 KPH)

MODEL 34-D 1½ to 2½ TONS

GROSS LADEN WEIGHT: 12,500 Lbs.

CHASSIS WT. STANDARD WHEELBASE: 3950 Lbs.

WHEELBASE — STANDARD: 138", OPTIONAL 160" & 180"

ENGINE-TYPE: BUDA 4-Cylinder Full Diesel, Displacement 196 Cu. In. (3.2 Liters)

BORE & STROKE: 3⅝" × 4¾"

TAX HORSEPOWER: 21.03

MAXIMUM BRAKE HORSEPOWER: 60 at 2600 RPM

MAXIMUM TORQUE-FOOT Lbs.: 130 at Peak

LUBRICATION: Full Pressure

ELECTRICAL EQUIPMENT: 12 Volt

FUEL INJECTION — MECH. PUMP: Bosch or Excello

CLUTCH-SIZE & TYPE: 11" Single Plate

TRANSMISSION — STANDARD TYPE: Underdrive, 4 Speeds Forward, 1 Reverse

TRANSMISSION — EXTRA: Overdrive

UNIVERSAL JOINTS: Needle Bearing

FRONT AXLE-TYPE: Drop Forged I-Beam

REAR AXLE — STAND. TYPE: Full Floating-Bevel

REAR AXLE — OPTIONAL-EXTRA: 2 Speed and Double Reduction

SERVICE BRAKE — STANDARD: 4 Wheel Hydraulic, Front 16" × 2¼", Rear 16" × 2¼"

POWER BRAKE — OPTIONAL, EXTRA: B.K. Vacuum Booster

EMERGENCY BRAKE-TYPE-SIZE: 9½" × 3"

SPRINGS: Front 40" × 2½", Rear 50" × 3"

HELPER SPRINGS: Standard

AIR SPRINGS — OPTIONAL-EXTRA: Gruss Cleco

STEERING GEAR-CAM & LEVER: Roller Mounted Type

RADIATOR-TYPE: Flat Fin & Copper Tube

FRAME-DIMENSIONS: 8" × 2¾" × ³⁄₁₆"

FUEL TANK CAPACITY: 30 U.S. Gallons, 25 Imperial Gallons, 94 Liters

WHEELS — STANDARD-TYPE: Cast Steel Spoke, Optional: Budd-Michelin

TIRES: Front 6.50 × 20, Rear 6.50 × 20 Dual

MAXIMUM ROAD SPEED: 42 MPH (68 KPH)

MODEL 44-D 2 ½ to 4 TONS

GROSS LADEN WEIGHT: 15,000 Lbs.

CHASSIS WT. STANDARD WHEELBASE: 4,970 Lbs.

WHEELBASE — STANDARD: 138", OPTIONAL 160", 180" & 190"

ENGINE-TYPE: HERCULES 6-Cylinder Full Diesel, Displacement 275 Cu. In. (4.5 Liters)

BORE & STROKE: 3½" × 4¾"

TAX HORSEPOWER: 29.4

MAXIMUM BRAKE HORSEPOWER: 86 at 2600 RPM

MAXIMUM TORQUE-FOOT Lbs.: 204 at Peak

LUBRICATION: Full Pressure

ELECTRICAL EQUIPMENT: 12 and 24 Volt

FUEL INJECTION — MECH. PUMP: Bosch or Excello

CLUTCH-SIZE & TYPE: 13" Single Plate

TRANSMISSION — STANDARD TYPE: Underdrive, 4 Speeds Forward, 1 Reverse

TRANSMISSION — EXTRA: Overdrive, 5 Speed

UNIVERSAL JOINTS — TYPE: Needle Bearing

FRONT AXLE-TYPE: Drop Forged I-Beam

REAR AXLE-STAND. TYPE: Full Floating-Bevel

REAR AXLE — OPTIONAL-EXTRA: 2 Speed and Double Reduction

SERVICE BRAKES — STANDARD: 4-Wheel Hydraulic, Front 16" × 2¼", Rear 16" × 3"

POWER BRAKE — OPTIONAL,EXTRA: B.K. Vacuum Booster

EMERGENCY BRAKE-TYPE-SIZE: 9½" × 3"

SPRINGS: Front 40" × 2½", Rear 50" × 3"

HELPER SPRINGS: Standard

AIR SPRINGS — FRONT — OPTIONAL-EXTRA: Gruss Cleco

STEERING GEAR — CAM & LEVER: Roller Mounted Type

RADIATOR-TYPE: Flat Fin & Copper Tube

FRAME-DIMENSIONS: 9" × 2¾" × ¼"

FUEL TANK CAPACITY: 30 U.S. Gallons, 25 Imperial Gallons, 94 Liters

WHEELS — STANDARD-TYPE: Cast Steel Spoke, Optional: Budd-Michelin

TIRES: Front 6.50 × 20, Rear 6.50 × 20 Dual

MAXIMUM ROAD SPEED: 45 MPH (72 KPH)

MODEL 75-D 3 ½ to 5 TONS

GROSS LADEN WEIGHT: 18,000 Lbs.

CHASSIS WT. STANDARD WHEELBASE: 6,980 Lbs.

WHEELBASE — STANDARD: 138", OPTIONAL 165", 180", 190", 200" & 210"

ENGINE-TYPE: BUDA 6-Cylinder Full Diesel, Displacement 275 Cu. In.

BORE & STROKE: 3½" × 4¾"

TAX HORSEPOWER: 29.4

MAXIMUM BRAKE HORSEPOWER: 86 AT 2600 RPM

MAXIMUM TORQUE-FOOT Lbs.: 204 at Peak

LUBRICATION: Full Pressure

ELECTRICAL EQUIPMENT: 12 and 24 Volt

FUEL INJECTION — MECH. PUMP: Bosch or Excello

CLUTCH-SIZE & TYPE: 13" Single Plate

TRANSMISSION — STANDARD TYPE: Overdrive, 5 Speeds Forward, 1 Reverse

TRANSMISSION — EXTRA: 2 or 3 Speed Auxiliary

UNIVERSAL JOINTS — TYPE: Needle Bearing

FRONT AXLE-TYPE: Drop Forged I-Beam

REAR AXLE STAND. TYPE: Full Floating Bevel

REAR AXLE — OPTIONAL-EXTRA: 2 Speed and Double Reduction

SERVICE BRAKES — STANDARD: 4 Wheel Hydraulic, Front 16" × 2¼", Rear 16" × 3½"

POWER BRAKE — OPTIONAL, EXTRA: B.K. Vacuum Booster

EMERGENCY BRAKE-TYPE-SIZE: 9½" × 3"

SPRINGS: Front 40" × 2½" Rear 50" × 3"

HELPER SPRINGS: Standard

AIR SPRINGS — FRONT: Gruss Cleco-Standard

STEERING GEAR-CAM & LEVER: Roller Mounted Type

RADIATOR-TYPE: Flat Fin & Copper Tube

FRAME-DIMENSIONS: 9" × 2 ¾" × ¼"

FUEL CAPACITY: 30 U.S. Gallons, 25 Imperial Gallons, 94 Liters

WHEELS — STANDARD-TYPE: Cast Steel Spoke, OPTIONAL: Budd-Michelin

TIRES: Front 7.50 × 20, Rear 7.50 × 20 Dual

MAXIMUM ROAD SPEED: 63 MPH (101 KPH)

MODEL 80-D 5 to 7 TONS

GROSS LADEN WEIGHT: 24,000 Lbs.

CHASSIS WT. STANDARD WHEELBASE: 6,980 Lbs.

WHEELBASE — STANDARD: 138," OPTIONAL 165", 180", 190", 200" & 210"

ENGINE-TYPE: BUDA 6 Cylinder Full Diesel, Displacement 315 Cu. In.

BORE & STROKE: 3¾" × 4¾"

TAX HORSEPOWER: 30.1

MAXIMUM BRAKE HORSEPOWER: 96 at 2600 RPM

MAXIMUM TORQUE-FOOT LBS.: 225 at Peak

LUBRICATION: Full Pressure

ELECTRICAL EQUIPMENT: 12 and 24 Volt

FUEL INJECTION MECH-PUMP: Bosch or Excello

CLUTCH SIZE & TYPE: 13" Single Plate

TRANSMISSION — STANDARD TYPE: Overdrive, 5 Speeds Forward, 1 Reverse

TRANSMISSION — EXTRA: 2 or 3-Speed Auxiliary

UNIVERSAL JOINTS — TYPE: Needle Bearing

FRONT AXLE-TYPE: Drop Forged I-Beam

REAR AXLE STAND. TYPE: Full Floating-Bevel

REAR AXLE — OPTIONAL-EXTRA: 2 Speed and Double Reduction

SERVICE BRAKES — STANDARD: 4 Whl. Hyd. & Vac. Booster, Frt. 16" × 2¼", Rear 17¼" × 4"

POWER BRAKE — OPTIONAL, EXTRA: Westinghouse-Air

EMERGENCY BRAKE-TYPE-SIZE: 9½" × 3"

SPRINGS: Front 44" × 2½", Rear 54" × 3"

HELPER SPRINGS: Standard

AIR SPRINGS — FRONT: Gruss Cleco-Standard

STEERING GEAR-CAM & LEVER: Roller Mounted Type

RADIATOR-TYPE: Flat Fin & Copper Tube

FRAME-DIMENSIONS: 10" × 2¾" × ¼"

FUEL TANK CAPACITY: 30 U.S. Gallons, 25 Imperial Gallons, 94 Liters

WHEELS — STANDARD-TYPE: Cast Steel Spoke, OPTIONAL: Budd-Michelin

TIRES: Front 8.25 × 20, Rear 8.25 × 20 Dual

MAXIMUM ROAD SPEED: 57 MPH (92K)

MODEL 90-D 5 to 7 TONS

GROSS LADEN WEIGHT: 24,000 Lbs.

CHASSIS WT. STANDARD WHEELBASE: 6,980 Lbs.

WHEELBASE — STANDARD: 140", OPTIONAL 165", 180", 210" & 220"

ENGINE-TYPE: BUDA 6-Cylinder Full Diesel, Displacement 415 Cu. In.

BORE & STROKE: 4" × 5½"

TAX HORSEPOWER: 40.8

MAXIMUM BRAKE HORSEPOWER: 106 at 2200 RPM

MAXIMUM TORQUE-FOOT Lbs.: 306 at Peak

LUBRICATION: Full Pressure

ELECTRICAL EQUIPMENT: 24 Volt

FUEL INJECTION — MECH PUMP: Bosch or Excello

CLUTCH-SIZE & TYPE: 14", Single Plate

TRANSMISSION — STANDARD TYPE: Overdrive, 5 Speeds Forward, 1 Reverse

TRANSMISSION — EXTRA: 3 Speed Auxiliary

UNIVERSAL JOINTS — TYPE: Needle Bearing

FRONT AXLE-TYPE: Drop Forged I-Beam

REAR AXLE STAND. TYPE: Full Floating-Bevel

REAR AXLE — OPTIONAL-EXTRA: 2 Speed and Double Reduction

SERVICE BRAKES — STANDARD: 4 Whl. Hyd. & Vac. Booster, Frt. 16" × 2¼", Rear 17¼" × 4"

POWER BRAKE — OPTIONAL, EXTRA: Westinghouse-Air

EMERGENCY BRAKE: 10" × 3½"

SPRINGS: Front 44" × 2½" Rear 54" × 3"

HELPER SPRINGS: Standard

AIR SPRINGS — FRONT: Gruss Cleco-Standard

STEERING GEAR-CAM & LEVER: Roller Mounted Type

RADIATOR-TYPE: Flat Fin & Copper Tube

FRAME DIMENSIONS: 12" × 2¾" × ¼"

FUEL TANK CAPACITY: 30 U.S. Gallons, 25 Imperial Gallons, 94 Liters

WHEELS — STANDARD-TYPE: Cast Steel Spoke, OPTIONAL: Budd-Michelin

TIRES: Front 9.00 × 20, Rear 9.00 × 20 Dual
MAXIMUM SPEED: 60 MPH (97KPH)

MODEL 105-D 7 to 9 TONS

GROSS LADEN WEIGHT: 28,000 Lbs.
CHASSIS WT. STANDARD WHEELBASE: 7,300 Lbs.
WHEELBASE — STANDARD: 140", OPTIONAL 165", 190", 210" & 220"
ENGINE-TYPE: BUDA 6 Cylinder Full Diesel, Displacement 468 Cu. In.
BORE & STROKE: 4¼" × 5½"
TAX HORSEPOWER: 43.3
MAXIMUM BRAKE HORSEPOWER: 118 at 2200 RPM
MAXIMUM TORQUE-FOOT Lbs.: 346 at Peak
LUBRICATION: Full Pressure
ELECTRICAL EQUIPMENT: 24 Volt
FUEL INJECTION — MECH. PUMP: Bosch or Excello
CLUTCH-SIZE & TYPE: 14" Single Plate
TRANSMISSION — STANDARD TYPE: Overdrive, 5 Speeds Forward, 1 Reverse
TRANSMISSION — EXTRA: 3 Speed Auxiliary
UNIVERSAL JOINTS — TYPE: Needle Bearing
FRONT AXLE-TYPE: Drop Forged I-Beam
REAR AXLE STAND. TYPE: Full Floating Double Reduction
REAR AXLE — OPTIONAL-EXTRA: Worm Drive
SERVICE BRAKES — STANDARD: 4 Wheel Vacuum Boost, Front 16" × 2¼", Rear 17¼" × 5"
POWER BRAKE — OPTIONAL, EXTRA: Westinghouse-Air
EMERGENCY BRAKE-TYPE-SIZE: 16" Single Shoe
SPRINGS: Front 44" × 2½", Rear 54" × 3"
HELPER SPRINGS: Standard
AIR SPRINGS — FRONT: Gruss Cleco-Standard
STEERING GEAR-CAM & LEVER: Roller Mounted Type
RADIATOR-TYPE: Flat Fin & Copper Tube
FRAME DIMENSIONS: 12" × 2¾" × ¼"
FUEL TANK CAPACITY: 60 U.S. Gallons, 50 Imperial Gallons, 227 Liters
WHEELS — STANDARD-TYPE: Cast Steel Spoke, OPTIONAL Budd-Michlein
TIRES: Front 9.75 × 20, Rear 9.75 × 20 Dual
MAXIMUM ROAD SPEED: 54 MPH (87 KPH)

MODEL 125-D 9 to 12 TONS

GROSS LADEN WEIGHT: 35,000 Lbs.
CHASSIS WT. STANDARD WHEELBASE: 8,600 Lbs.
WHEELBASE — STANDARD: 145", OPTIONAL 165", 190", 210" & 220"
ENGINE TYPE: HERCULES 6 Cylinder Full Diesel, Displacement 468 Cu. In.
BORE & STROKE: 4¼" × 5½"

TAX HORSEPOWER: 43.3

MAXIMUM BRAKE HORSEPOWER: 118 at 2200 RPM

MAXIMUM TORQUE-FOOT Lbs. 346 at Peak

LUBRICATION: Full Pressure

ELECTRICAL EQUIPMENT: 24 Volt

FUEL INJECTION — MECH. PUMP: Bosch or Excello

CLUTCH-SIZE & TYPE: 14" Single Plate

TRANSMISSION — STANDARD TYPE: Overdrive, 5 Speeds Forward, 1 Reverse

TRANSMISSION — EXTRA: 3 Speed Auxiliary

UNIVERSAL JOINTS — TYPE: Needle Bearing

FRONT AXLE-TYPE: Drop Forged I-Beam

REAR AXLE STAND. TYPE: Full Floating Double Reduction

REAR AXLE — OPTIONAL-EXTRA: Worm Drive

SERVICE BRAKES — STANDARD: Westinghouse Air, Front 17¼" × 3", Rear 17¼" × 5"

EMERGENCY BRAKE-TYPE-SIZE: 16" Double Shoe

SPRINGS: Front 44" × 3", Rear 56" × 4"

HELPER SPRINGS: Standard

AIR SPRINGS — FRONT: Gruss Cleco-Standard

STEERING GEAR-CAM & LEVER: Roller Mounted Type

RADIATOR-TYPE: Flat Fin & Copper Tube

FRAME-DIMENSIONS: 12" × 2¼" × ¼"

FUEL TANK CAPACITY: 60 U.S. Gallons, 50 Imperial Gallons, 227 Liters

WHEELS — STANDARD-TYPE: Cast Steel Spoke, OPTIONAL: Budd-Michlein

TIRES: Front 10.50 × 20, Rear 10.50 × 20 Dual

MAXIMUM ROAD SPEED: 50 MPH (80 KPH)

MODEL 150-D 12 to 20 TONS

GROSS LADEN WEIGHT: 40,000 Lbs.

CHASSIS WT. STANDARD WHEELBASE: 10,200 Lbs.

WHEELBASE — STANDARD: 148", OPTIONAL: 165", 200", 220" & 240"

ENGINE TYPE: BUDA 6 Cylinder Full Diesel, Displacement 691 Cu. In.

BORE & STROKE: 4¾" × 6½"

TAX HORSEPOWER: 54.1

MAXIMUM BRAKE HORSEPOWER: 162 at 2000 RPM

MAXIMUM TORQUE-FOOT Lbs.: 501 at Peak

LUBRICATION: Full Pressure

ELECTRICAL EQUIPMENT: 24 Volt

FUEL INJECTION — MECH. PUMP: Bosch or Excello

CLUTCH-SIZE &TYPE: 13" Double Plate

TRANSMISSION — STANDARD TYPE: Overdrive, 5 Speeds Forward, 1 Reverse

TRANSMISSION — EXTRA: 3 Speed Auxiliary

UNIVERSAL JOINTS — TYPE: Needle Bearing

FRONT AXLE-TYPE: Drop Forged I-Beam

REAR AXLE STAND. TYPE: Full Floating Double Reduction

POWER BRAKE — OPTIONAL EXTRA: Westinghouse-Air

SPRINGS: Front 44" × 3", Rear 56" × 4"

HELPER SPRINGS: Standard

AIR SPRINGS — FRONT: Gruss Cleco-Standard

STEERING GEAR-CAM & LEVER: Roller Mounted Type

RADIATOR TYPE: Flat Fin & Copper Tube

FRAME-DIMENSIONS: 12" × 2¾" × ⁵⁄₁₆"

FUEL TANK CAPACITY: 60 U.S. Gallons, 50 Imperial Gallons, 227 Liters

WHEELS — STANDARD-TYPE: Budd-Michelin

TIRES: Front 10.50 × 22, Rear 10.50 × 22 Dual

MAXIMUM ROAD SPEED: 48 MPH (77KPH)

NOTE: Standard Chassis Equipment Includes: Front Bumper, "V" Radiator Grille; Head, Parking, Stop and Tail Lamps; Cowl, Front Fenders and Short Running Boards; Instrument Panel with Ammeter, Oil Gauge, Fuel Gauge, Temperature Indicator, Speedometer, Tachometer, All Indirectly Lighted; Dash Mounted Light Controls, Cigar Lighter and Instrument Panel Switch; Kit of Tools and Jack. Standard Painting-Chassis-Clydesdale Golden Tan. Wheels — Yellow.

"SPECIFICATIONS SUBJECT TO CHANGE WITHOUT NOTICE"

Appendix C: Export Packing and Shipping Guide

Much of the Clydesdale Motor Truck Company's inventory was exported to countries outside the United States, particularly during World War I. The company gained a reputation for managing an extensive international sales network, as well as for efficiently packaging a truck chassis. While there are no export details from the company available for the years during World War I, there are details available for later years, for diesel trucks. The packing and shipping chart on the next page shows measurements and pricing for exported chassis. Something like this would have been used by Clydesdale engineers in charge of shipping finished chassis. It provides a window into the packing and shipping materials, weights, measures, and prices that were central to the company's success.

CLYDESDALE MOTOR TRUCK COMPANY — EXPORT SHIPPING DATA AND PRICES

MODEL	Wheelbase Inches	Capacity Tons	Export Boxing	Net Weight Chassis Pounds	Net Weight Chassis Kilos	Gross Weight Boxed Pounds	Gross Weight Boxed Kilos	Volume of Box Cu. Ft.	Volume of Box Cubic Meters	Approx. Frt. to New York Carload Unboxed	Approx. Frt. to New York Boxed	List Price	Discount	Net Price F.O.B. Clyde
30-D	140	1½	40.00	3650	1655	4400	1996	145	4.1	61.20	30.60	2795	35%	1817
	160	1½	42.00	3750	1701	4550	2063	160	4.5	61.20	30.60	2825	35%	1836
	170	1½	45.00	3850	1746	4675	2121	170	4.8	61.20	30.60	2835	35%	1843
	180	1½	50.00	3900	1768	4775	2166	180	5.1	61.20	30.60	2845	35%	1849
70-D	140	2	45.00	4800	2176	5600	2540	170	4.8	61.20	38.08	3865	35%	2512
	170	2	50.00	5000	2268	5850	2654	180	5.1	61.20	39.78	3865	35%	2512
	180	2	50.00	5100	2313	6000	2722	195	5.5	61.20	40.80	3865	35%	2512
75-D	140	2½	50.00	5230	2372	6030	2735	175	5.0	61.20	41.00	4070	35%	2645
	170	2½	55.00	5430	2463	6330	2871	185	5.2	61.20	43.04	4070	35%	2645
	180	2½	60.00	5530	2508	6430	2917	200	5.7	61.20	43.72	4070	35%	2645
	200	2½	70.00	5680	2575	6630	3007	210	5.9	61.20	45.08	4170	35%	2710
80-D	140	3	70.00	7200	3266	8640	3919	250	7.0	61.20	58.75	5355	40%	3213
	160	3	75.00	7300	3310	8760	3974	285	8.0	61.20	59.57	5355	40%	3213
	170	3	80.00	7350	3333	8820	4001	290	8.2	61.20	59.97	5355	40%	3213
	180	3	85.00	7400	3356	8880	4028	300	8.5	61.20	60.38	5355	40%	3213
	210	3	100.00	7500	3402	9060	4082	330	9.3	61.20	61.20	5455	40%	3273
90-D	140	4	75.00	7400	3356	8840	4010	250	7.0	61.20	60.11	5465	40%	3279
	160	4	80.00	7500	3402	8960	4065	285	8.0	61.20	60.93	5465	40%	3279
	170	4	80.00	7550	3425	9020	4091	290	8.2	61.20	61.34	5465	40%	3279
	180	4	85.00	7600	3447	9080	4118	300	8.5	61.20	61.74	5465	40%	3279
	210	4	100.00	7700	3493	9200	4173	330	9.3	61.20	62.56	5565	40%	3339
100-D	145	5-7	75.00	8400	3809	9920	4500	300	8.5	61.20	67.46	7760	40%	4656
	170	5-7	100.00	8600	3900	10150	4603	330	9.3	61.20	69.02	7760	40%	4656
	180	5-7	110.00	8700	3945	10370	4704	350	9.9	61.20	70.52	7760	40%	4656
	210	5-7	125.00	8850	4013	10640	4826	375	10.6	61.20	72.53	7860	40%	4716
	220	5-7	140.00	8900	4036	10900	4944	400	11.3	61.20	74.12	7860	40%	4716
105-D	145	5-7	75.00	7800	3536	9320	4227	260	7.3	61.20	63.38	6650	40%	3990
	170	5-7	100.00	8000	3627	9550	4332	300	8.5	61.20	64.94	6650	40%	3990
	180	5-7	110.00	8100	3672	9770	4432	330	9.3	61.20	66.44	6650	40%	3990
	210	5-7	125.00	8200	3717	9930	4531	350	9.9	61.20	67.93	6750	40%	4050
	220	5-7	140.00	8450	3831	10450	4740	375	10.6	61.20	71.06	6750	40%	4050
125-D	145	7-10	80.00	9750	4423	11270	5111	260	7.5	66.30	76.63	8495	40%	5097
	170	7-10	105.00	9950	4513	11590	5216	300	8.5	67.66	78.20	8495	40%	5097
	180	7-10	115.00	10100	4581	11770	5339	330	9.3	68.68	80.04	8495	40%	5097
	210	7-10	135.00	10200	4627	11990	5439	350	9.9	69.36	81.53	8595	40%	5157
	220	7-10	145.00	10300	4672	12800	5806	375	10.6	70.04	87.04	8595	40%	5157

Where trucks are shipped unboxed, add $10.00 per unit to the carload freight rate for lighterage or towing to steamer at New York.

Chapter Notes

Chapter 1

1. The establishment of the Clydesdale Motor Truck Company was widely publicized within the truck manufacturing industry. Press releases appeared in several places, including: "Krebs Company Reorganized," *Clyde Enterprise*, March 22, 1917; "Change of Firm Name," *Clyde Enterprise,* May 1, 1917; "The Clydesdale Trucks," *Clyde Enterprise,* May 17, 1917; "Three Truck Firms Merge," *The Automobile*, May 17, 1917, 947; "Six Clydesdale Truck Models," *The Automobile*, May 24, 1917, 984; "Three Trucks in Merger," *Motor World*, May 23, 1917, 34; and "Merger of Commercial Car Companies," *Horseless Age*, June 1, 1917, 45.

2. "Clyde Now Clydesdale," *Automotive Industries*, December 4, 1919, 1147; "Advertising Makes Clyde Company Change Name," *Printer's Ink,* January 15, 1920, 193.

3. "Is Now the Clydesdale Company," *New York Herald*, November 30, 1919.

4. *Catalogue D*, Clyde Cars Company, May 20, 1918, 2.

5. Thomas Sugrue, "From Motor City to Motor Metropolis: How the Automobile Industry Reshaped Urban America," Automobile in American Life and Society, website from the University of Michigan, http:// www. autolife. umd. umich. edu/ Race/ R_ Overview/ R_ Overview1. htm#popsugrue (accessed March 18, 2013).

6. "Commercial Club," *Clyde Enterprise*, January 5, 1911.

7. J.C.L. "Louis" Krebs is profiled in Nevin Otto Winter, *History of Northwest Ohio*, vol. 2 (Chicago: Lewis, 1917), 841.

8. "Krebs Company Reorganized," *Clyde Enterprise*, March 22, 1917.

9. "New Elmore Building," *Clyde Enterprise*, April 13, 1911.

10. *The Car that has no Valves*, Elmore Manufacturing Company, 1908, 5.

11. This is noted in an untitled article that appeared in the *Clyde Enterprise*, December 21, 1911. The two-cycle engine is U.S. Patent number 880,958. Patent was granted on March 3, 1908.

12. "An Elmore for France," *Clyde Enterprise*, April 27, 1911.

13. Elmore Manufacturing Company advertisement appeared in *Review of Reviews,* 1905, 81.

14. *The Car that has no Valves*, Elmore Manufacturing Company, 1908, 8.

15. In 1912, the distinction between "car" and "truck" was not as clearly defined as it is today. Automobiles may have been referred to as "cars" generally, even if they had what we now recognize as truck characteristics. Likewise, truck manufacturers referred to their products as "cars," or sometimes "motor trucks."

16. "The Krebs Commercial Car," *Clyde Enterprise*, May 16, 1912.

17. This is noted in an untitled article that appeared in the *Clyde Enterprise,* June 27, 1912.

18. This is noted in an untitled article that appeared in the *Clyde Enterprise,* June 27, 1912.

19. The Automatic Controller, or Engine Governor, is U.S. Patent #1,117,759. Patent was granted November 17, 1914. Text of patent included in Appendix A.

20. Clydesdale Motor Truck Company advertisement appeared in *Literary Digest*, December 29, 1917, 56.

21. Clydesdale Motor Truck Company advertisement appeared on page 6 of the print edition of *New York Times*, February 13, 1919.

22. Brian Hanley, "Motor Transport: World War I," *World at War: Understanding Conflict and Society* in the ABC-CLIO digital library, 2012 (accessed March 18, 2013).

23. Quoted in William Scheck, "World War I: American Expeditionary Forces Get Motorized Transportation," *Military History*, June 1997. Available online from the Weider History Group, http:// www. historynet.com/ world-war-i-american-expeditionary-forces-get-motorized- transportation. htm (accessed April 28, 2013).

24. "News and Notes of the Great Automobile at the Coliseum," *Chicago Daily Tribune*, January 30, 1918.

25. "The Trucks are Coming: What the Motor Industry Has Done and is Doing to Meet the Need for Efficient Transportation," *The Independent*, March 16, 1918, 459; also Steven Titchenal's website, Rails and Trails. com: Transportation History Primary Sources, 2013. Available online at http://www.railsandtrails. com/ AutoFacts/1920p20–100–8.jpg (accessed April 28, 2013).

26. "Army Not Likely to Commandeer Trucks," *The Commercial Vehicle*, April 15, 1917, 11.

27. Hugh Rockoff, "U.S. Economy in World War

I," *Economic History Association*, February 10, 2008, available online at: http://eh.net/encyclopedia/article/ Rockoff.WWI (accessed March 18, 2013); also "New Record in Foreign Commerce," *Dun's International Review*, February 1919, 92.

28. Quoted in Scheck.

29. Bill Hudgins, "When Johnny Came Trucking Home," *Land Line*, November 2012, 58.

30. "Burch shows how trucks save steel," *Motor Record*, December 1918, 344.

31. *Model 6X,* Clydesdale Motor Truck Company, c. 1918.

32. Birger Jacobsson, "The American Motor Industry," *Sweden-America*, New York, 1918, 44.

33. Ibid.

34. Robert Whitney Imbrie, *Behind the Wheel of a War Ambulance*, 1918, 14–15.

35. "Clydesdale Trucks in Red Cross Service in France," *Clyde Enterprise,* October 24, 1918.

36. "Survival of the Fittest," Clydesdale Motor Truck Company advertisement appeared in *Evening Post*, New York, January 8, 1918.

37. "The Era of the Motor Truck," *Dun's International Review*, April 1918, 36–37.

38. "A World-Proven Motor Truck," Clydesdale Motor Truck Company advertisement appeared in *Saturday Evening Post*, February 15, 1919, 128; "Proof of a Truck's Worth," Clydesdale Motor Truck Company advertisement appeared in *Motor Age*, November 28, 1918, 83; and Clydesdale Motor Truck Company advertisement appeared in *Literary Digest*, December 29, 1917, 56.

39. Clydesdale advertisement, *Literary Digest*, December 29, 1917, 56.

40. "Upholding an enviable reputation," *Chicago Tribune*, January 27, 1918.

41. "Cars Company Spreading Out," *Clyde Enterprise*, October 31, 1918.

42. Letter from A.C. Burch to authorized Clydesdale Motor Truck dealers, August 1, 1918. A.C. Burch's move from Signal Truck Company to Clydesdale Motor Truck Company is noted on page 41 in the June 25, 1918, issue of *Automobile Journal*.

43. Descriptions of the Sixteenth Annual Boston Automobile Show drawn from the Official Program, 1918.

Chapter 2

1. *Model 6X,* Clydesdale Motor Truck Company, c. 1918.

2. "European Features in the New Clydesdale," *Automobile Trade Journal*, October 1917, 233.

3. *Tested in the Crucible of War — and Found Fit*, Clydesdale Motor Truck Company, October 29, 1917.

4. "Six Clydesdale Truck Models," *The Automobile*, May 24, 1917, 984.

5. *Burden Bearers of Business*, Clydesdale Motor Truck Company, 1919, 32.

6. Clydesdale Motor Truck Company advertisement appeared in *Motor Age*, December 26, 1918, 72.

7. "Fourteen Points," Clydesdale Motor Truck Company advertisement appeared in *Chicago Tribune*, May 25, 1919.

8. Ibid.

9. Many Clydesdale truck chassis specifications are outlined in the 1919, 1920, and 1921 editions of the *Official Handbook of Automobiles,* published annually by the Automobile Manufacturers Association and the National Automobile Chamber of Commerce. In the 1919 edition, Clydesdale trucks appear on pages 185–187; in the 1920 edition, Clydesdale trucks appear on pages 240–241; and in the 1921 edition, Clydesdale trucks appear on pages 210–211.

10. *Catalogue D*, Clyde Cars Company, May 20, 1918, 27.

11. *Burden Bearers of Business*, Clydesdale Motor Truck Company, 1919, 6.

12. *Clydesdale Model 90 3-ton Truck*, Clydesdale Motor Truck Company, no date, 7.

13. "European Features in New Clydesdale," *Automobile Trade Journal*, October 1917, 234.

14. *Model 6X*, Clydesdale Motor Truck Company, c. 1918.

15. W.W. Wells, "Variable Speed Governors," *Society of Automotive Engineers* 4, no. 5 (May 1919): 375.

16. *Burden Bearers of Business*, Clydesdale Motor Truck Company, 1919, 9.

17. Clydesdale Driver Under the Hood postcard, Clydesdale Motor Truck Company, no date.

18. "Unique Motor Adjustment Keeps Trucks at One Speed," *Syracuse Herald*, October 5, 1919.

19. Clydesdale Driver Under the Hood postcard.

20. "Automatic Controller on the Clydesdale," *The Sun*, February 18, 1919.

21. "Clydesdale trucks travel steadily uphill or downhill without attention to the throttle," Clydesdale Motor Truck Company advertisement, no date.

22. "Why didn't you tell me it would do this?" Clydesdale Motor Truck Company advertisement appeared in *Literary Digest*, November 29, 1919, 72.

23. "Put your driver behind the wheel and let him tell you," Clydesdale Motor Truck Company advertisement appeared in *Literary Digest*, December 27, 1919, 129.

24. "You Will Believe When You See It," Clydesdale Motor Truck Company advertisement appeared in *Motor Truck*, January 1920, 37.

25. "Try to induce your driver to run a truck without it," Clydesdale advertisement appeared in *Literary Digest*, January 3, 1920, 71.

26. "I Wish I Could Buy Them to Install on My Other Trucks," Clydesdale Motor Truck Company advertisement appeared in *Literary Digest*, January 24, 1920, 123.

27. "You probably won't believe it until you see it work," Clydesdale Motor Truck Company advertisement appeared in *Literary Digest*, February 28, 1920, 61.

28. "Two drivers on your truck are better than one," Clydesdale Motor Truck Company advertisement appeared in *Literary Digest*, May 29, 1920, 109.

29. "Why drivers swear *by* the truck, not *at* it," Clydesdale Motor Truck Company advertisement appeared in *Scientific American*, December 4, 1920, 577.

30. "Chapter XI: Motor Truck Governors," *Motor Truck Manual,* produced by the editorial Staff of *American Automobile Digest*, 1921, 141.

31. Ibid.

32. "Krebs Automatic Controller," *Motor Age*, June 20, 1918, 4.
33. "New Mechanism Aids Truck Sales," *New York Evening Telegram*, January 3, 1920.
34. "What does the Clydesdale Controller do?" Clydesdale Motor Truck Company advertisement appeared in *Motor Age*, March 1919, 115.
35. "European Features in New Clydesdale," *Automobile Trade Journal*, October 1917, 233.
36. *Clydesdale Model 90 3-ton Truck*, 3.
37. *Catalog D*, 21.
38. Clydesdale Motor Truck Company advertisement appeared in *American Lumberman*, October 9, 1920, 139.
39. "Chapter II: Motor Truck Engines," *Motor Truck Manual*, 18.
40. *Clydesdale Model 90 3-ton Truck*, 4.
41. *Burden Bearers of Business*, 6–7.
42. "Controller Feature of Clydesdale," *Motor Truck*, July 1921, 386.
43. *Catalog D*, 19–20.
44. Ibid.
45. "Facts About 1922 Auto Industry Told Briefly," *Chicago Commerce*, February 3, 1923, 34; and Zay Jeffries, "Aluminum Alloys," *Journal of the Society of Automotive Engineers* 7, no. 3 (September 1920): 205.
46. "Motor Truck Bodies—Their Design and Use," *Power Wagon Reference Book*, 1920, 498.
47. *Burden Bearers of Business*, 26.
48. "Making Dump Bodies for Motor Trucks," *Iron Age*, October 6, 1921, 937.
49. Van Dorn Iron Works Company also produced armor plates for vehicles during World War I and, later, World War II. At the time of publication, the company was still doing business, as the Van Dorn Demag Corporation, a producer of plastic injection molding machines. "Van Dorn Demag Corp.," Encyclopedia of Cleveland History, Case Western Reserve University, available online at http://ech.case.edu/cgi/article.pl?id=VDDC (accessed April 20, 2013).
50. "Motor Truck Bodies," *Motor Truck Manual*, 142.
51. Ibid.
52. *Burden Bearers of Business*, 40.
53. "Motor Truck Bodies—Their Design and Use," *Power Wagon Reference Book*, 1920, 501–507.
54. *Burden Bearers of Business*, 42.
55. Charles Dickens, "Motor Truck Operation and Accounting XXXII," *Municipal Engineering*, April 1918, 29.
56. Ibid.
57. "Use of Motor Trucks by Sand and Gravel Producers," *Engineering World*, July 1921, 47–50.
58. "Motor Truck Bodies—Their Design and Use," *Power Wagon Reference Book*, 1920, 517.
59. "Agni Motor Fuel Company to Sell Gas Substitute," *Petroleum Age*, April 1920, 68.
60. "The only Clydesdale," *Clyde Enterprise*, April 13, 1994.

Chapter 3

1. "Motor Cars and Trucks for All the World," *Duns International Review*, February 1919, 70.

2. "The Eternal Triangle," *Motor Record*, September 1919, 38.
3. "Motor Cars and Trucks for All the World," 72.
4. *Model 6X*, Clydesdale Motor Truck Company, c. 1918.
5. "Big Clydesdale Foreign Market," *The Sun*, February 16, 1919, 9.
6. "Clydesdale Motor Truck Company Notable Industry at Clyde," *Sandusky Register*, December 31, 1922.
7. "Rural Motor Express on Long Island," *New York Times*, February 9, 1919.
8. Hi Sibley, "Automotive Future of Japan Looms Big Despite Poor Traveling Conditions," *Commercial Car Journal*, February 15, 1921, 21.
9. Hi Sibley, "Japan—An Empire with 21 Motor Trucks," *The Automobile and Automotive Industries*, August 9, 1917, 237.
10. "Announcement," *Dun's International Review*, June 1919, 159.
11. "Clydesdale Increases its Capitalization," *Motor West*, December 15, 1919, 66.
12. "Clydesdale: A World-Proven Motor Truck," Clydesdale Motor Truck Company advertisement appeared in *Saturday Evening Post*, January 4, 1919.
13. "Big Clydesdale Foreign Market."
14. "Clydesdale Trucks Make Fine Record," *The Sun*, September 29, 1918.
15. "A Service Worth Talking About," Clydesdale Motor Truck Company advertisement appeared in *Commercial Car Journal*, November 15, 1920, 110.
16. "Hans Lochen & Son adept at handling the big moves," *Milwaukee Sentinel*, November 19, 1979.
17. "How Chickopee Picked a Truck," Clydesdale Motor Truck Company advertisement appeared in *Telephony: The American Telephone Journal*, April 1920, 47; and "A Studebaker Power Pressure Sprinkling-Flushing Unit on the Clydesdale: A World-Proven Motor Truck," Clydesdale Motor Truck Company advertisement appeared in *The American City*, February 1919, 84.
18. Noted in *Automobile Trade Journal*, August 1, 1920, 249.
19. "Henderson is New England Clydesdale Truck Agent," *Motor Truck*, June 1918, 228.
20. Letter from Clydesdale to Motor Truck Dealers of America, appeared in *Automobile Topics*, June 29, 1918, 795.
21. "In comes Ed," Clydesdale Motor Truck Company advertisement appeared in *Evening Public Ledger-Philadelphia*, February 5, 1919.
22. "New Clydesdale Service Station at Philadelphia," *The Accessory and Garage Journal*, 42.
23. "Clydesdale Trucks Make Fine Record."
24. "Institute 24 Hour Service," *Motor Age*, December 16, 1920, 25.
25. "Courtesy of the Unwritten Obligation of the Service Station," *American Garage and Auto Dealer*, September 1920, 32.
26. New York Girl Succeeds Selling Motor Trucks," *American Garage and Auto Dealer*, February 1919, 22; and "Girl Phenom at Selling Trucks," *Washington Times*, February 1, 1919, 6.
27. "Motor Trucks on Farms," *New York Times*, September 14, 1919.

28. "Decline of the Horse in New York City," *Motor West*, October 15, 1919, 48; and "Stable Census," *Municipal Record* 13, no. 13 (March 25, 1920): 99.

29. U.S. Department of Agriculture, "Increase of Horses," *Weekly Newsletter* 5, no. 37 (April 17, 1918): 15.

30. Herbert Newton Cassons, et al., *Horse, Truck and Tractor: The Coming of Cheaper Power for City and Farm* (Chicago: F.G. Browne, 1913), 12.

31. "Getting the Most of Every Acre with the Aid of a Motor Truck," Clydesdale Motor Truck Company, 1920, 3.

32. Ibid., 7.

33. Ibid., 5.

34. Allan Campbell, "Motor Trucks in Demonstration Tour," *Power Farming*, October 1919, 36.

35. A.V. Comings, "Four Hundred Mile Truck Tour of St. Louis Motor Truck Dealers is a Wonderful Success," *Commercial Car Journal*, July 15, 1919, 7.

36. Ibid.

37. Ibid., 9.

38. "Motor Trucks in Demonstration Tour," 34.

39. A.V. Comings, "National Motor Truck Development Tour is Making Progress on Long Trip," *The Commercial Car Journal*, August 15, 1919, 25.

40. "Motor Trucks in Demonstration Tour," 34.

41. Ibid.

42. The National Motor Truck Development Tour of 1919 was covered heavily in the national trade press. Coverage included: "National Motor Truck Development Tour ends at Milwaukee," *Tractor World*, October 1919, 21; A.V. Comings, "National Motor Truck Development Tour is Making Progress on Long Trip," *Commercial Car Journal*, August 15, 1919, 25–30; "Truck Train Demonstrating Haulage to Farmers of Northwest," *Tractor World*, August 1919, 31–34.

43. "They are Interested in Clydesdale," Clydesdale Motor Truck Company advertisement appeared in *Motor West*, February 1, 1920, 63.

44. "Trucks Exhibited at Dairy Show," *Commercial Car Journal*, October 15, 1919, 28.

45. "Thirty Trucks Participate in Des Moines Tour," *Commercial Car Journal*, October 15, 1919, 24.

46. "Milwaukee Farm Truck Tour Proves Highly Successful," *Motor Age*, July 8, 1920, 22.

47. Clydesdale Motor Truck Company, *Instructions for Care and Operation*, p. 4.

48. "Motor Trucks, Tractors, and Trailers," *Oil Trade Journal*, February 1920, 28.

49. "Full Clydesdale Line on Exhibition," *The Sun*, February 11, 1919.

50. "The 19th Annual Automobile Show," *Motor Travel*, March 1919, 7–17; and "New York Truck Show Will Cram Garden," *Automobile Topics*, February 8, 1919, 83–85.

51. "Chicago Truck Show Vindicates Dealers," *Automobile Topics*, February 8, 1919, 80.

52. "You can buy an airplane at the Detroit Auto Show," *Michigan Manufacturer and Financial Record* 23, no. 4 (January 25, 1919): 22.

53. Ibid.

54. "Dayton Truly Automotive," *Motor Age*, March 13, 1919, 16.

55. "Motor Truck Displays," *American Wool and Cotton Reporter*, March 20, 1919, 957.

56. "Iowa Motor Show Draws Record Crowds," *Automotive Industries*, September 4, 1919, 494.

57. "Motor Trucks, Tractors, and Trailers," *Oil Trade Journal*, February 1920, 28.

58. "New York Ready for 20th National Motor Show," *Motor West*, January 1, 1920, 34.

59. Harry Griffiths, "An American Auto Show," *Commercial America*, February 1920, 49.

60. "Chicago Show Big Indication of 1920," *American Garage and Auto Dealer*, February 1920, 11–12.

61. Ibid.

62. F. Ed Spooner, "Echoes of the Chicago Show," *Motor West*, February 15, 1920, 48.

63. Ibid.

64. Ibid.

65. "Clydesdale Truck Sells on Appearance," *Motor West*, February 15, 1920, 66.

66. "San Francisco Show a Practical and Artistic Feast," *Motor West*, March 1, 1920, 34.

67. "Stage Set for Opening of Fourth Pacific Show," *Motor West*, February 15, 1920, 44.

68. "The Boston Truck Show Expected to Attract Many Dealers," *Commercial Car Journal*, March 15, 1920, 59; also "Magnificent Display of Trucks at the Boston Show, *Commercial Car Journal*, April 15, 1920, 56–57.

69. "Los Angeles Motor Truck Show Opens," *Motor West*, April 1, 1920, 54.

70. "Another 'Still' Truck Show Fails to Arouse Interest," *Motor World*, January 12, 1921, 28.

71. "The Annual Milwaukee Show Presented a Novel Setting in Its 'Trucktown,'" *Commercial Car Journal*, September 15, 1920, 40.

72. "Clydesdale Guarantees Price," *Motor Age*, October 21, 1920, 17.

73. "Another 'Still' Truck Show Fails to Arouse Interest."

74. Ibid.

75. Ibid.

76. "Spirit of Optimism Very Much Alive at Boston Show," *Accessory and Garage Journal*, March 1921, 27.

77. "Representative Dealers Boost Boston Show," *Accessory and Garage Journal*, March 1921, 29.

78. "British Truck Show Finds Trade Quiet," *Automobile Topics*, November 5, 1921, 965.

79. "Problem of the Short Haul," *American Contractor*, January 3, 1920, 66.

80. Title XII, Democratic Party Platform, June 14, 1916, provided by the American Presidency Project, University of California Santa Barbara, available online at http://www.presidency.ucsb.edu/ws/?pid=29591 (accessed April 28, 2013).

81. P.M. Gunsaulus, "What 'Ship by Truck' Has Done," *Michigan Manufacturer and Financial Record* 26, no. 3 (July 17, 1920): 11

82. Ibid.

83. "Buffalo Dealers Tour a Huge Success," *The Commercial Car Journal*, October 15, 1919, 23.

84. Ibid.

85. "California Dealers Promote Truck Tours," *Motor West*, October 15, 1919, 30.

86. Ibid., 34.

87. "Truck Manufacturer Spurns Railroad," *Motor West*, October 15, 1919, 48.

88. "Coast to Cost, Canada to Gulf, truck tours,

parades, and public meetings in hundreds of cities combined to observe national Ship by Truck Good Roads Week," *Pittsburgh Gazette*, May 23, 1920.

89. P.M. Gunsaulus, "What 'Ship by Truck' Has Done," *Michigan Manufacturer and Financial Record* 26, no. 3 (July 17, 1920): 11–12.

Chapter 4

1. *Model-10 All Steel Truck with Speed*, Clydesdale Motor Truck Company, 1922.

2. Announcements appeared in many trade and press outlets, including: "Clydesdale Motor Truck Company Builds New Model," *Highway Engineer Contractor*, May 1922, 64; "Clydesdale Motor Truck Company Builds New Model," *Engineering World*, June 1922, 401; "New Clydesdale Truck," *Motor World*, April 19, 1922, 39; "New Clydesdale Truck," *Automotive Industries*, April 13, 1922, 838; and "Clydesdale 1½ ton Truck," *Power Wagon*, June 1922, 23.

3. "Clydesdale Motor Truck Company Builds New Model."

4. "Clydesdale Motor Truck Company Builds New Model."

5. "Clydesdale Adds an All-Steel Speed Truck," *Commercial Vehicle*, June 1, 1922, 22.

6. "Interesting British Truck Bodies," *Automotive Manufacturer*, June 1922, 16.

7. "Coach Body made by Fremont Metal Bodies Company, *Fremont Daily News*, December 23, 1922.

8. "Clydesdale Bus Has Six-Cylinder Engine," *Automotive Industries*, April 26, 1923, 946; also "New Clydesdale Bus," *Motor Age*, May 3, 1923, 30.

9. "Clydesdale Brings Out New Coach Chassis," *Commercial Car Journal*, September 15, 1923, 72.

10. "Trackless Street Pictured," *Motor West*, March 15, 1920, 48b.

11. Ibid.

12. J. Kenneth Ballinger, *Miami Millions: The Dance of the Dollars in the Great Florida Land Boom of 1925* (Miami: Franklin Press, 1936), 25.

13. "Trackless Street Pictured."

14. Interview with Milton Opper, age 98, February 20, 2013, Huron, Ohio.

15. "Clydesdale Changes," *Motor Transport*, May 15, 1923, 219.

16. "New Clydesdale Models," *Power Wagon*, January 1923, 28.

17. "New Road Laws Forced Upon Eastern States," *Popular Mechanics*, August 1921, 218.

18. "Clydesdale Fixes Prices on Full Line of Trucks," *Automotive Industries*, October 18, 1923, 815.

19. Clydesdale Motor Truck Company advertisement appeared in *Management*, June 1, 1923, 96–97.

20. Clydesdale Motor Truck Company advertisement appeared in *Management*, August 1, 1923, 96–97.

21. Clydesdale Motor Truck Company advertisement appeared in *Management*, September 1, 1923, 104–105.

22. Clydesdale Motor Truck Company advertisement appeared in *Management*, October 1, 1923, 96–97.

23. Clydesdale Motor Truck Company advertisement appeared in *Management*, February 1, 1924, 96–97.

24. Ibid.

25. "The New Clydesdale Model 10," *Commercial Car Journal*, January 15, 1923, 21.

26. F.W. Hershey, "Driving Adversity to Cover," *Michigan Manufacture and Financial Record*, November 19, 1921, 3.

27. "Seasonal Decline in Demand Bound up in Price Reductions," *Motor Age*, June 2, 1921, 25.

28. "What is the Outlook for 1922?" *Automobile Trade Journal* 26, no. 7 (January 1, 1922): 18.

29. M.H. Hoepli, "Truck Exports Exceed Those of the Last War Year," *Power Wagon*, November 1923, 26.

30. *Continental Motors Corporation v. Clydesdale Motor Truck Company (1925)*, Case 589; Equity Case Files, compiled 1912–1938; U.S. District Court for the Western (Toledo) Division of the Northern District of Ohio. (06/08/1878 —); Records of the District Courts of the United States, Record Group 21; National Archives at Chicago.

31. "The Clydesdale Operating Company," *Clyde Enterprise*, February 5, 1925.

32. "Clydesdale Notes," *Clyde Enterprise*, January 29, 1925.

33. "The Clydesdale Operating Company," *Clyde Enterprise*, February 19, 1925.

34. Ibid.

35. In 1925, the Clydesdale Motor Truck Company entered what is now recognized as a common alternative to formal bankruptcy known as equity receivership. This legal procedure was commonly used with companies when the creditors had an interest in reorganizing and continuing business.

36. "The Clydesdale Situation," *Clyde Enterprise*, December 10, 1925.

37. *Continental Motors Corporation v. Clydesdale Motor Truck Company.*

38. *Continental Motors Corporation v. Clydesdale Motor Truck Company.*

39. Industrial Plants Corporation, *Public Auction: Land, Buildings, Service Parts, Business, Machinery, Equipment, and Small Tools of Clydesdale Motor Truck Company*, 1926.

40. Ibid.

41. "Clydesdales are Popular Abroad," *Clyde Enterprise*, June 4, 1925.

42. Ibid.

43. "Will Auction Clydesdale Plant," *Clyde Enterprise*, January 14, 1926.

44. "Clydesdale Factory May Again be Operated," *Clyde Enterprise,* January 21, 1926.

45. Ibid.

46. Ibid.

47. "Prospects at the Clydesdale Factory," *Clyde Enterprise*, February 11, 1926.

48. "Factories Busy," *Clyde Enterprise*, February 25, 1926.

49. Noted in the *Clyde Enterprise*, March 12, 1926.

50. "Clydesdale to Resume Truck Production," *Automotive Industries*, October 4, 1930, 504; and "Truck Industry News," *Commercial Car Journal*, October 1930, 40.

51. "Clydesdale to Resume Truck Production."

52. Ibid.

53. Sources in the Ford Motor Company archives indicate that local assembly plants were closed and re-opened throughout the 1930's. Referenced in Timothy Bresnahan and Daniel M.G. Raff, "Intra-Industry Heterogeneity and the Great Depression: The American Motor Vehicles Industry, 1929–1935," *Journal of Economic History* 51, no. 2 (June 1991): 324.

54. Arlena Sawyers, "Even During the Depression, GM Managed to Make Money," *Automotive News*, September 15, 2008, 84.

55. Ibid.

56. Ibid.; Bresnahan and Raff, "Intra-Industry Heterogeneity and the Great Depression: The American Motor Vehicles Industry, 1929–1935," 317–318.

57. Harold Barger, *The Transportation Industries, 1889–1946: A Study of Output, Employment, and Productivity* (New York: National Bureau of Economic Research, 1951), 221–242.

58. Meyer Fishbein, "The Trucking Industry and the National Recovery Administration," *Social Forces*, December 1955, 171.

59. Ibid.

60. Ibid.

61. Barger.

62. James Newcomb, "Depression Auto Styling," *Winterthur Portfolio* 35, no. 1 (Spring 2000): 81–82.

63. Ibid., 82.

64. Ibid., 90.

65. Ibid., 83, L. Clayton Hill speech recorded from January 25, 1930.

Chapter 5

1. "Clydesdale Diesel Engine Motor Trucks," Clydesdale Motor Truck Company advertisement appeared in *Commercial Car Journal*, April 1937, 145.

2. Charles Morrow Wilson, "Fire Under Your Hood," *Popular Mechanics*, July 1938, 22.

3. "Diesel Motor as Auto Power Forecast to Save Fuel," *Popular Mechanics*, August 1925, 289.

4. Jeffrey Cruikshank and David Sicilia, *The Engine that Could: Seventy-Five Years of Values-Driven Change at Cummins Engine Company* (Boston: Harvard Business Press, 1997), 58.

5. "A Bourgeois Engine," *Fortune*, June 1930, 64ff.

6. Ibid.

7. *The Engine that Could*, referring to: Phillip H. Smith, "Diesels Stride Ahead," *Scientific American*, December 1934, 285, 287; and "Diesels on Wheels," *Fortune*, December 1934, 106ff.

8. "Diesel Sales Mount," *Business Week*, February 9, 1935, 24.

9. "Big Tractors Go Diesel," *Popular Mechanics*, June 1935, 869.

10. C.L. Cummins, "Herr Diesel Started It," *The Rotarian*, October 1936, 27.

11. Ibid., 61.

12. "The Use of Diesel Engines," *Science Supplement*, November 27, 1936, 12–13.

13. "Local Industry Specializes on Diesel Engine Trucks," *Clyde Enterprise*, November 1, 1934.

14. "Diesel Motors, Inc.," Clydesdale Motor Truck Company advertisement appeared in *Michigan Trucking News*, May 1937, back cover.

15. "Clydesdale Diesel Engine Motor Trucks" advertisement.

16. "Local Industry Specializes on Diesel Engine Trucks," *Clyde Enterprise*, November 1, 1934.

17. Ibid.

18. "Clydesdale Camiones y Omnibus con Motor Diesel," Clydesdale Motor Truck Company advertisement, November 1935.

19. *Hercules Diesel*, Clydesdale Motor Truck Company, c. 1937.

20. U.S. Patent and Trademark Office, "Diesel and Gasoline Motor Trucks, Diesel and Gasoline Buses, Trailers, and Commercial Truck Bodies, Clydesdale Motor Truck Company, Clyde, Ohio," filed June 14, 1937, granted October 12, 1937, trademark registration #394,021.

21. *Clydesdale Diesel Engine Motor Trucks*, Clydesdale Motor Truck Company, 1937, 1–3.

22. Ibid.

23. Ibid., 7.

24. Ibid., 5.

25. Clydesdale Motor Truck Company advertisement appeared in *Commercial Car Journal*, September 1937, 175.

26. "Diesel Motors, Inc."

27. "Clydesdale Gets Large Government Truck Order," *Clyde Enterprise*, February 25, 1937.

28. Ibid.

29. "Diesel Motors, Inc. Named Michigan Distributors for Clydesdale," *Michigan Trucking News*, May 1937, 23.

30. Ibid.

31. "Diesel Motors, Inc."

32. Ibid.

33. "Clydesdale Model-80," Clydesdale Motor Truck Company advertisement, no date.

34. "Clydesdale Diesel Trucks," Clydesdale Motor Truck Company advertisement appeared in *Michigan Trucking News*, June 1937, back cover.

35. "Clydesdales At Big Truck Show," *Clyde Enterprise*, September 30, 1937.

36. Ibid.

37. The Ex-Cell-O fuel pump was standard on all domestic Clydesdale diesel trucks, but optional on export models.

38. The Newark Motor Truck Show of 1937 was covered extensively by the trade press, including "Exhibit of Commercial Vehicles," *Commercial America*, December 1937, 14; "Important Truck Shows at Newark and Louisville in November," *Power Wagon*, October 1937, 8; "National Motor Truck Show," *Motor Truck*, October 1937, 4; as well as in the local press, including "Clydesdales Go To Truck Show," *Clyde Enterprise*, October 28, 1937.

39. "National Motor Truck Show."

40. Ibid.

41. Ibid.

42. Ibid.

43. "Important Truck Shows at Newark and Louisville in November."

44. "List of Exhibitors National Motor Truck Show," *Motor Truck News*, December 1937, 27.

45. "4,000 Truckers at Louisville ATA Convention, Nov. 15–18, *Power Wagon*, November 1937, 8.

46. "Important Truck Shows at Newark and Louisville in November."

47. "Clydesdale Gets Large Government Truck Order," *Clyde Enterprise*, February 25, 1937.

48. Ibid.

49. Ibid.

50. "Clydesdale Gets Government Test," *Clyde Enterprise*, September 23, 1937.

51. "Company Has New Program," *Clyde Enterprise*, May 12, 1938.

52. Ibid.

53. Ibid.

54. Ibid.

55. Ibid.

56. Ibid.

57. "Manufacturers Forecast Good Business Here for 1939," *Clyde Enterprise*, January 5, 1939.

Chapter 6

1. "Sue to Close Up Clydesdale Co.," *Clyde Enterprise*, September 21, 1939.

2. Ibid.

3. *F.D. Huffer v. Clydesdale Motor Truck Company (1939)*, Case 23373; Case Files, compiled 1939–1942; Court of Common Pleas of Sandusky County (Fremont, Ohio); obtained from the records of the Court of Common Pleas, Fremont, Ohio.

4. Ibid.

5. "Sale at Clydesdale," *Clyde Enterprise*, October 19, 1939.

6. "New Clydesdale Goes to Finland," *Clyde Enterprise*, August 5, 1939.

7. Edward D. Kennedy, *The Automobile Industry: The Coming of Age of Capitalism's Favorite Child* (New York: Reynal & Hitchcock, 1941), 306.

Epilogue

1. "Search for Clydesdale Fire Truck Ends as Chardon Man Donates It to Clyde Village, *Clyde Enterprise*, July 20, 1967.

2. "Clydesdale was Driving Force in City," *News-Messenger*, Fremont, Ohio, October 5, 2010.

Bibliography

Books

Cassons, Herbert Newton, et al. *Horse, Truck and Tractor: The Coming of Cheaper Power for City and Farm.* Chicago: F.G. Browne, 1913.

Cruikshank, Jeffrey, and David Sicilia. *The Engine that Could: Seventy-Five Years of Values-Driven Change at Cummins Engine Company.* Boston: Harvard Business Press, 1997.

Georgano, George N., ed. *The Complete Encyclopedia of Commercial Vehicles.* Minneapolis: Motorbooks International, 1979.

Karolevitz, Robert. *This Was Trucking: A Pictorial History of the First Quarter Century of the Trucking Industry.* Seattle: Superior Publishing, 1966.

Kennedy, Edward D. *The Automobile Industry: The Coming of Age of Capitalism's Favorite Child.* New York: Reynal & Hitchcock, 1941.

Mroz, Albert. *American Cars, Trucks, and Motorcycles of World War I: Illustrated Histories of 225 Manufacturers.* Jefferson, NC: McFarland, 2009.

Ontario Trucking Association. *The Golden Years of Trucking.* Ontario, Canada: Ontario Trucking Association, 1976.

Van Horn, Lloyd. *Early American Motor Trucks.* Macon City, IA: Lloyd Van Horn, 1994.

Wager, Richard. *Golden Wheels: The Story of the Automobiles Made in Cleveland and Northeastern Ohio.* Cleveland, OH: Western Reserve Historical Society, 1975.

Watts, Steven. *The People's Tycoon: Henry Ford and the American Century.* Vancouver, WA: Vintage, 2006.

Whirlpool Corporation. *These Things Stay By You.* Clyde, OH: Whirlpool Corporation, 1966.

Winter, Nevin Otto. *History of Northwest Ohio*, vols. 1 & 2. Chicago: Lewis, 1917.

Wren. Genevieve J., and James A. Wren, for the Motor Vehicles Association of America. *Motor Trucks of America: Milestones, Pioneers, Roll Call, Highlights.* Ann Arbor: University of Michigan Press, 1980.

Popular and Trade Magazines

The Automobile
Automobile Trade Journal
The Commercial Car Journal
The Commercial Vehicle
Dun's International Review
Engineering World
Horseless Age
Iron Age
Literary Digest
Motor Age
Motor Record
Motor Truck
Motor West
Motor World
Popular Science (1930–1935)
Power Wagon
Saturday Evening Post
Scientific American (1930–1932)
Telephony

Other Resources

American Truck Historical Society. http://www.aths.org (accessed May 25, 2013).

Historical Vintage Truck Association. http://www.htva.net (accessed May 25, 2013).

Ohio Memory Project. Digital archive maintained by the Ohio Historical Society. http://www.ohiomemory.org (accessed May 25, 2013).

Sponholtz, Shirley. Old Time Trucks. http://www.oldtimetrucks.org (accessed November 13, 2013).

Sugrue, Thomas. "From Motor City to Motor Metropolis: How the Automobile Industry Reshaped Urban America." Automobile in American Life and Society. Website from the University of Michigan. http://www.autolife.umd.umich.edu/Race/R_Overview/R_Overview1.htm#popsugrue (accessed March 18, 2013).

Index